THE MARXIST MINSTRELS

A HANDBOOK ON COMMUNIST SUBVERSION OF MUSIC

BY

DAVID A. NOEBEL

"Even music may be intoxicating. Such apparently slight causes destroyed Greece and Rome, and will destroy England and America."

Henry David Thoreau

American Chris
Tulsa, Oklahoma
January, 1974

Post Office Box 42, Tulsa, Oklahoma 74102

Library of Congress Catalog Card Number 76-186601.

First Edition

Manufactured in the United States of America

To Alice, my wife,
who not only knows what it means,
but what it meant.

PREFACE

Karl Marx in his 1848 *Manifesto* said, "The Communists disdain to conceal their views and aims."

Following the example of their phrenological master, the Communists have openly declared culture (music, art and literature) to be in their sphere of weaponry. Moshe Decter, in *The Profile of Communism*, admits, "The Communists endeavor to capture men's minds through the cultural offensive."[1] And J. Edgar Hoover, the late director of the Federal Bureau of Investigation, stated that the Communists "have infiltrated every conceivable sphere of activity; youth groups, radio, television, and motion picture industries; church, school, educational and cultural groups; the press; nationality minority groups and civil and political units."[2] He stated elsewhere, "The war between communism and the free world is not fought with bombs or other tangible weapons. It is being fought now by subversion through the medium of ideas. It is not an accident that the greatest concentration of Communist workers has been found in three fields — education, union, entertainment. These are the areas where ideas flourish and thinking patterns are formed."[3]

In the musical arena the radicals have to be congratulated for their successful *use of music*, for they have inflicted upon the American people a program persistently pursued until near perfection and completion. The Communist infiltration into the subversion of American music has been nothing short of phenomenal and in some areas, e.g., folk music, their control is fast approaching the saturation point under the able leadership of Pete Seeger, *Sing Out!* Folkways Records and Oak Publications, Inc. One need only consult R. Serge Denisoff's *Great Day Coming* for corroborating evidence.

The subverter's use of music is a refined two-edged subversive sword, cutting deeply into our nation's will to resist a "Soviet America."

One cutting edge is aimed at removing the barrier between classical music and certain types of popular music by substituting perverted form (e.g., jungle noises) for standardized classical form.

The other edge is more psychological than cultural and consists of the Communist use of music directed at destroying the mental and emotional stability of America's youth through a scheme capable of producing mass neurosis.

The father of the Bolshevik Revolution, V.I. Lenin, speaking to the Third All-Russian Congress of the Young Communist League on October 2, 1920, insisted that they must "rework culture," for only by so doing could they hope to build "a proletarian [Communist] culture."[4] He also appreciated the findings of Ivan Pavlov and his experiments regarding "conditioned reflexes."

In 1929, the ideological platform of the Russian Association of Proletarian Musicians was written. In its class war interpretation of music, the comrades were assured that classical music was "bourgeois," whereas folk music was the music of the "exploited and oppressed classes."[5] The ultimate aim of the Association was the extension of the proletarian Communist influence to the musical masses, reeducation and reorganization of these masses in order to direct their work and creative talents toward socialist upbuilding."[6] To accomplish this, "new musical forms [must be] created and will be created by the proletariat. Proletarian music must penetrate into the innermost masses of workmen and peasants, unite the thought and the will of these masses and raise them for further struggle and construction, organizing their class consciousness in the direction of the ultimate victory of the proletariat as builder of a Communist society."[7]

The subversive International Music Bureau, with its headquarters in Moscow, published its aims in the magazine *Soviet Music* in 1933. The publication announced, "We should not verge one single iota from a program of progressive class struggle. We can be successful in our efforts only if we know how to transplant our political slogans to the sphere of music . . . We should prove that the only right road for artistic creations, which include also that of musicians, is the service to the objectives of proletarian revolution." Hanns Eisler, one of the founders of the International Music Bureau, frankly admitted, "Communist music becomes heavy artillery in the battle for Communism."[8]

On November 18, 1945, the National Council of American-Soviet Friendship[9] held an American-Soviet cultural conference at the Engineering Societies Building in New York

City. Scores of Communists and their followers attended, together with others interested in revolutionary, leftist cultural activities.[10]

Less than six months later an "Arts as a Weapon" symposium was held in New York City on April 15, 1946. It was headlined by Communist Party chief William Z. Foster, Howard Fast, Dalton Trumbo, Arnaud E'Usseau and Elizabeth Cattlett. It was decided at this time that the cultural section of the revolutionary field was to be rebuilt; that "art was to become a weapon." Only a few months earlier, Moscow had purged its cultural fronts of the so-called "weaklings" who had permitted the "vibrations of world unity for victory to dull their drums for revolution."[11]

In July 1946 a cultural front congress was held in Moscow. Norman Corwin, American writer and radio commentator, was the "honored guest." He presented the Moscow International Convention with two recordings from the American-Soviet Music Society, on which were reproduced special messages from the Red leaders in the United States to the Soviet heads.[12] In this same year the Communists established a number of recording companies here in the United States, aimed not only at proletariatizing our culture, but also seeking to make a generation of our youth mentally ill. This program will be examined in detail in this work.

Sidney Finkelstein, "the cultural spokesman for the Communist conspiracy"[13] in the United States, in his book *How Music Expresses Ideas,* made Lenin's "rework culture" speech the heart of his work.[14] Finkelstein called for breaking down the barrier between classical music and "popular" music. He termed this barrier chauvinistic,[15] and proposed to smash it by inundating the American public with the "music of the Negro people."[16] One can be sure Mr. Finkelstein was not referring to "Negro spirituals" but rather to African "beat" music. His proposed method of eliminating the barrier seems to be quite successful since America is presently submerged in jungle "beats" and "noises."

Even *Time* magazine's article on rock 'n' roll[17] more than substantiated Finkelstein's fondest dreams. Finkelstein concludes, "works will come forth which will inspire the American people in their collective struggles for peaceful progress, express their solidarity with all other struggling peoples and be a historic contribution to world culture."[18]

And now Jerry Rubin in his modern day "Communist Manifesto" *Do It!* admits that "rock 'n' roll marked the beginning of the revolution."[19] He says, "We see sex, rock 'n' roll and dope as part of a Communist plot to take over Amerika."[20] And concludes, "We've combined youth, music, sex, drugs and rebellion with treason — and that's a combination hard to beat."[21]

Perhaps this is why Alfred G. Aronowitz commented, "If the establishment knew what today's popular music really is saying, not what the words are saying, but what the music itself is saying, then they wouldn't just turn thumbs down on it. They'd ban it, they'd smash all the records and they'd arrest anyone who tried to play it."[22] Or again, "While American radio kept busy trying to keep its turntable clean of records that dealt with sex and drugs, American songwriters kept busy outwitting the censors with lyrics that had double, triple and sometimes multiple meanings. America's new generation was creating its own culture and as part of that culture it was creating its own music and its own language."[23]

This study is concerned with both the cultural and the psychophysiological, i.e., the Communist use of music capable of producing a generation of neurotic and emotionally unstable youth. The study is, in part, "unbelievable," but then so is $E = MC^2$, and since knowledge is the irreducible requirement for intelligent action, the following material is offered with the sincere prayer that those concerned will take the proper action to assure a free Republic based on Christian precepts and Constitutional concepts.

TABLE OF CONTENTS

PART ONE

Introduction

"Music is a curiously subtle art with innumerable, varying emotional connotations. It is made up of many ingredients and, according to the proportions of these components, it can be soothing or invigorating, ennobling or vulgarizing, philosophical or orgiastic. It has powers for evil as well as for good."

— Dr. Howard Hanson, *The American Journal of Psychiatry*, Volume 99, p. 317.

Chapter I

COMMUNIST USE OF MIND WARFARE

The Communists, according to Dr. Leon Freedom, have originated nothing in brainwashing, or in any other phase of psychiatry. "All that they have done is to take what free science has developed and use it in a manner that would ordinarily be considered mad . . . there isn't anything original about what they are doing, only in the way they are doing it. Their single innovation has been to use what they copy in a diabolical order. Their objective is solely to make minds sick, not healthy, to create frustrations . . ."[1]

Dr. Freedom, a prominent Baltimore neuropsychiatrist,[2] charges that "the methods devised by the Free World to combat illness are used by the Communists to create it."[3] The world's greatest subverters are using highly specialized knowledge of medical science to unbalance normal minds. This is their contribution to modern thought.

Edward Hunter characterized the Communist operation of mind-tampering with the comment: "The most diabolical intrigues of the past never descended to such dark, unstirred depths. There is something repulsive and against nature in it. This is not easy for the normal mind to grasp."[4] Is it any wonder the United States' first ambassador to the Soviet Union said, "The great tragedy of the West is that its leaders — and they are all good, Christian patriotic men — simply are incapable of grasping or understanding the nature of the enemy bent upon their destruction."[5]

It is no secret that the Communists have determined in their innermost councils to destroy the United States of America.[6] The methods to achieve our destruction have varied from time to time but the goal has never changed. One method concocted to bring about the demise of the United States is a little known weapon termed menticide,[7] a lethal psychological process that produces a literal suicide of the mind! One University of Illinois professor stated that "the Communist Conspiracy . . . conducts scientifically planned attacks on the human mind on many levels with techniques adapted to the circumstances."[8] It is true that methods vary in this field, but the object is the same — to create a sick mind!

The Communists, through their scientists, educators and entertainers have contrived an elaborate, calculated and scientific technique directed at rendering a generation of American youth neurotic, through nerve-jamming, mental deterioration and retardation.[9] The plan involves certain types of music, hypnotism and Pavlovian psychiatry. The results, designed to destroy our nation, are precise and exact. No wonder the Kremlin maintains it will not raise the Red flag over America — the Americans will raise it themselves! If the following scientific program, destined to create mental illness in our children, is not exposed, degenerated Americans will indeed raise the Communist flag over their own nation.

Chapter II

POWER OF MUSIC FOR GOOD OR EVIL

The knowledge that certain kinds of music can be destructive is not new. As early as 2500 years before Christ, observations on the effects of music on the composite of mind, body and emotion were written on papyri by the Egyptians. David certainly had a telling effect on King Saul as recorded in I Samuel 16:16-23. Pythagoras discovered that music was an exact science which exercised a profound influence on the senses and emotions. Plato understood the destructive qualities of certain kinds of music. In *The Republic* he states that "the introduction of a new kind of music must be shunned as imperiling the whole State; since styles of music are never disturbed without affecting the most important political institutions."[1] Emil Neuman, in his *History of Music*, summarizes the opinions of Plato: "He insisted it was the paramount duty of the Legislature to suppress all music of an effeminate and lascivious character, and to encourage only that which was pure and dignified; that bold and stirring melodies were for men, gentle and soothing ones for women."

Aristotle likewise understood the destructiveness of certain kinds of music. He states that "emotions of any kind are produced by melody and rhythm," and that "music has the power to form character," the manner of its arrangement being so important that "the various modes may be distinguished by their effects on character ... one, for example, working in the direction of melancholy, another of effeminacy; one encouraging abandonment, another self-control, another enthusiasm; and so on through the series."[2]

Dr. Howard Hanson, former director of the Eastman School of Music, University of Rochester, commented, "Music is a curiously subtle art with innumerable, varying emotional connotations. It is made up of many ingredients and, according to the proportions of these components, it can be soothing or invigorating, ennobling or vulgarizing, philosophical or orgiastic. It has powers for evil as well as for good."[3]

Dr. Norman Rosensweig, of Mount Sinai Hospital in Detroit, Michigan, more than substantiates Dr. Hanson's observations. His research has been centered in the area we have come to call "brainwashing" — the experience of sensory deprivation used so successfully by the Communists to break down prisoners and force confessions or cooperation. His study convinced him that "it is meaningless noise which wears people's nerves to a frazzle."[4]

In an experiment with three groups of volunteers each listening to different types of noise, Dr. Rosensweig found the first group could easily listen to eight hours of meaningful stories and plays. The second group, listening to the sound of a rushing waterfall for eight hours, found it twice as difficult to withstand the time as the first group. The third group was fed the first tape backwards, and thirty volunteers underwent the ordeal before ten were found who could withstand the eight hours. Among those who did last the grueling experience, Dr. Joyce Brothers points out that "there were many near-psychotic symptoms for a time afterwards." Her conclusion was that most "people cannot long endure a steady onslaught of 'meaningless' noise."[5]

Unfortunately, the noise that millions of our youth call music is analogous to the story tape played backwards. It is invigorating, vulgarizing and orgiastic. It is destroying our youth's ability to relax, reflect, study, pray, and meditate, and is in fact preparing them for riot, civil disobedience and revolution.

Chapter III

COMMUNIST USE OF HYPNOTISM

The Communist scientists and psycho-politicians have devised a method of combining music, hypnotism and Pavlovianism to nerve-jam the children of our nation without our leaders, teachers, or parents being aware of its shocking implications.[1]

"An ideology, so ruthlessly materialistic as Communism," says Edward Hunter, "would be at variance with its own philosophy if it failed to make use of drugs and hypnotism."[2] During the Korean War, the North Korean and Chinese psycho-politicians used hypnotism as a means of brainwashing our captured soldiers. Colonel Donald B. Peterson, chief of Army Psychiatry in the Far East, commented that "These young expatriots spoke and acted as if they were under a hypnotic spell."[3] In an interview with Mr. Hunter, he said, "The indoctrination techniques in certain elements resembles some techniques of hypnotism." Mr. Hunter concludes, "The information I had been gathering convinced me that at least some form of mass hypnosis was part of the Red technique."[4]

The laboratory work involving rhythm, hypnosis and conditional reflexes was accomplished by a number of Russian scientists, but the important ones were Ivan P. Pavlov,[5] A.R. Luria[6] and K.I. Platonov.[7]

Chapter IV

PAVLOV, LURIA AND PLATONOV

Pavlov, experimenting with animals and human beings, popularized the expression "conditioned reflex." He found at least three areas of the human body conditionable, viz., muscles, glands and skin area. His famous experiment with dogs is well known. Edward Hunter, in his excellent book *Brainwashing*, summarizes the experiment: "The central theme [of the film *The Nervous System*] was indicated by a scene showing a dog in harness, standing on what looked like an operating table, in a room full of mechanical gadgets and curious meters. What immediately attracted attention was the glass container inserted into the side of the dog's lower jaw. This was supposed to have been painless; it did not seem to annoy the dog. Unsmiling doctors busied themselves with the experiment. One held the bulbous end of a rubber tube. By squeezing it, air pressure moved a circular tray bringing a bowl of food within reach of the harnessed canine. As soon as this happened, a light flashed. The dog hungrily eyed the approaching food, and its saliva began to drip into the test tube attached to its jaw. Each drop was counted and carefully tabulated on a graph.

"The dog," continues Hunter, "at first paid no attention to the light. Sometimes the rotary table brought an empty bowl to the dog's mouth, but whenever that happened, the light did not go on and no saliva flowed. A routine was established. When the light flashed, food appeared and saliva appeared. When an empty bowl approached, the light did not go on and there was no saliva.

"After a while, the dog hardly glanced at the bowl. It had identified the light with the food. The light was sufficient sign; it had 'learned'.[1] The crucial point in the experiment was now reached. A white-gowned doctor pressed a push button, the light flashed, but this time the round table did not bring the dog any food. Its saliva dripped just the same. The light had replaced the food in the mind of the dog, the way a slogan or label can replace a thought in a man's mind. The caption merely read 'Reflex caused by flashing light.' "[2]

Pavlov experimented with animals in other areas as well, e.g., in an area known as artificial neurosis. Here the scientist took healthy animals and, using two conditioned reflexes, the excitatory reflex and the inhibitory reflex, caused these healthy animals to break down mentally with cases of artificial neurosis. As we shall see, this is nearly what hard rock 'n' roll is doing to our teenagers!

In the years 1924-1929 A.R. Luria conducted extensive experiments with children[3] in the area of hypnotism and rhythm.[4] In 1932 he published *The Nature of Human Conflicts: An Objective Study of Disorganization and Control of Human Behaviour*. This Communist explains in great detail the nerve-jamming[5] of children and how younger children can be retarded mentally by: (1) subjecting them to severe nervous tension (explained by numerous diagrams and charts), (2) creating artificial degrees of neurosis,[6] (3) interfering with the normal maturation of the nervous system of the cortical or reasoning portion of the brain (as contrasted with the subcortical or the impulsive, uncontrolled section with animal instincts), (4) destroying the normal inhibitory mechanism of the cerebral cortex, and (5) hypnotic induction of sleep.[7] Luria, conducting one of his experiments, stated, "The conflict which we bring out very often causes in the subject a considerable shock of the higher speech processes, which are accompanied by a rupture of the 'functional barrier' . . ."[8] The discoveries of Luria and Platonov (to whom we now turn) have been extensively applied in American homes and schools.

The final scientist to be mentioned in this brief introduction is K.I. Platonov, author of *The Word As A Physiological and Therapeutic Factor*. The English translation was published in 1959 by the Foreign Languages Publishing House in Moscow. Platonov's "Word" in the title of the book refers to the hypnotic Word.[9] His work is a basic study in the field of hypnotism. Many of the techniques mentioned by Dr. William J. Bryan, Jr. in his analysis of the Communist records for children in the USA can be traced directly back to Platonov, who in turn acknowledges his dependence on Pavlov.

Platonov introduces his study with the following frank

admission: "Soviet psychotherapy has developed under conditions entirely different from those in foreign countries and in pre-revolutionary Russia. It is being built on the basis of dialectical materialism, a materialist mind and body, and the determination of the consciousness by the conditions of life."[10]

This Russian scientist not only describes the three stages of hypnotism and the various possibilities of each stage, but also most revealingly admits, "A weakening of the volitional traits may occur only if a special verbal suggestion aimed precisely in this direction is made; which, of course, is opposed to the basic moral principles of a physician."[11]

Since Communist psychopoliticians have no such moral scruples, the admitted possibility becomes of ultimate concern.

Now, according to Pavlov, the subcortical is not the executive organism, but a receptor organism. In fact, the subcortical can receive suggestions and impulses, arousing emotion and even bodily actions, without the master of the house (the executive organism) realizing that his body-temple has been invaded. This, as we shall see, is exactly what the Communists have capitalized on, and, at present, they are using this knowledge of the various stages of hypnotism and music[12] to invade the privacy of our children's minds,[13] to render them mentally incompetent and neurotic.

Chapter V

COMMUNIST INFILTRATION

Following the laboratory experiments, the Communists contacted educators and procured entertainers to convert this devilish scheme into a program scientifically designed to destroy American youth — mentally and emotionally! Evidently, the intermediary between the scientists, educators and entertainers was Norman Corwin.[1] This psychopolitical[2] plot was hatched in the United States of America in 1946.

"In July of 1946 a 'cultural' congress was held in Moscow. Norman Corwin, writer and radio commentator,[3] was the 'honored guest.' He presented the Moscow International Convention with two recordings from the American-Soviet Music Society. Following this convention in Moscow, renewed activity in the recording field for Communist causes and objectives became apparent. A few of the fronts which resulted are . . . Young People's Records . . . Challenge Records . . . Charter Records . . . Compass Records . . . People's Songs. . . ."[4]

Young People's Records, with its subsidiaries, Pram Records and the Children's Record Guild, is directed specifically toward young children. In fact, Pram Records are "for babies and one and two-year-olds."[5]

People's Songs, People's Artists, Inc., Sing Out! Inc., and Oak Publications with its publication *Sing Out!* in conjunction with Folkways Records, Vanguard Records and Elektra Records, are aimed specifically at our college and university students. The style is basically folk music.

And our high school students are still being swept off their feet by hard rock. As we shall see in context, not only is the "beat" of the music harmful, but many of the lyrics are promoting drugs, promiscuous sex and revolution.

PART TWO
COMMUNIST USE OF RHYTHMIC-HYPNOTIC MUSIC

"The methods devised by the Free World to combat illness are used by the Communists to create it."

— Dr. Leon Freedom
Edward Hunter, *Brainwashing*,
Pyramid Books, 444 Madison Avenue,
New York 22, New York, Paperback
edition, second printing, April 1961,
p. 229.

"Alexander E. Kabaleski, an Austrian physicist, escaped from the Kharkov Institute of Physics, Kharkov, Russia, and told then that they [the Communists] had research projects going on with hypnotic techniques and brainwashing . . ."

— Dr. William J. Bryan, Jr.
See Appendix[1]

Chapter VI

NATURE OF RED RECORD COMPANIES

Boris Morros, counterspy for the United States, testified under oath that "some of the fronts for Communist machinations and operations in the United States have been *certain record companies . . .*"[1]

One of these record companies established by the Communists in the United States, employing the techniques of the Russian scientists and discing records geared to nerve-jam our children, was (and still is) known as Young People's Records, Inc. (YPR). It was established in 1946 and its president for many years, Horace Grenell (one time instructor at the subversive Jefferson School of Social Science[2]) when called before the House Committee on Un-American Activities, submitted four solid pages of First and Fifth Amendments.[3]

In an official H.C.U.A. report, "100 Things You Should Know About Communism and Education," the American people were alerted to a number of subversive organizations. The report stated, "Here are a few [organizations] which have been declared subversive by the Attorney General, the Committee on Un-American Activities, or some other official investigating agency." Listed as one of the cited subversive organizations was Young People's Records.[4]

In the Government's *Guide to Subversive Organizations and Publications*, Young People's Records was again cited as subversive.[5]

Dr. Bella Dodd, one time member of the Communist Party, testified to the effect that the Communists were extremely interested in financially supporting YPR.[6]

For some time Young People's Records was, according to the press, a subsidiary of the Traffic Publishing Company.[7] The manager of the company was identified as Herman Singerman, who not only engaged in Communist political subversion,[8] but was also engaged in a union (United Office and Professional Workers of America) which was expelled from the C.I.O. in 1950 for being Communist dominated.[9] Interestingly enough, this very union was YPR's representative (Local Fifty), and Herman Singerman was Local Fifty's representative.

Karl Prussion, for many years a member of the Communist Party and a former agent for the F.B.I. within the Party, stated, "...I can definitely state under oath that, within the cell apparatus of the Communist Party, both of these organizations (Young People's Records and Traffic Publishing Company) were known about, accepted and supported by the Communist cell members."[10]

At present Young People's Records is closely related to the Franson Corporation and Greystone Press. Employed by Franson Corporation is none other than Local Fifty's Herman Singerman as evidenced by the Torrance School Board of Torrance, California, which received a letter from Franson signed by Mr. Singerman himself. The corporation was chartered in 1960 with a capital listing of $2,000. Its president and director is Fred Breismeister and the corporation, besides its involvement with YPR, sells a fourteen-volume set of encyclopedias.

The Greystone Corporation seems to be the controlling influence among a number of enterprises active at 100 Sixth Avenue, New York. This particular corporation was established in 1942 by John Stevenson. Mr. Stevenson, still its president and treasurer, bought into the YPR undertaking, according to *Counterattack*, sometime in 1951. Henry Goldsmith is the vice-president and Will Baronoff is its secretary. Greystone publishes the order forms for YPR and CRG records. Many of these records are identically the same that were disced when Young People's Records was originally accused by the California Fact-Finding Subcommittee on Un-American Activities of discing records promoting the "Communist Party('s) . . . indoctrination of children."[11]

It should be noted that at no time in the past twenty years has Young People's Records requested a re-evaluation by the California Senate Subcommittee on Un-American Activities.[12] The California committee first labeled YPR subversive in 1948,[13] and in 1961 the California committee in its eleventh report again mentioned YPR.[14] There is some possibility that YPR will be fully investigated by the California Fact-Finding Subcommittee on Un-American Activities under Senate Resolution Number 270.[15]

Since the late Paul Coates of the *Los Angeles Times* contended that Young People's Records came under new management and turned over a new leaf in 1951,[16] it is important to observe that the same individuals and the same records disced and copyrighted in 1947, 1948 and 1949 were sold in 1965. For example, Leone Adelson, Raymond Abrashkin, Margaret Wise Brown, Tom Glazer, Will Geer, Peter Gordon, Walter Hendl, John Michaels, Norman Rose and Jay Williams were all involved with YPR in the late 1940s, but as of July 1, 1965, these same individuals were still listed on products of YPR and CRG.

The following records were all disced in the late 1940s just prior to the *Guide to Subversive Organizations*' citation of subversion of YPR, and yet these same records with the same catalog numbers are presently being sold and can be purchased through an order form of the Greystone Corporation: Chisholm Trail (copyrighted 1948); Daniel Boone (1949); Muffin in the City (1948); Muffin in the Country (1948); Sleepy Family (1948); The Little Fireman (1948); The Little Cowboy (1948); Out-Of-Doors (1949); and When I Grow Up (1949). Tom's Hiccups was copyrighted in 1951, the same year YPR was cited subversive and a full year before its Fifth-Amendment president, Horace Grenell, took leave of the record company. Only time and space prohibit a complete listing of all the records that are presently being sold which were disced when YPR was cited subversive.

At present six corporations and/or companies occupy the same address with YPR and most with the same telephone number and bank account: (1) Young People's Records, (2) Children's Record Guild, (3) Greystone Press, (4) Living Language Courses, (5) Traffic Publishing Company and (6) Franson Corporation.

Established as a subsidiary to Young People's Records were two extremely popular record companies: Pram Records and the Children's Record Guild (CRG). The latter records were also scientifically calculated to nerve-jam the minds of our children. Pram Records, disced for babies one and two years old, are, no doubt, preparatory to the music heard in the rhythmic activity records of CRG and YPR. On the back side of both Pram Records and Children's Record Guild records one finds, "A product of YPR" or "A product of Young People's Records, Inc." Also established as a subsidiary of YPR was Living Languages Courses whose records can be found prominently displayed in Communist book stores, particularly, "Living Russian."

It is obvious that the Communists have not entered into the children's recording field for any humanitarian purpose. As the California Senate Fact-Finding Committee put it: "The Communist Party does not overlook the indoctrination of children.[17] The Communist book stores recently have been handing out folders advertising Young People's Records. One of these folders, distributed by the Communist Party Progressive Book Shop,[18] located at 1806 West Seventh Street in Los Angeles, is entitled 'Help Your Child Discover the Fascinating World of Music' —. The records, announced the folder, are on 'permadisc' and sell for only $1.49 plus tax. The folder declares that 'Critics and Teachers Hail Young People's Records.' "[19]

The address given for YPR and CRG is 100 Sixth Ave., New York 13, N.Y. In Canada the address is 1184 Castlefield Ave., Toronto. Also printed on some of the jackets is the comment: "Approved by boards of education and in daily use in thousands of schools in all 50 states and Canada." Consistently enough, the members of the Pavlovian Society[20] here in the United States are affiliated with many of the same Communist fronts[21] as the educators on the editorial board of Young People's Records[22] and the entertainers, artists, writers and promoters of these Communist recordings.[23]

Chapter VII

ANALYSIS OF RED RECORDS

One of the records disced by the Children's Record Guild Co. is entitled *The Little Puppet.* It is to be played to children in the home and in the elementary classroom supposedly to promote music appreciation or creative rhythm activity. "It contains," according to Dr. William J. Bryan, Jr., "a certain power of suggestion and musical arrangements designed to be frustrating and hypnotic."[1] It also contains such background effects as a ticking clock, a metronome[2] and properly placed wind sounds — all elements used in the process of hypnotism.[3]

Children's Record Guild records have been analyzed by experts in the fields of medicine and hypnosis. The conclusions reached by these doctors are the same as those envisioned by the Communists who perpetrated the records — both in the laboratory and in the classroom and home.

Dr. Granville F. Knight, a prominent physician, stated unambiguously: "There is no question in my mind about the hypnotic effects of the so-called 'sleepy songs' found among these records. Hypnotic induction by means of these records could easily place young children in a most receptive mood for suggestions about world citizenship, against patriotism and nationalism or anything which the teacher felt should be inculcated in the minds of young children."[4]

When one considers the endorsement by the United Nations of both Young People's Records and Children's Record Guild,[5] the conclusions reached by Dr. Knight are not too inconceivable.

Dr. Granville F. Knight also graciously arranged a meeting in Santa Monica, California, in March 1965 between the board of the Los Angeles County Medical Association and this writer. At this luncheon some Young People's Records were played and analyzed. Approximately 15 or 20 seconds into one record, a Los Angeles physician commented, "there's no doubt about it — it's hypnotic all right."

One of Canada's authorities in the field of hypnotism, Dr. J.A.

Boucher, commented as follows regarding these Communist records: "I have played these at length and found they are certainly something to give plenty of thought and consideration to. I would certainly agree . . . that they are in the hypnosis category."[6]

Dr. William J. Bryan, Jr., an American authority in the field of hypnosis, analyzed these records. Dr. Bryan, a Duke graduate, received his B.S. Degree in 1949 and his Doctorate in Medicine from the University of Illinois in 1952. During the Korean War he was director of medical survival training for the U.S. Air Force. Following his honorable discharge from the Air Force, he was a member of his local county and state medical societies and the A.M.A., while doing general practice. He was elevated to the American Academy of General Practice, was state chairman of the U.S. Committee of the World Medical Association and operated a flying medical service.

In 1955 Dr. Bryan organized the American Institute of Hypnosis to spur interest in training physicians and dentists in the use of this new medical and dental diagnostic and therapeutic tool. He has been a guest lecturer at St. Ann's Psychiatric Hospital Faculty of Medicine, University of Paris (Sorbonne), France, is an honorary member of the British Society of Medical Hypnosis, and is past president, founder, fellow and executive director of the American Institute of Hypnosis.

Dr. Bryan also edits the *American Institute of Hypnosis Journal*, a professional medical and dental publication devoted exclusively to the use of hypnosis in the respective professions.

One of few M.D.'s in the United States specializing full time in the practice of hypnosis in medicine, since the approval of hypnosis by the A.M.A. in 1958, Dr. Bryan has taught the use of these techniques to over 5,000 physicians and dentists all over the world under the sponsorship of the American Institute of Hypnosis. He has written numerous articles on the use of hypnosis for various medical journals, and two books, *Legal Aspects of Hypnosis* and *Religious Aspects of Hypnosis*, which are the first of their kind in the field.

The following analysis of *The Little Puppet*[7] is included in a stenographic transcript of Dr. Bryan's authoritative testimony regarding these records.

"In the first place, the thing that strikes me immediately is that the tempo is the same as the pulse rate,[8] approximately 82 beats per minute.[9] Hans Sutermeister, I believe I'm correct, in the *British Medical Journal of Hypnotism*, commented on a research program of this very thing. When sound stimuli are presented at the same rate as the average pulse rate, they tend to make the suggestion given at the same time — they seem to greatly increase the force with which the suggestions are given at that particular time."[10]

Dr. Bryan continues, "I'm sure I could use this record 'The Little Puppet' very definitely as an induction record for children, and I would be happy to take ten children,[11] and with a few words . . . play that record for them, and show you that you can induce every one of them into a state of hypnosis.[12] The children are being hypnotized without their knowledge and that's the real insidious part about these records." And, it is even more insidious when one realizes ". . . the more often hypnotization is repeated, the higher the suggestibility of the subject."[13]

In "The Little Puppet" record, the musician sings "lower, still lower." Dr. Bryan comments, ". . . this is just like 'down deeper and deeper'; it's obvious induction, a deepening technique. Every one of these things, and the exact fact that the person, as soon as he says 'drop them' and 'boo' and you then get the reaction of the drum following as though the thing is well on its way to completion. This is strictly an induction record, it's the only thing you can say about it, an absolute hypnotic induction."

Even a non-expert can grasp the word content of the record although Dr. Bryan warns that "the devices used in these records are so subtle that they very well may pass inspection by a well-meaning committee of physicians untrained in hypnosis, brainwashing and other such fields."[14] As long as the puppeteer pulls the strings, the puppet does fine; otherwise the puppet can do nothing by himself. Dr. Bryan puts it, "when you loosen up the strings and [the puppet] falls down — it's . . . obviously placing the idea in the subconscious of the child that unless the string puller is there he can't do anything by himself without the specific directions of the Communist boss, or whoever it happens to be . . .

and it really takes the entire control away from the child, and then after he gets through three or four of these deepening techniques he says, 'I can make you jump much higher than that' and then he goes on to prove it."

Dr. William J. Bryan, Jr., then remarks that according to Dr. Van Soulstead, speaking at the 4th International Psychiatric Congress, Barcelona, one of the "tremendous increases in mental illnesses in this country today is by virtue of the fact that . . . there is a tremendous increase in the 'accidental' hypnosis that is going on."[15]

Remembering Dr. Leon Freedom's opening remarks, ". . . Their objective is to solely make minds sick . . .," Dr. Van Soulstead's alarming statement isn't entirely surprising.

Other records produced by the Children's Record Guild include sleepy time records for children.[16] The record is supposed to induce natural sleep, but in reality the child is placed into a "state of hypnotic sleep." Dr. Bryan remarks: "Now when a suggestion is placed in your mind under such circumstances, you accept it, and you accept it with such a force that this can become a compulsion with you,[17] and that's one of the reasons why we see so much compulsive behavior, and this is the cause of a lot of juvenile delinquency . . . the symptoms can be as varied as life itself. But the underlying cause is the same, mainly the accidental hypnosis that resulted in the acceptance of the subconscious suggestion which the patient is acting out."[18]

In his analysis of a Young People's Record production entitled "Tom's Hiccups,"[19] Dr. Bryan comments: "Well, you've got a number of things here, in the first place, every bit of this has appeared both in the American and Russian psychiatric literature. First, you have symptom substitution. I think every psychiatrist is familiar with this. In other words, we can remove any symptom and another takes its place and you are placing in the child's mind the idea that this is exactly what's going to happen to him. As he has symptoms of things happening to him in the future, for instance, if he gets asthma or something, you remove asthma and he'll get migraine. If you remove the migraine, he'll get something else. In other words, it's placing difficulty in the way of treatment in any type of illness in the future. Whenever the child becomes ill, he will immediately have a sense of substitution occur so that he does become ill again. It's very isidious! The second thing here is that you have (the hiccups) right at the end to show that he never really gets over any of it; that he always is going to go around and around. The third thing he has told you is that the only real way to get rid of this is to forget it, in other words, to repress whatever started this to begin with which, of course, is another way of saying that you should forget it; then you're not able to remember the cause of your illness, and if you're unable to remember the cause, the illness goes on and on by itself as if you were unable to bring out the cause from the subconscious mind. The fourth thing bad about this is that it ties in all these things that actually produce the disease[20] in people with songs which we all know,[21] so that every time the child hears these familiar tunes, he will be tempted to fall into one of these categories of illness, each one representing to the child the child's illness, but as he grows up and becomes an adult,[22] then he will take on adult illnesses in the same fashion. What is now a harmless snore or yawn will turn into insomnia. What is now only sneezing as a child will turn into hay fever or asthma as an adult. And what is merely a shaky voice as a child will turn into a chronic stutterer later on who is unable to get along, etc. And the hiccups may lead to alcoholism."[23]

Concluding his analysis of these Communist records, Dr. Bryan states that these records are "breeding a tremendous race of people who are going to be mentally ill — it's terrible, really horrible, the scope of this thing is fantastic — this is for the age group two to five.[24] This is terrible, I've never seen anything so bad as this; scares you to death. You can see why when Khrushchev says, "We're going to bury you . . . we won't need to go to war . . . we're going to have you in seven or eight years,' well, obviously, when these school pupils grow up, we won't be able to defend America. When you control the minds of the people that push the button on the A-bomb, what good is the bomb? Nothing. Well, it's very well known that illness has always been a great incapacitator, accounting for a greater percentage of any Army in any war than all the bombs and everything in the history of wars. And it's obvious that they're approaching it from this standpoint. And, if that's true, then why not make everybody sick[25] and unable to defend themselves? And the easiest way to cause it insidiously is through mental illness programs."[26]

Chapter VIII

SOCIAL PSYCHOLOGY AND BERTRAND RUSSELL

In his book, *The Impact of Science on Society*, Bertrand Russell[1] says, "The social psychologists of the future will have a number of classes of school children on whom they will try different methods of producing an unshakable conviction that snow is black. Various results will soon be arrived at. First, that the influence of home is obstructive. Second, that not much can be done unless indoctrination begins before the age of ten. Third, that verses set to music and repeatedly intoned are very effective."[2] In apparent expectation he says, "It is to be expected that advances in physiology and psychology will give governments much more control over individuals' mentality than they now have even in totalitarian countries."[3]

Verses set to music and repeatedly intoned are very effective — so effective, in fact, that such music can be used to control ("The Little Puppet") as well as mentally destroy ("Tom's Hiccups") our youth. Russell fully understands the impact of such records, and when one remembers the statement by Lecron and Bordauz, "one interesting modern development (1947) in the induction of hypnosis is the use of the phonograph record,"[4] the Communist plan to destroy us from within through menticide should be apparent.

Chapter IX

DISTRIBUTION OF COMMUNIST RECORDS IN THE UNITED STATES

The Communists' ingenuity, however, does not end with the production of these records. The placing of these records in hundreds of thousands of American homes and in thousands of schools in all fifty states and Canada is likewise ingenious. Since neither the American family nor the American teacher would knowingly purchase Communist recordings designed to produce mentally sick children, the Communists crawled into the woodwork and allowed others to do their subversive work for them.

The Book-of-the-Month Club promoted and recommended these Communist recordings put out by the Children's Record Guild.[1]

The *San Francisco Chronicle* praised Young People's Records with, "These are highly superior productions, done with great intelligence, skill and simplicity, and infinitely finer than the drivel commonly purveyed on discs for children."[2]

The New York Times gave its endorsement of these Communist recordings. On the jackets of some Young People's Records is printed the *New York Times* recommendation, stating these Communist records to be "Best in Children's Records." On others is found the following endorsement: "No company has surpassed the consistently high standards that Young People's Records has maintained for its product.[3]

Music Teachers' Quarterly goes so far as to state: "Deserves all praise and cooperation from every music teacher, every musician and every parent . . . Far-reaching educational value . . . One of the most wholesome developments in the history of recordings."[4]

This Week Magazine[5] enthuses, "Young People's Records do an inspired job. Recommended are all their releases."[6]

Good Housekeeping and *Parents' Magazine* have also guaranteed and endorsed both Young People's Records and Children's Record Guild records. Both endorsements are reproduced on the jackets of the records for all to see. As Dr.

William J. Bryan, Jr. remarked: "And here it is, recommended by *Parents' Magazine* and guaranteed by *Good Housekeeping,* how in the devil can they do this?" Dr. Bryan concludes, "*Parents' Magazine*, boy, they certainly are all duped, aren't they?"[7]

Good Housekeeping and *Parents' Magazine* have, however, in more recent times informed their inquirers that Young People's Records, Inc. has been using their seals of approval "unrightfully" and "illegally."

G. Harry Chamberlaine, *Good Housekeeping's* director of Consumers Guaranty Administration, in a letter to Mr. Bruce S. Glenn, wrote, "They [YPR] may not rightfully make use of *Good Housekeeping's* Guarantee Seal."[8] Likewise, Dr. Marjorie B. Keiser, Director of Consumer Service Bureau, *Parents' Magazine,* informed Mr. Glenn that, "If they [YPR] are currently using our Seal, they do so illegally."[9] Dr. Keiser further informed Mr. Glenn that "Young People's Records and the Children's Record Guild were awarded the Parents Magazine Commendation Seal in July 1950. Their products were officially removed from our list of Seal holders a few years later." *Good Housekeeping* authorized Young People's Records and the Children's Record Guild to use its Seal in 1951, but according to Mr. Chamberlaine, "Their right to use the Seal expired within a year."

With Young People's Records boasting that its records "are approved by Boards of Education and in daily use in fifty states and Canada," it is quite obvious that the record jackets were printed after August 21, 1959, when President Eisenhower proclaimed Hawaii the fiftieth state.[10]

Since many school boards of education have purchased, and even the National Council of Churches has recommended, YPR records on the basis of these two seals of approval, this revealing fact should have beneficial consequences for the cause of freedom. Parents and even school boards of education who purchased YPR records on the basis of these two companies' approval have the legal right to file a protest with the Federal Trade Commission for YPR's misrepresentation of the product. In fact, the Federal Trade Commission in a letter, September 2, 1965, from its Division of Legal and Public Records, stated, "The type of violation mentioned re: the *Good Housekeeping* Seal is covered by the

Federal Trade Commission Act." In a Federal Trade Commission publication, "Trade Practice Rules for the Phonograph Record Industry," promulgated October 9, 1964, Rule Eighteen reads, "In the sale, offering for sale, or distribution of any industry products, members of the industry shall not represent or imply, through advertising or otherwise, that such products conform to any standards recognized in or applicable to the industry when such is not the fact." And Rule Twenty reads, "Members of the industry shall not use any trade name, trademark, or other trade designation, which has the capacity and tendency or effect of misleading or deceiving purchasers or prospective purchasers as to the name, nature, or origin of any product of the industry, or of any material used therein, or which is false, deceptive, or misleading in any other material respect." Young People's Records and Children's Record Guild's illegal usage of these two Seals should certainly fall under one or both of these two rules.

The National Council of Churches[11] urged the continued use of Children's Record Guild records on the recommendation of *Good Housekeeping* and *Parents' Magazine.* In answering an inquiry about the use of CRG records in a Sunday School class, the inquirer was told, "It would seem to this writer that the good names of *Good Housekeeping* and *Parents' Magazine'* would be sufficient guarantee for your church to continue using their records."[12]

Even the Southern Baptist Convention, a non-National Council of Churches denomination, has been guilty of displaying YPR and CRG records in its catalog,[13] selling these Communist nerve-jamming records to Southern Baptist Churches. This writer personally found these records in the Sunday School classroom of his son in a Southern Baptist Sunday School. The finale of finding such records was the church's refusal to dispose of these mentally diseased discs as long as the Southern Baptist Convention endorsed them. In fact, outside the Communist bookstores, Southern Baptist bookstores have become the largest distributors of these records.

One record displayed for some time in the Southern Baptist catalog was entitled "The Carrot Seed." On the jacket of this CRG record one finds the following comment: "leaves anxiety to the parents, competition to the big brother and wins for himself [i.e., the child] real satisfaction in his success and knowledge that he is right and the grown-ups wrong." Instead of teaching respect for mother and father, the record very cleverly raises doubts in the child's mind about the wisdom and veracity of his parents. Hardly a commendable procedure to strengthen the family unit, but then CRG can't be expected to fan revolution and the destruction of the United States by binding together the family unit. The technique is admittedly an excellent revolutionary device in psychological warfare, but why the Southern Baptist catalog should assist its sworn enemy in promoting and using these discs is difficult to understand. Doubtless the ones behind this were also behind the recommendation of James Baldwin's filthy and vile *Another Country*,[14] and the *Playboy* morality seminars.

The Southern Baptist Convention is not, however, the only denomination afflicted with these records. A Presbyterian lay leader wrote recently, "I am a Church officer in the First Presbyterian Church, Gainesville, Fla. My wife teaches a Sunday School kindergarten age group. It has come to my attention that Young People's Records and Children's Record Guild records are recommended by our new Covenant Life Curriculum and are on hand to be used by our Church."

In the Methodist Church's *Nursery 1 Storybook* for the Fall Quarter of 1965, Young People's Records sung by Tom Glazer are recommended. When brought to the attention of the Methodist Board of Education, Evelyn M. Andre replied, "It has been our understanding that this has always been a reliable and respected company among educators. However, we will look into it more fully and we will review very carefully our records from them."

Harriet Johnson's Bank Street Schools[15] play these records to their children. Commenting on the effects of this music on these children,[16] one publication stated: "The children are reacting to a train song. A look at their faces shows that they are not pretending to be trains — they are trains! The right kind of musical material — in this case a train song with strong rhythmic accent and simple, image-provoking words[17] — communicates itself right to their muscles."[18] When one recalls that conditioning affects three areas of the human body — muscles, glands and skin area —

the conclusions to be drawn from this comment are apparent.[19]

Grade Teacher, a magazine for grade school teachers, has recommended these Communist recordings put out under the Young People's label.[20]

Dr. Felix Guenther, professor of music, wrote glowingly: "It gives me great pleasure to report to you that all the records submitted by the Children's Record Guild have been chosen by my teacher-students as the finest and most valuable material in the field of children's musical education."[21]

A catalog for teachers, "Phonograph Records and Filmstrips for Classroom and Library," lists these Communist records. The teacher could be easily misled right from the start since in the foreword one reads: "Most of the listings are the products of RCA Victor, Columbia, Encyclopedia Britannica Films and other leading companies."[22] Some of the records not included in the "most" but forming an impressive minority collection are the Communist recordings of Young People's Records and Children's Record Guild. These Communist records, subsidized no doubt by Moscow, sell for $1.24.

In the Department of Music Education for the State of Texas, a work entitled "Materials List and Course Outlines for Music Education," prepared by Dr. Walter E. Purdy and published by the University of Houston, is replete with references to Young People's Records and Children's Record Guild. In another publication, produced by the Texas Education Agency and entitled "Music for Elementary Schools," we find numerous references to YPR and CRG.

An elementary school catalog published by Lyons, "the name that merits your confidence," openly endorses both Children's Record Guild records and Young People's Records. Under the caption, Children's Record Guild, the catalog states: "This listing has been carefully prepared to be used as a tool by the teacher, supervisor or librarian who is looking for the finest on Records as Educational aids."[23] One of the recommended records is "The Little Puppet." Concerning this record, the catalog explains, "Child imagines he's a puppet, imitates puppet gestures to rhythmic music of the French folk song 'La Petite Marionette.' Delightful lyrics suggest what he's to do."[24] In another school catalog, "Tools of Teaching," published by a firm in Los Angeles, California, and extremely popular among California school teachers, both Young People's Records and Children's Record Guild records are recommended.[25]

Recently a member of the Florida State Textbook Committee informed us that at least three textbooks presently proposed for usage in the State of Florida recommended Young People's Records as a source for teaching aids. He said, "The following are the books that listed the recording companies. Bear in mind that these are usually used as a series which includes First through Sixth or Eighth Grades.

"*Enjoying English 4*, Wolfe, Hamilton, Howard, Popofsky, The L.W. Singer Company, A Division of Random House, Inc., Syracuse, Atlanta, etc. *Language for Daily Use, Harbrace Edition*, Dawson, Zollinger, Elwell, Johnson, Harcourt, Brace and World, Inc., New York, Chicago, Atlanta, etc. *English Your Language*, Wolfe, Wright, Donovan; Allyn and Bacon, Inc., Boston, Chicago, Atlanta, etc."

Chapter X

"COUNTERATTACK," YOUNG PEOPLE'S RECORDS AND TORRANCE, CALIFORNIA

The Torrance, California, Unified School District Trustees voted 3-1 to keep records produced by Young People's Records in the Torrance Schools and to continue purchasing records from the company. Not only did the trustees vote to keep and purchase more records, but one of the trustees, Mr. Bert Lynn, states, "It is time we clear the name of the company we have marred for the past weeks."[1]

Another trustee, Dr. Donald E. Wilson, said the movement opposing the recordings of Young People's Records "smacks of censorship" and ". . . the same as book-burning."[2]

The opposition Dr. Wilson was referring to included Mrs. Frances Slater, a long-time music teacher, who made an extensive study of the recordings. Mrs. Slater found the records to be "written and designed to produce a jangling effect in children's nervous systems."[3]

In spite of this and other material presented, Dr. Wilson further stated, "Here we are asked to deny a freedom — the freedom academic personnel have in choosing materials. This country was also founded on faith, yet some people show little faith in the board members they select. And this country was founded on the belief that a person is innocent until proven guilty. The evidence presented is inconclusive."[4]

The school board seemed to possess a predilection for two points which at first blush seem to justify its retention of these diseased records.

It was pointed out that *Good Housekeeping* and *Parents' Magazine* both recommended and endorsed the records since their Seals of approval appeared on the back side of the record jackets. It was also made clear, especially by the late Mr. Paul Coates of the *Los Angeles Times,* that *Counterattack,* a conservative, anti-Communist publication, had fully undermined *Communism, Hypnotism and the Beatles,* since, according to *Counterattack,*

Young People's Records changed ownership in 1951 and henceforth came clean.

The answer to the first point is that both *Good Housekeeping* and *Parents' Magazine* have, as previously mentioned, sought clearance from the charge. *Parents' Magazine* stated, "If they [YPR] are currently using our Seal, they do so illegally."[5]

Good Housekeeping, in a similar vein wrote, "It is also a matter of public information that they have not been advertising in *Good Housekeeping* since the early 1950s and that therefore they have not had the right to use our Guaranty Seal for well over a decade."[6]

Such perfidy on the part of Young People's Records falls into the jurisdiction of the Federal Trade Commission. In a letter from Joseph E. Forch, Attorney for the Bureau of Industry Guidance for the Federal Trade Commission, we have been assured of an investigation into the illegal usage of both seals by Young People's Records.[7]

According to *Counterattack's* defense of Young People's Records, *Counterattack* contends basically, that since 1951, Young People's Records has changed ownership and therefore product. However, this can be simply disproven, i.e., that the product changed, by comparing the records copyrighted before or during 1951 with the records being sold by Young People's Records in 1965. The conclusive proof is that the records are the same. For example, "Chisholm Trail" was copyrighted in 1948, but is presently being offered for sale by the Greystone Corporation, one of many corporations occupying the same address with Young People's Records. Other records copyrighted before or during 1951 and presently being sold in 1965 were listed earlier.

However, since *Counterattack's* letter was intended to be public, we are publishing both the letter and its answer. Since we have never received even an acknowledgment for having sent our rebuttal, and no reply to any of our lesser letters to *Counterattack* asking for an explanation of their hasty behavior, we leave it to the reader to judge for himself the weakness or strength of *Counterattack's* position.

June 15, 1965

Rev. David Noebel
Christian Crusade Publications
P. O. Box 977
Tulsa, Oklahoma
Re: Young People's Records and Children's Record Guild
Dear Rev. Noebel:

I have read with interest your booklet, "Communism, Hypnotism and the Beatles," copyrighted 1965. I get many of the other publications of the Christian Crusade and have admired the Rev. Billy James Hargis for many years but my interest in this subject was sparked by the many letters we received from Tennessee, the Torrance School District in California and Orcutt, California, where controversies are raging about Young People's Records and the Children's Record Guild. I purposely do not say the "records" of the YPR and the CRG as it seems only the organizations are being questioned.

Many of us agree about the hypnotic and therapeutic effect some music has and your comments about the Beatles are hardly strong enough. Even they have been quoted as having said that what they do is hardly music but it makes money.

I was engaged in this same controversy over YPR and CRG in 1952 and thought the matter had been laid to rest. While I agree with what you write I cannot help but point out that the facts you mention were true and the footnotes you base your booklet on were accurate, but I think you do a disservice to our cause by implying that the situation is the same today as it was around 1948.

This letter is written in a friendly vein to help right a wrong caused by someone falling into a trap. I refer to only a few footnotes in your booklet.

On page 4, after explaining how the Communists executed their plans to capture the minds of the young through musical fronts, you state:

> "... The Communist bookstores recently have been handing out folders advertising Young People's Records. One of these folders, distributed by the Communist Party Progressive Book Shop ..." (Footnote 43)

The inference is clear that these actions are taking place the year your booklet was copyrighted — 1965.

The fact is that your Footnote 43 is to "House Report No. 259, Report on the Southern California District of the Communist Party," April 3, 1959.

However, that report is a review of the:

> "... intensive staff investigations supplemented by a series of hearings in that State during September 1958 and February 1959.

Communist activities in this area have, of course, been subject to continuous investigation by this committee for more than a dozen years . . ." (Emphasis mine.)

To prove the point, the same report on page 4 quotes a practicing attorney who quit the local party organization in disgust, in 1940. (p. 52)

Too often your remarks do not consider the time element as your Footnote No. 43 is a review of the background of Frank Spector, "Manager, Progressive Book Shop," going as far back as 1895, the year he was born.

You also state on page 4:

> "One of the records disced by this Communist Record Company, the Children's Record Guild . . ."

The facts are that Young People's Records and the Children's Record Guild were purchased by the late Milo Sutliff and John Stevenson in 1951. Horace Grenell, former president, has had no connection with either Young People's Records nor with the Children's Record Guild since 1952. Yet your Footnote No. 35 refers to his testimony before the Senate Internal Security Subcommittee in 1958, when he had other employment.

Your Footnote No. 38 mentions ". . . educators on the editorial board of Young People's Records . . ." None of the names mentioned have been connected with Young People's Records nor the Children's Record Guild since 1951.

Unfortunately, you could have known this had you read the reference completely. Your Footnote No. 29 refers to the testimony of Harvey M. Matusow who identified Irwin Silber, of People's Songs, as a member of the Communist Party. Did you know that Matusow also testified on March 1, 1955, before the Senate Internal [Security] Subcommittee, (The significance of the Matusow Case) Part 4? This testimony referred to a memorandum dated October 19, 1951 (Exhibit No. 24) made by Matusow in which this pertinent passage is contained on page 353 of the Committee report:

> ". . . I have never known Grenell more than to just say hello to. As for his party membership, I don't know of that either, but from the treatment of Young People's Records by the Party Bookshops and People's Songs I can say that YPR had party backing of the Party . . . Some of the first recording artists were booked out of the People's Songs Office and members of the Party (Betty Sanders, Ernie Leiberman, Pete Seeger, and the Weavers). YPR has since been sold and to the best of my knowledge has no connection to the party. I think they changed when they fired all the UOPWA employees and tried to break the union contract, there was a picket line and some name calling. Here we found a party controlled union being kicked out by a

party set up organization . . ." (Emphasis mine.)

I happened to have had no small part in effecting these changes to which he refers and they also included changes in the advertising on the record jackets, the editorial board, the artists, composers, singers, etc.

The Party constantly disposes of its fronts one way or another once they no longer serve its purpose. By so doing they sometimes catch the unwary off guard. What makes this present situation so awfully confusing is that the normal Party front is not usually a going business firm as in this case. Here, the assets were sold and the buyers chose to keep the names because they considered, at that time (1951), that there was value in the good will in the names. This present confusion only aids the enemy.

I hope this helps to clear up that confusion.

Sincerely,

John G. Keenan
Publisher

* * *

July 14, 1965

Mr. John G. Keenan, Publisher
Counterattack
250 West 57th St.
New York 19, N.Y.

Dear Mr. Keenan:

Harbored here in Manitou Springs, Colorado, training High School and College students on the evils and present dangers of Communism as well as the basics of Christianity and Americanism, I was shocked to have received a telephone call from Los Angeles informing me that the A.C.L.U., the A.D.L., Paul Coates of the *Los Angeles Times* and the Pacifica Foundation (pro-Communist radio network) were using your materials to defeat a citizens' demand for removal of the Young People's Records and Children's Record Guild records from the Torrance School District.

When this gentleman called, I had never heard of said material originating with *Counterattack*, much less have had the opportunity to answer such material. He stated that the A.C.L.U. and A.D.L. were extremely active at the Torrance meeting and that Pacifica Foundation was granted permission to tape the proceedings. He could not understand why you would publicly distribute such a critique without first giving me an opportunity to see the material privately (which I now find to be a three-page letter), and seek to correct any misunderstandings accordingly. I told him I didn't know and was concerned myself since I have always had a high regard for *Counterattack*.

On June 23, 1965, I finally received a copy of your "personal" letter, as well as a copy of the reprint of the letter. You must have made public the reprints the same day you sent me the original letter since California received the reprints before I saw the letter. Why the rush?

Instead of a private exchange of letters, Mr. Keenan, you have placed me in the most unfortunate position of publicly defending "Communism, Hypnotism and the Beatles." For combatants on the same side this is a *faux pas*, to say the least.

Everything in your letter could have been handled without fanfare. Why didn't you give me an opportunity to return a reply to your opening thrust before turning the letter loose to the public? All pertinent points could have been corrected with a simple exchange of materials; correcting misunderstandings, etc., but now that your reprint of a personal letter is being used by the enemies of our Republic to keep hypnotic records in our public school systems, disced and sung by pro-Communists, I feel it is my Christian responsibility to set the record straight — for the sake of our children and our nation.

Let me first state, however, that those who interested me in this situation were parents whose children were coming home from school "sick." Upon investigation the parents learned that records were being used during class periods, and upon checking these records found them to be Young People's Records and Children's Record Guild records. This was not 1948 or even 1951 but 1961. These good people were not aware of your previous research into this matter, but were only concerned with their children's welfare. Therefore, any failure to recognize your earlier part in this situation was purely unintentional.

In analyzing your letter, nine specific points have been raised against our material on Young People's Records and the Children's Record Guild. Each of your points will be stated fully with a complete answer immediately following your charge.

Charge Number One by Counterattack: "I purposely do not say the 'records' of the YPR and the CRG as it seems only the organizations are being questioned." (page 1, paragraph 1)

Answer: The organizations of YPR and CRG were not alone questioned as anyone reading the booklet, "Communism, Hypnotism and the Beatles," would quickly see. The "records" of these two organizations were definitely called in question with comments from two medical doctors and a lengthy analysis of these "records" by one of America's outstanding experts in the field of hypnosis, Dr. William J. Bryan, Jr. Dr. Bryan found these records to be mentally destructive (and even physically harmful). Why should *Counterattack* ignore such a powerful indictment of the "records" of these two companies in question, and make out that only the organizations are in question?

Charge Number Two by Counterattack: "While I agree with what you write I cannot help but point out that the facts you mention were true and the footnotes you base your booklet on were accurate, but I think you do a disservice to our cause by implying that the situation is the same today as it was around 1948." (page 1, paragraph 3)

Answer: The booklet, "Communism, Hypnotism and the Beatles," does not imply that the situation is the same today as it was around 1948. The situation today is much worse since the promoters of these evil records have had a great deal more time to implant these records in our public school systems "in every state of the union." In 1948 the Communists were just pushing off the ground and probably suffered a few setbacks, e.g., being declared subversive in 1951; but today YPR and CRG's hypnotic discs are being used in practically every school system in America!

Charge Number Three by Counterattack: " '. . . The Communist bookstores recently have been handing out folders advertising Young People's Records. One of these folders, distributed by the Communist Party Progressive Book Shop . . .' The inference is clear that these actions are taking place the year your booklet was copyrighted — 1965. The fact is that your Footnote 43 is to House report No. 259 . . . April 3, 1959. However, that report is a review of the . . . 'continuous investigation by this committee for more than a dozen years.' " (page 1, paragraph 5, and page 2, paragraphs 1,2,3)

Answer: It is true that my footnote was dated and that at a specific time, the Senate Fact-Finding Committee of the State of California pointed out that the Progressive Book Shop was handing out YPR literature and folders. The context of this statement was to point up the fact that the Communists have not entered into the children's recording field for any humanitarian purpose. The fact, therefore, remains that at one time the Communist book shop in Los Angeles pushed YPR records. *Counterattack*, however, has overlooked one simple but very important point — the Progressive Book Shop in the year of our Lord, 1965, is still selling YPR records! I personally purchased some in January of this year. And when I asked Mr. Spector why he didn't have a complete listing of the records for sale he informed me that he just didn't have room to stock them. When I returned to the Book Shop in April, the records were still there in the side room.

Charge Number Four by Counterattack: "Too often your remarks do not consider the time element as your Footnote No. 43 is a review of the background of Frank Spector, 'Manager, Progressive Book Shop,' going as far back as 1895, the year he was born." (page 2, paragraph 5)

Answer: "Communism, Hypnotism and the Beatles" does not include the history of Mr. Spector, going as far back as 1895. The booklet only mentions the fact that Mr. Spector is manager of the Progressive Book Shop in 1965 (selling YPR records as well as YPR's subsidiary LIVING LANGUAGES along with the other works of Communist and pro-Communist authors). Also, the booklet pointed out that this same Mr. Frank Spector was identified under oath as a former "organizer for the Communist Party in the San Francisco County" area.

Charge Number Five by Counterattack: "The facts are that Young People's Records and the Children's Record Guild were purchased by the late Milo Sutliff and John Stevenson in 1951." (page 2, paragraph 7)

Answer: It makes little difference if the company has changed hands a thousand times if the records being presently distributed in 1965 are still detrimental to the mental health of our children. Mr. Sutliff and Mr. Stevenson might have been the best of Americans, but if they were unaware of the destructive nature of these records which are still being distributed, then it makes little difference who owns the company. The truth of the matter is that these records that school teachers have been sending me from all areas of the country are the same records being sold today in the Progressive Book Shop of Los Angeles. And "The Little Puppet" and "Tom's Hiccups" are very prominent on the list. It no doubt will take the House Committee on Internal Security to fully straighten out the situation as a number of other organizations are using the same address as YPR and CRG. It only stands to reason that since the Communists have spent so much time and energy on developing this technique of combining hypnosis and music to destroy a generation of our youth that they would never surrender such a potent scheme at such a cheap price.

Charge Number Six by Counterattack: "Horace Grenell, former president, has had no connection with either Young People's Records nor with the Children's Record Guild since 1952. Yet your Footnote No. 35 refers to his testimony before the Senate Internal Security Subcommittee in 1958, when he had other employment." (page 2, paragraph 7)

Answer: On June 19, 1958, Mr. Horace Grenell was subpoenaed to appear before the H.C.U.A. When Mr. Arens asked Mr. Grenell whether or not he was the President of Young People's Records, Mr. Grenell took sanction behind the Fifth Amendment. Grenell also took the Fifth Amendment when asked about his relationship with People's Songs, Inc., the Jefferson School of Social Science and the Communist Party. *Counterattack* contends that YPR changed colors when it was sold to Mr. Sutliff and Mr. Stevenson in 1951.

Yet even *Counterattack* admits that Grenell did not leave YPR until 1952 which could have been a year or more since it changed hands; and even *Counterattack* must admit that Grenell is or was something more than a Fifth Amendment "patriot." YPR could have easily changed owners and even shifted a few of its Red singers, but the hypnotic-producing discs could have just as easily been sung by other "innocent singers." Mr. Horace Grenell could have seen to this before he left the organization!

Charge Number Seven by Counterattack: "Your Footnote No. 38 mentions '. . . educators on the editorial board of Young People's Records . . .' None of the names mentioned have been connected with Young People's Records nor the Children's Record Guild since 1951." (page 2, paragraph 8)

Answer: One of the educators on the editorial board of Young People's Records which we listed in Footnote 38 was Mr. Douglas Moore. According to *Counterattack*, "none of the names mentioned have been connected with YPR and CRG since 1951," yet on July 1, 1965, Douglas Moore's name appears on record jackets distributed by YPR! Tom Glazer who sings the insidious "Tom's Hiccups" was connected with Pete Seeger's subversive People's Songs, Inc. in 1946. Yet YPR still sells Glazer's destructive little disc.

Charge Number Eight by Counterattack: "YPR has since been sold and to the best of my knowledge has no connection to the party." Harvey M. Matusow — (page 3, paragraph1)

Answer: Mr. Matusow predicates his opinion on whether or not YPR is Communist Party connected with "to the best of my knowledge." However, for the following reasons, we must respectfully disagree with Mr. Matusow.

(1) The Pavlovian psychiatrists, Communist psychopoliticians and scientists who labored hard and long on this project would never forsake it with such apparent ease when it offers untold consequences.

(2) The very fact that Communist book stores carry YPR materials in 1965 would strongly suggest that Communist book stores know their friends. Also a YPR subsidiary, "Living Language Courses," is presently being sold in Communist book stores, with "Living Russian" prominently displayed.

(3) YPR was cited as subversive by the House Committee's *Guide to Subversive Organizations* on May 14, 1951. This same year YPR conveniently sold out to Greystone Press, but did not release Mr. Horace Grenell until sometime in 1952. Is one to believe that Mr. Grenell changed anything but a few outward and obvious mistakes?

(4) YPR was cited as subversive in the eleventh report of the Senate Fact-Finding Committee of the State of California, 1961. Yet according to Mr. Richard Combs, counsel for the committee, YPR has never asked for a re-evaluation of its announced subversive status.

(5) YPR at the present time is a subsidiary of Traffic Publishing Company [according to *Torrance Daily Breeze*, January 13, 1966].[9] In fact, six corporations and/or companies occupy the same address of YPR and most with the same telephone number. According to the manager of Traffic Publishing Company, YPR has been a subsidiary for nearly 15 years. The manager, Herman Singerman, was active in Communist political subversion in 1949 as head of Local 50 of the United Office and Professional Workers of America. In a letter dated June 30, 1965, Robert J. Wentworth, Assistant Director of Public Relations Department of the AFL-CIO, states that, "Your information — 'that the United Office and Professional Workers of America were forced out of the organized labor movement in 1950 because they were adjudged to be a "Communist-dominated union" ' — is correct." Interestingly enough, Local 50 was the YPR's union! Mr. Singerman is identified in Exhibit 185c at page 7427, Part 1, *Communist Political Subversion* hearings of the H.C.U.A., 1956, as active in Communist political subversion.

(6) Karl Prussion, former FBI agent within the Communist Party (1947-1960), states in a letter of June 15th, 1965, ". . . I can definitely state under oath that, within the cell apparatus of the Communist Party, both of these organizations [Young People's Records and Traffic Publishing Company] were known about, accepted and supported by the Communist cell members."

(7) When writing to Herman Singerman of Traffic Publishing Company, one receives a reply from Mr. Fred C. Breismeister, president of the Franson Corporation. Franson occupies the same address with YPR and Traffic. Mr. Breismeister will express "shock" and "outrage" that anyone could doubt the good intentions of the mentally diseased records, "The Little Puppet" and "Tom's Hiccups." Mr. Breismeister contends that his whole staff and management are not in sympathy with any Communist doctrine or objective! An official representative of one of the Congressional committees of Los Angeles stated that he felt this letter from Franson "was not on the up and up." Obviously, a full hearing by one of our Government's committees designed to uncover subversion will prove Mr. Breismeister right or wrong. However, since Herman Singerman also uses Franson Corporation stationery, it is difficult to believe that Mr. Breismeister wasn't writing with tongue in cheek.

Charge Number Nine by Counterattack: "I happened to have had no small part in effecting these changes to which he (Matusow) refers and they also included changes in the advertising on the record jackets, the editorial board, the artists, composers, singers, etc." (page 3, paragraph 2)

Answer: One of the early members of the editorial board prominently displayed on the jackets of YPR records was Douglas Moore. On July 1,

1965, in the Children's Music Center, Inc., 5373 W. Pico Blvd., Los Angeles 19, California, Douglas Moore's full name still appears on the jackets of YPR! His Communist-front record appears in footnote 38 of "Communism, Hypnotism and the Beatles." In a preliminary check of the "artists, composers, singers, etc." appearing on YPR and CRG records as of July 1, 1965, 20 per cent have Communist-front records. One, Algernon Black, has been cited as having 60 Communist-front affiliations. Further checking will no doubt raise the percentage, but this should be enough evidence to cause you, Mr. Keenan, and *Counterattack*, to cease attacking its friends and begin attacking the enemy!

From our observations it would appear that YPR has undergone changes in similar fashion as People's Songs, Inc. (See Senate Document No. 117.) People's Songs has changed its name a number of times as well as a few faces, but is essentially the same organization that was set up in 1946 by Pete Seeger. Today it goes under the guise of *Sing Out!* or Oak Publications.

YPR has six companies to confuse the issue with all using the same address and nearly all the same telephone number: (1) Young People's Records; (2) Children's Record Guild; (3) Greystone Press; (4) Living Language Courses; (5) Traffic Publishing Company and (6) Franson Corporation. Perhaps the sooner some official committee on Communist subversion investigates the goings on at 100 Sixth Avenue, New York, the better!

In a telephone interview, Mr. Keenan, you admitted to Mr. Bruce S. Glenn, "maybe there is something here I don't know about." We could not agree more and only pray that *Counterattack* will cease giving the ACLU, the ADL, Paul Coates, and the Pacifica Foundation further ammunition.

Sincerely in Christ Jesus,

David A. Noebel
Executive Assistant to Dr. Hargis

In the Senate Document mentioned above (No. 117) entitled, *The Communist Party of the United States of America, 1956*, a number of important points were set forth concerning Communist fronts. To begin with the document states, "It would be well for alert Americans to be aware of the tricks employed by Communist fronts when faced with the threat of exposure or prosecution. We list some of these which have previously been employed." The report then follows with a listing of Communist tricks and gimmicks to assure their misdetection. (1) "After lengthy and arduous investigation the front will suddenly change its name so that the job will have to be done all over again. Front organizations change their names from time to time and are variously labeled in different cities and neighborhoods. Sometimes fronts will merge to avoid exposure or prosecution. At times they have been known to assume a name similar to some well-known and respectable organization . . ." (2) "The names of prominent citizens who have been duped into the organization who are usually inactive and unaware of what is going on will be cited as proof of the organization's respectability." (3) "Individuals who expose the character of Communist fronts will be treated with libel suits, smears, physical assault, blackmail and ouster from positions. Legal advice is always valuable as a safeguard." (4) "The organization will claim a membership which cannot be accurately verified." (5) "Communist fronts, when identified as such, will immediately and vigorously deny the charge." (6) "A favorite device is to arrange for the defense of the particular front by a non-Communist publication . . ." (7) "Ofttimes, after a Communist front has been successfully launched by a provisional committee, a new committee will be substituted to conceal the origin of the organization." (8) "A favorite Communist gambit is to claim that since an individual belonged to a given front organization prior to its citation as such by the Attorney General, the individual should not be held responsible. This asks us to ignore the fact that a front organization is by definition subversive and, except in the very few cases where organizations originally formed by non-Communist forces were taken over by the Communists thereafter, all front organizations were subversive from their inception. The important date is not when the organization was cited, for its subversive character does not date from the day of its listing by the Attorney General." (9) "Recently there has developed a tendency to decry references to defunct organizations. This is unrealistic because the fact of membership in an organization which was subversive loses none of its evidentiary value when the organization goes out of existence. No information about a live and active conspirator should be considered as dead or irrelevant . . ."

Needless to say, many of the above nine articles are pertinent to Young People's Records with its many subsidiaries.

Chapter XI

RESPONSIBILITY TO OUR CHILDREN

Since these Communist records were designed to nerve-jam children, create frustration and induce hypnotism leading to mental and even physical illness, and since two and a half to four and a half million of our children at the present time stand in need of psychiatric help,[1] it is peculiar to find elementary school catalogs endorsing them. And, since these Communist record companies have been declared subversive in a number of different investigations by Federal and State legislative committees, there appears little excuse for these catalog companies to be ignorant of the facts. Whatever the excuse, the time to clean out these destructive little discs of mental illness is now! Our children are our sacred trust. Our Lord Jesus Christ said, "But whoso shall offend one of these little ones which believe in me, it were better for him that a millstone were hanged about his neck, and that he were drowned in the depths of the sea."[2] If someone attempted to molest our children physically, we would be the first to repel such perversion. We would stand with the Apostle Paul, "if any provide not for his own, and specifically for those of his own house, he hath denied the faith, and is worse than an infidel."[3] But we confront no mere attempt, for the Communists are actually molesting the minds of our children by the most cunning, diabolical conspiracy in the annals of human history. Dr. William J. Bryan, Jr. said, "it's not only possible, it's happening; not only possible, it's being done all the time. This started clear back in 1938. Alexander E. Kabaleski, an Austrian physicist, escaped from the Kharkov Institute of Physics, Kharkov, Russia, and told then that they had research projects going on with hypnotic techniques and brainwashing . . ."[4]

Edward Hunter, in referring to this type of insidious mind attack, very carefully says: "Surely there can no longer be a trace of doubt that brainwashing is sheer evil. The fight against it is the culminating issue of all time, in which every human being is a protagonist. There can be neither escape nor neutrality where such responsibilities lie."[5]

Christians, and all real Americans who love their sons and daughters, cannot remain silent. To do so would be un-Christian, cowardly and a sign of utter capitulation to the enemy. Our immediate action, tempered with knowledge, wisdom and love, is of the utmost urgency.

PART THREE

COMMUNIST USE OF BEAT MUSIC

"Now, in our popular music, at least, we seem to be reverting to savagery. And the most dramatic indication of this is the number of occasions in recent years when so-called concerts of rock 'n' roll have erupted into riots."

— Dimitri Tiomkin
Los Angeles Herald-Examiner
August 8, 1965, p. J-9.

"We've combined youth, music, sex, drugs and rebellion with treason — and that's a combination hard to beat."

— Jerry Rubin
Do It!
New York: Simon and Schuster, 1970, p. 249.

Chapter XII

TAMPERING WITH OUR TEENAGERS

America's children are not the only targets of the Communists. Also included in their ingeniously conceived master music plan are America's teenagers. Since rhythmic activity music ceases to be effective by early adolescence, the music designed for high school students is extremely effective in aiding and abetting demoralization among teenagers; effective in preparing them for riot and ultimately revolution to destroy our American way of life and the basic Christian principles governing that way of life.

The music has been called a number of things, but today it is best known as rock 'n' roll, beat music or simply Beatle-music. Even *Time* magazine admitted that "there was obviously something visceral" about the music since it has caused riots in countless communities.[1] Riot-causing it is, but it is also a noise which causes teenagers to experience countless side effects, detrimental not only to the community, but also to the individual and the country.

Henry David Thoreau predicted in 1854 that music would some day destroy England and America.[2] With today's beat "music" churning destruction throughout the length and breadth of England and America, Thoreau's prophecy could be fulfilled sooner than most would care to contemplate.

It took Lenin little time to realize that music played a vital part in the cohesion of society. He also realized that one sure way to destroy an enemy society was to destroy that society's music. This is exactly what his disciples have set out to do.

In his *How Music Expresses Ideas*, Sidney Finkelstein, the recognized cultural spokesman for the Communists in the USA,[3] sets forth the program with little ambiguity. Finkelstein calls for the destruction of the barrier between classical music and popular music[4] and insists that African music is the true epitome of popular music. The goal is to inundate the American people with African music and disparage the importance of good classical and standard musical forms!

Time magazine's analysis of the origin and influence of rock 'n' roll could hardly please Finkelstein more. The only mistake in *Time's* analysis was its failure to mention Africa. It stated, "The origins of rock 'n' roll go deep — Deep South, U.S.A."[5] The full truth is that it goes still deeper — the heart of Africa, where it was used to incite warriors to such a frenzy that by nightfall neighbors were cooked in carnage pots! The music is a designed reversion to savagery!

Race-conscious *Time* admitted that "One of the first white disc-jockeys to play these 'race records,' as they were known in the industry, was Cleveland's Alan Freed, a flamboyant, rapid-fire pitchman who sang along with the records, slamming his hand down on a telephone book to accentuate each beat!"[6]

Alan Freed has been recognized as the father of rock 'n' roll. Upon his death at forty-three in a Palm Springs, California, hospital, a UPI dispatch commented, "Freed's career went downhill after a payola scandal." *Time* magazine detailed the UPI dispatch, "Freed was indicted for accepting $30,000 in bribes from six record companies for pushing their releases."[7] According to the District Attorney's office of the County of New York, "Freed was accused of the crimes of requesting and accepting gifts and gratuities, was agent and employee of another, in violation of Section 439 of the Penal Law of the State of New York, from the following companies: (1) Action Records, Inc., (2) Alpha Distributing Co., (3) Superior Record Sales Co., Inc., (4) United Artists Records, Inc., (5) Cosnot Distributing Corporation, (6) Cosnot Distributing Corp. of Cleveland and (7) Roulette Records."[8]

Freed was fired by radio station WABC (New York City) for refusing to answer questions concerning a possible payola scandal. He self-righteously answered that such an investigation was "an insult to my reputation for integrity."[9]

Today all major record companies are flooding (nearly 800 releases per week) our teenagers with a noise that is basically un-Christian, mentally unsettling, revolutionary and a medium for promiscuity and the drug culture. The consequences of this type of "music" have been staggering. In Jacksonville, Florida, 6,700 rock 'n' roll fans were sent into a "screaming, fighting frenzy in the Jacksonville coliseum . . . Twenty police officers on duty at the show were swamped and called for reinforcements . . . they (according to one police officer) were like a herd of cows stampeding."[10]

In Long Beach, California, "a mob of more than 4,000 teen-age girls poured out of the Long Beach Arena Sunday afternoon after a 'Beatles-type' rock 'n' roll performance, and caused a melee which injured three police officers, damaged three vehicles and sent seven of the girls to the hospital."[11]

In an earlier incident in Long Beach, the newspapers reported that "More than a dozen policemen fought a valiant but losing 'battle' with 5,000 frenzied, screaming teen-age girls in the Long Beach Arena Friday night before halting the show in self-defense."[12]

Further up the coast in San Francisco, "A mob of howling teen-age boys and girls, at least 1,000 strong, rampaged through Mission district last night, inflicting heavy damage to automobiles and shops . . . The trouble, theorized Police Sergeant William Mikulik, can be attributed to the strange powers of a rock 'n' roll singer."[13]

Subsequent to the above melee in San Francisco, another rock 'n' roll entourage plagued that city with the following disease: "Four teenagers were stabbed, another was kicked until bloody and a policeman was mauled last night after a performance by the British rock 'n' roll group The Animals. Police riot squads with dogs took an hour to break up gang fights outside the Cow Palace after The Animals played to about 3,500 young fans. The gangs fought with knives and tire chains. Three teen-age boys suffered deep stab wounds while outside the arena. Another was stabbed while in front of the bandstand." One police officer said The Animals "wound up the crowd so tight they snapped."[14]

In Los Angeles, *the Herald-Examiner* reported, "some 15,000 teenagers kept a date with mass hysteria at the Sports Arena, bowling over police officers and gatecrashing to see England's newest singing group, the Rolling Stones."

Lt. T. E. Barnes commented that the "girls just develop mass hysteria." Some had to be ejected because they were "uncontrollable" and others fainted. One girl, according to the press report, "ripped off her blouse and threw it over a ten-foot partition." But another "wild-eyed teenager topped that performance by taking off her bellbottomed slacks and tossing them in the dressing room. A long coat kept her decent."[15]

When the Beatles presented one of their earlier "concerts" in Vancouver, a hundred persons were stomped, gouged, elbowed and otherwise assaulted during the twenty-nine minute performance. Nearly 1,000 were injured in Melbourne, Australia. In Beirut, Lebanon, fire hoses were needed to disperse hysterical fans.[16] In the grip of Beatle fever, we are told, the teenagers weep, wail and experience ecstasy-ridden hysteria that has to be seen to be believed.[17] Also, we are told, teenagers "bite their lips until they bleed and they even get overexcited and take off their clothes."[18] To understand what rock 'n' roll in general and the Beatles in particular have been doing to our teenager, it is necessary to return to Pavlov's laboratory. The Beatles' ability to make teenagers weep and wail, become uncontrollable and unruly, and take off their clothes and riot is laboratory tested and approved. It is scientifically induced artificial or experimental neurosis.[19]

Chapter XIII

PAVLOV'S CONDITIONED REFLEX TECHNIQUE

Ivan P. Pavlov, the eminent Russian physiologist, was invited to Moscow as the personal house guest of Nikolai Lenin, the father of the Bolshevik revolution. Pavlov expressed confidence that his findings on conditioned reflexes and inhibitions would be a blessing to mankind someday in its struggle against human ailments. Lenin had other plans. Remaining in Lenin's home for three months, Pavlov penned a 400-page manuscript for the Communist dictator regarding his findings. Upon reading the manuscript, Lenin exclaimed to Pavlov, you have "saved the Revolution."[1]

"What Lenin did not tell Pavlov," commented Edward Hunter, "was that he had come to realize how impossible it was that he would ever obtain the people's willing cooperation in changing human nature and creating the 'new Soviet man.' He saw in Pavlov's discoveries a technique that could force it upon them."[2]

Mr. Hunter observes the interesting fact that "Pavlov's manuscript, which became the working basis for the whole Communist expansion-control system, has never left the Kremlin."[3]

Much overt Pavlovian material has, however, been inflicted upon the unsuspecting American public. Herbert A. Philbrick, nine years an undercover agent for the Federal Bureau of Investigation and author of *I Led Three Lives*, remarked in one of his many speeches, "I learned as a member of the Communist Party — sitting in these deeply conspiratorial meetings night after night — that the Communists concentrate a great deal on something which they call Pavlovian psychiatry. Sometimes they refer to it as Soviet psychiatry."[4]

Pavlov, in his many experiments with animals and human beings, discovered specific scientific procedures to produce artificial neuroses in dogs and men. In studying and relating these experiments, one is immediately impressed with the almost perfect analogy between what our youngsters experience under

Beatlemania and the technique inflicted on Pavlov's dogs to develop "artificial neurosis."

For example, Dr. Bernard Saibel, child guidance expert for the State of Washington, in his account of a Beatle "concert," declares that the hysteria experienced by these teenagers caused many of them to become "frantic, hostile, uncontrolled, screaming, unrecognizable beings."[5]

These characteristics are all mentioned by Pavlov in his account of producing an artificially neurotic state in his animals. In one experiment, he writes, "this excitation could not be stopped in any way, whether by shouting, petting or striking the animal, which became absolutely unrecognizable."[6] In another experiment, the Russian physiologist relates, "Now we produce the neurosis . . . during the experiment the dog was extremely excitable . . . [experiencing] chaotic condition of the nervous activity . . . the animal was intolerant and uncontrollable."[7] In still a third experiment, Pavlov observes, "Its weakening results in an abnormal predominance of delay and other normal phenomena of which inhibition is a part, expressed also in the general behavior of the animal, struggling, impatience, unruliness and finally as pathological phenomena."[8]

All these experiments were related to the production of neuroses in dogs. The human parallel is described in his Lecture XXIII, "Application to Man."[9]

Pavlov found that his dogs generally fell into the four classical types or temperaments of Hippocrates: the extremely excitable, the extremely inhibited, and the two moderate types: quiet and lively.[10]

He generally refers to the above as three main groups: (1) the excitatory group; (2) the inhibitory group and (3) the central group with two types.[11]

He devised three scientific methods (two basic) to produce neurosis in animals. One method involved overstraining or overexciting the excitatory group of dogs with extremely strong stimuli. A second method involved overstraining the inhibitory group with a strong or a very protracted inhibition. Finally a third method involved a clashing or collision of the excitatory and inhibitory processes, thereby producing neurosis.[12] In Pavlovian terminology, "The conditions for the transition into a morbid state are quite definite. Two of these are well known. These are: very strong external stimuli and the collision of the excitatory and inhibitory process."[13]

To emphasize the seriousness of the resultant mental disorder, Pavlov carefully observes, "Experimental neuroses are usually permanent, affecting an animal for months and even years." Elsewhere he states, "In both cases the normal relation between excitation and inhibition has disappeared. We call this a nervous breakdown, and these destructions of equilibrium in the nervous system we consider as neuroses. They are real neuroses, one showing a predominance of excitation, the other of inhibition. It is a serious illness, continues months, and is one for which treatment is necessary."[14]

Rock and Neurosis

We contend that rock 'n' roll, certainly a strong external stimulus, is producing this artificial type of neurosis in our teenagers, and causing teenage mental breakdowns to reach an all time high.[15] And, no more scholarly statement of the relation between "wild" music and neurosis can be found than Dr. Howard Hanson's comment in *The American Journal of Psychiatry*, "The music ... is frequently crass, raucous and common-place, and could be dismissed without comment if it were not for the radio whereby hour after hour, night after night, American homes are flooded with vast quantities of the material. To its accompaniment our youngsters dance, play and even study. Perhaps they have developed an immunity to its effects — but if they have not, and if the mass production of this aura drug is not curtailed, we may find ourselves a nation of neurotics which even the skill of your profession (psychiatry) may be hard-pressed to cure."[16] And since this violent, orgiastic type of music is aired nearly twenty-four hours a day across this nation, his comment on mental sanity and radio is most important: "For in this day when through the radio the country is literally flooded with sound it seems logical to assume that music is destined to play an important part in helping to preserve mental sanity on the one hand or, if misused, to add to the emotional strain of an age already over-taxed by disruptive forces."[17]

Considering Dr. Hanson's statements in the context of current conditions, the following quotation from Edward Hunter's work on corticovisceral psychiatry merits attention: "If brainwashing can make a single individual neurotic, what about the inhabitants of a village, or a city, or even a country? . . . The only possible conclusion is that a long-range program is being pursued which, if left unhindered over a long period, will make whole populations just as neurotic as a single individual."[18] We are contending that perverted music is one major contributing factor in this long-range program!

Now, in the constant, destructive noises called hard rock or "Beatle music," our teenagers could well be experiencing all three of the neurotic techniques discovered by Pavlov.

In the first place, artificial neurosis is produced by a "continually increasing tension of the excitatory process."[19] Rock 'n' roll is just such a cumulative, tension-producing stimulus. Teenagers are thrown into a tremendous frenzy as the tension is built up through the beat of the drum and other instruments, and it is just such a stimulation of tension that is causing many teenagers in the so-called excitatory group to suffer artificially induced neurosis. In pre-Freudian terminology, the disease would be termed neurasthenia and hysteria.[20]

Secondly, "The inhibitory process likewise may be weakened either through strain or through collision with the excitatory process. Its weakening results in an abnormal predominance of delay and other normal phenomena of which inhibition is a part, expressed also in the general behavior of the animal, struggling, impatience, unruliness, and finally as pathological phenomena, e.g., neurasthenic irritability; in man as a hypomaniac or manic condition."[21] From this description there seems little doubt that teenagers in the inhibitory group are also affected, since rock 'n' roll "concerts" are producing this behavior!

The final method of causing artificial neurosis consists in the clashing or collision of the excitatory and inhibitory reflexes. Pavlov relates two experiments in which metronomes were used to bring about just such a collision. In one experiment he used 30 beats a minute to establish the excitatory reflex and 15 beats per minute to establish the inhibitory reflex.[22] In the other experiment he used 120 beats per minute to establish the excitatory reflex and 60 beats to establish the inhibitory reflex.[23]

Pavlov's Dogs

Pavlov conditioned his dog to secrete saliva while a metronome beat 120 per minute. To accomplish this, the scientist used the same technique as in the earlier discussed experiment with the flashing light. Each day, as food was placed before the animal, the scientist would activate the metronome at 120 beats per minute. Finally merely setting the metronome at 120 beats per minute caused the salivary gland of the dog to secrete. Normally, a sound stimulus does not cause such a secretion, but through a synthetic path (the conditioning process) in the central nervous system of the animal the sound stimulus now calls forth abnormally the same response that the normal stimulus, i.e., the sight or smell of food, would bring forth. This conditioning process implanted in the animal was termed the excitatory reflex.

Using the same animal, Pavlov then implanted another reflex designated as the inhibitory reflex. Here he conditioned the animal never to secrete saliva when the metronome operated at 60 beats per minute. This inhibitory reflex was firmly implanted in the animal by never feeding her while the metronome beat at that rate. The salivary gland of the dog was, of course, finally conditioned never to secrete saliva with the metronome set at 60 beats per minute.

The animal, conditioned with two reflexes, the excitatory and the inhibitory, was then exposed to both metronomes at the same time or in rapid alternation. One metronome, beating 120 beats a minute, induced the gland of the dog to secrete saliva. The controlled situation, with its capacity to produce tremendous, internal, conflicting tensions, caused a breakdown which was termed by Pavlov artificial neurosis. "All these experiments," says Pavlov, "clearly bring out the fact that a development of a chronic pathological state of the hemispheres can occur from one or another of two causes; first, a conflict between excitation and inhibition which the cortex finds itself unable to resolve; second, the action of extremely powerful and unusual stimuli."[24]

The last experiment, the clashing of the two reflexes, like the other two experiments of overstraining the excitatory or the inhibitory process, explains the process by which our young teenagers are being criminally seduced into this neurosis.[25] Attending a Beatle "concert," these young people already possess what Pavlov would term a built-in inhibitory reflex.[26] This has been implanted by their parents, churches, and society. It entails such things as decent behavior, prohibiting the coed from taking off her dress in public, tearing up the auditorium, creating havoc and battling with the authorities.

Rock and Hypnosis

However, within twenty-nine minutes, the Beatles or any other rock group can have these young people doing these very things. Rock 'n' roll, with its perverted music form,[27] dulls the capacity for attention and creates a kind of hypnotic monotony which blurs and makes unreal the external world. "Earthly worries are submerged in a tide of rising exaltation . . . the whole universe is compressed into the medium of the beat, where all things unite and pound forward, rhythmic, and regular."[28] In the area of morals, "rock 'n' roll treats the concept of love with a characteristic doubleness. The lyrics generally [in 1964] capitulate to the concept [of true love], but the music itself expresses the unspoken desire to smash it to pieces and run amuck."[29] This was precisely what Dr. Ronald Sprenger, chief school medical officer of Nottingham, England, had in mind when he referred to rock 'n' roll as the cause of sexual delinquency among teenagers. He also said, "Mass hysteria affects many to the stage of loss of consciousness and lack of thought for their immediate welfare."[30]

With the previously instilled inhibitions prohibiting the teenager from committing acts of sexual and other delinquency, the external excitatory music creates exactly the opposite desires. The ensuing internal conflict causes a severe clash or collision of the two forces and the teenager breaks down with a mental condition identifiable as artificial neurosis.

And, the frightening aspect of this mentally conditioned process is the fact that these young people, in this highly excited, hypnotic state, can be told to do practically anything — and they will.[31]

One can scarcely conceive of the possibility, but nevertheless the method exists, wherein the enemies of our Republic could actually use television and the Beatles (or any other rock 'n' roll/folk group) to place thousands of our teenagers into a frenzied, hypnotic state and send them forth into the streets to riot and revolt.

Dr. Andrew Salter, in his work *Conditioned Reflex Therapy*, laid down the physiological laws for such a probability. He mentioned three ingredients that are both necessary and sufficient to control human behavior. He said, "Hypnosis, word conditioning and emotional conditioning are thoroughly interwoven. They do not operate by different laws. They are aspects of the same laws. To understand those laws is to understand how to control human behavior."[32]

Dr. Salter's statement unpacked could well contain the *modus operandi* for riot and revolution. The Beatles, Rolling Stones or any rock group, for example, need only mass-hypnotize thousands of American youth, condition their emotions through the beat of their "music" and then have someone give the word for riot and revolt. The consequences are imponderable. Watts, Detroit, Newark and its "Burn, baby, burn" would fade into insignificance.

And recently *Modern Medicine* stated that persons can be "hypnotized by television," according to Drs. Herbert Spiegel and James H. Ryan of Columbia University, New York City. These doctors contended that this technique "might be useful in mass education, group treatment, and research," but they also warned that "unscrupulous operators could confuse, exploit, and deceive hypnotizable persons."[33] Since the subversive Fair Play for Cuba Committee was organized by two CBS newsmen, Richard Gibson and Robert Taber,[34] and since J. Edgar Hoover admitted that Communists have infiltrated television,[35] the Communists would not have too much difficulty finding their "unscrupulous operators." If this should ever come to pass, Aldous Huxley's jewel, "Never before have so few been in a position to make fools, maniacs or criminals of so many,"[36] could be considered fulfilled.

Dr. William Sargant,[37] head of the Psychological Medicine Department at St. Thomas' Hospital, writes: "Once a state of hysteria has been induced in men and dogs by mounting stresses[38] which the brain can no longer tolerate, protective inhibition is likely to supervene. This will disturb the individual's ordinary conditioned behavior patterns."[39]

Sargant further states: "Normally, it seems, the human nervous system, like the dog's, is in a state of dynamic equilibrium between excitation and inhibition.[40] But if subjected to excessive excitation or excessive inhibition which Pavlov described in dogs, the brain then becomes incapable, for the time being, of its usual intelligent functioning."[41] Under such a condition, Sargant states, "belief can be implanted in people, after brain function has been sufficiently disturbed by accidentally or deliberately induced fear, anger, or excitement. Of the results caused by such disturbances, the most common one is temporarily impaired judgment and heightened suggestibility."[42]

In an address before the Royal Society of Medicine, Dr. William Sargant had the following to say concerning the Beatles: "Adolf Hitler, ancient Greek orators, the Beatles and African witch doctors all practiced a similar type of brainwashing. I believe the human brain has not altered since the Stone Age. It still behaves the same way under stress. People can be brainwashed to believe anything. The tragic thing is that it doesn't matter whether it's sense or nonsense. You should be warned when young, of the way people get at you when you are older. Rhythmic music and dancing are ways of getting at the nervous system. [I will show some] movies demonstrating how the primitive rhythms of a Stone Age tribe in Kenya and a band at a London ball produce the same trancelike emotions . . . Hitler got people into a tremendous state of excitement and then talked to them. This method can be used for either good or evil. Hitler used it and killed twenty million people."[43]

Rock and Hysteria

Dr. Howard Hanson, commenting on the relationship between

music and hysteria, remarks, "The mass hysteria present in recordings of the rhythmic chants of primitive peoples and the similar mass hysteria of the modern 'jam-session' indicates — at times, all too clearly — the emotional tension producible by subjecting groups of people to concentrated doses of rhythm."[44]

Dr. Bernard Saibel, child guidance expert for the Washington State division of community services, attended the Seattle performance of England's Beatles at the request of the *Seattle Times*. He reported:

"The experience of being with 14,000 teenagers to see the Beatles is unbelievable and frightening.

"And believe me, it is not at all funny, as I first thought when I accepted this assignment.

"The hysteria and loss of control go far beyond the impact of the music. Many of those present became frantic, hostile, uncontrolled, screaming, unrecognizable beings.

"If this is possible — and it is — parents and adults have a lot to account for to allow this to go on.

"This is not simply a release, as I first thought it would be, but a very destructive process in which adults allow the children to be involved — allowing the children a mad, erotic world of their own without the reassuring safeguards of protection from themselves.

"The externals are terrifying. Normally recognizable girls behaved as if possessed by some demonic urge, defying in emotional ecstasy the restraints which authorities try to place on them.

"The hysteria is from the girls and when you ask them what it is all about, all they can say is, 'I love them.'

"There are a lot of things you can say about why the Beatles attract the teenage crowd.

"The music is loud, primitive, insistent, strongly rhythmic, and releases in a disguised way (can it be called sublimation?) the all too tenuously controlled, newly acquired physical impulses of the teenager.

"Mix this up with the phenomena of mass hypnosis,[45] contagious hysteria, and the blissful feeling of being mixed up in an all-embracing, orgiastic experience, and every kid can become 'Lord of the Flies' or the Beatles.

"Why do the kids scream, faint, gyrate and in general look like a primeval, protoplasmic upheaval and go into ecstatic convulsions when certain identifiable and expected trademarks come forth, such as 'O yeah!,' a twist of the hips or the thrusting out of an electric guitar?

"Regardless of the causes or reasons for the behavior of these youngsters, it had the impact of an unholy bedlam, the like of which I have never seen. It caused me to feel that such should not be allowed again, if only for the good of the youngsters.

"It was an orgy for teenagers."[46]

According to Leonard Gilman,[47] Schonaur insisted "that an increasing volume of sound in modern life — without adequate control of its character — is one of the causes of growing emotional instability in contemporary society."[48] This is exactly what we are presently experiencing.

Chapter XIV

ROCK'S DESTRUCTIVE NATURE

"Rock 'n' roll has dominated the United States and England more than any other two nations in the civilized world," states Mr. Jack Staulcup, president of Local No. 200, American Federation of Musicians, Metropolis, Illinois. "Most every juke box, radio station and television station in these two countries has been loaded with this noise since 1953. By the same token these two nations have the highest juvenile delinquency rate of any other nation in the world."

Mr. Staulcup, after two years of research on rock 'n' roll, went on to say, "It is interesting to note that LaVahn Maesch, who is director of Lawrence University Conservatory of Music and vice president of our National Association of Music Schools, revealed recently at the NAMS national convention in St. Louis that Russia had outlawed rock 'n' roll completely in the Soviet Union (about 1960 or 1961). It is also very interesting to note that only this year our own American newspapers carried an Associated Press article stating that the juvenile delinquency rate in Russia decreased 16.2 per cent in 1962 and decreased another 18.6 per cent in 1963 . . . this is a total decrease of 34.8 per cent (over one third) in the short period of only three years since rock 'n' roll was outlawed.

"Right here in our own country it can be found that two small cities of approximately the same population can be used to prove what is happening. We have chosen two cities of approximately the same population that incidentally are only seventy miles apart. These two cities are in the Midwest. Each of these cities has approximately the same number of night clubs, radio stations and high schools. Each city has one college and one television station. In one of these cities rock 'n' roll music rules the roost. Two of its radio stations broadcast it almost all day long. Two of its three night clubs feature it almost all of the time. Its television station telecasts a teenage rock 'n' roll party once a week. Its two high schools use rock 'n' roll music for just about all dances such as junior-senior proms, Christmas dances, etc., and its one college does the same. Its one civic center features a teenage rock 'n' roll party most every Saturday night.

"In the other city one of its two radio stations broadcasts some rock 'n' roll, but the other station seldom broadcasts any. Its night clubs feature good music most of the time. Its two high schools use good music for most all school dances. Its one college does the same, and its television station never telecasts any rock 'n' roll parties.

"Now to prove the point it can be found that the city where the junk music rules, the combined rate of young unwed mothers, school dropouts, teenage deaths by automobile accidents, burglaries, store break ins, and general vandalism is more than 50 per cent higher than it is in the city where good dance music rules. To get this information only requires the checking of the schools, radio stations, television stations, night clubs, hospitals, ADC offices, sheriff and police departments in both cities. If any person or agency wishes to check it out, the names of the two cities are Paducah, Ky., and Cape Girardeau, Mo.

"A recent issue of *Parade* magazine revealed that in England the British Medical Association has become so alarmed at the rise in venereal disease rate in teenagers that they have placed booklets on the subject on sale in 1,400 British drug stores selling for one shilling (fourteen cents) each. The article went on to say that the television networks in this country killed programs pointing up the dangers of VD on the grounds that it is not a 'polite subject.' Please note that the VD rate in teenagers is now higher than it was even before we had the wonder drug penicillin.

"This year *Men Today* magazine revealed that illegitimate births have increased 57 per cent in the past ten years (since rock 'n' roll). Half of the unwed mothers are under twenty years of age. In New York State 95 per cent of the fathers did not marry the mothers. The article said nothing about the illegal abortion rate which has to be tremendously high.

"It is also interesting to note that this year the Metropolitan Life Insurance Co. through a statistical survey pointed out that the suicide rate among teenagers rose 50 per cent between the years of 1952 and 1962 (since rock 'n' roll). Also most druggists and pharmacists will tell us that the number of prescriptions for tranquilizers for teenagers has grown higher every year for the past ten years (again since rock 'n' roll).

"Here is something else that can be given some thought. For many, many years the teenagers of this country have enjoyed many segments of recreation such as swimming, tennis, skating, boating, basketball, football, picnicking, music, dancing and many others. The big question is why did music and dancing suddenly die eleven years ago when all of these other forms of recreation have lived on and are still living cleaner and better than ever? A rebellious teenager will quickly tell you that music and dancing aren't dead. He or she will try to tell you that we are going forward. We would like to say here that if three guitar players plunking three chords on an amplified guitar and an African beat drummer is progress in music, then we might as well abolish all musical instruments in our school systems now, because it certainly does not require music lessons to play what these boys are playing. What's more, if this sex wiggle they call dancing is progress, then we might as well concede to the fact that we are a nation going into paganism. There is no need to worry about topless bathing suits. Any person who does not believe this can read Samuel Grafton's article, 'The Twisted Age,'[1] and see what is happening."[2]

In a letter to the Office of Economic Opportunity, Mr. Staulcup protested the usage of federal anti-poverty funds for the development of rock 'n' roll groups[3] (*the St. Louis Globe Democrat* also protested) throughout the country. In the letter he asks eleven questions worth pondering:

"1. Why do we have a constant increase in teenage and college student riots at summer resorts all over this land originating chiefly in resort rock 'n' roll dance halls?

"2. Why has the illegitimate birth rate in this country risen 250 per cent since rock 'n' roll and the primitive, and in many cases, savage, sex stimulating dances came [sic] into existence?

"3. Why is the VD rate among teenagers in this country higher although we now have the wonder drug penicillin?

"4. Why has the suicide rate among teenagers increased 50 per cent just since rock 'n' roll became popular?

"5. Why did the juvenile delinquency rate in Russia decline 34.8 per cent in only a short time after rock 'n' roll was outlawed in that country?

"6. Why did a few of our highly respected senators in Washington protest against the foul CBS-TV rock 'n' roll show 'It's What's Happening Baby' which was supposed to be beamed to school drop-outs?

"7. Why have at least a dozen high schools in central Illinois banned rock 'n' roll completely from their Junior-Senior Proms?

"8. Why did a popular motel in Chicago recently bar all rock 'n' roll groups (regardless of their reputation) from staying at the motel?

"9. Why did a top law enforcement officer in the city of Bridgeport, Connecticut, on July 23, ask the city to prohibit rock 'n' roll entertainers of any kind from making personal appearances in that city?

"10. Why have many responsible civic groups in numerous cities all over America completely abolished sponsoring rock 'n' roll teenage dances?

"11. Can we find one single qualified psychiatrist or mental specialist who will tell us that the jungle beat of rock 'n' roll and some of these late dances is not stimulating savage, animal emotions in the minds of millions of our young people?"

Rock, An Insidious Weapon

As one writer put it: "This type of music, it appears, is just as dangerous and perhaps more insidious a weapon in the battle between Light and Darkness for the minds, bodies and souls of our young people, as are the salacious movies and pornographic literature on which the Parent-Teacher Associations, the clergy and other groups are waging an all-out attack."[4]

Offhand it would look as if *Teen Magazine* disagrees for it states, ". . . despite what your parents and music teachers may say, rock 'n' roll is a musical art form — and the Beatles are better at it than anybody in the business."[5]

But the evidence points in another direction. The music isn't "artform" at all, but a very destructive process — contrary to *Teen*

Magazine and even Dr. David Reisman, who sees it as no danger.[6]

Great musicians see the music as degenerative. Anna Marly, composer of France's second most popular song, "The Song of Liberation," which is now sung following the French national anthem at public gatherings, states that Beatle music is a "degenerating music." She says, "The Beatles don't exalt the best in people. They exalt the materialistic things. Youths are seeking something and they accept the Beatles because it is a cheap way of emotion — a low emotion."[7] Interestingly enough she commented, "It's not a music you could win a war with." Her song inspired French resistance fighters during German occupation, but this woman, who became a historical figure during World War II as a composer, is sure that Beatle music would not have done it.

Dimitri Tiomkin, famous composer and conductor, had the following to say concerning rock 'n' roll: "The big beat is deliberately aimed at exciting the listener. There is actually very little melody, little sense in the lyrics, only rhythm.

"The fact that music can both excite and incite has been known from time immemorial. That was perhaps its chief function in prehistory and it remains so in the primitive societies which still exist in the far reaches of the world. In civilized countries, music became more and more a means of communicating pleasurable emotions, not creating havoc.

"Now, in our popular music, at least, we seem to be reverting to savagery (emphasis added). And the most dramatic indication of this is the number of occasions in recent years when so-called concerts of rock 'n' roll have erupted into riots.

"Those riots, however, are only the obvious manifestations of what I mean. More to the point is the fact that youngsters who listen constantly to this sort of sound are thrust into turmoil. They are no longer relaxed, normal kids.

"They will tell you they get a 'charge' out of rock 'n' roll. So do the kids who smoke marijuana and shoot 'H.' "[8]

The Big Beat

Dr. Howard Hanson, in his speech before the American

Psychiatric Association, set down a few simple principles in his consideration of the effects of rhythm upon our youth. He said, "First, everything else being equal, the further the tempo is accelerated from the pulse rate toward the upper limit of practical tempo, the greater becomes the emotional tension. Second, as long as the subdivisions of the metric units are regular and the accents remain strictly in conformity with the basic pattern, the effect may be exhilarating but will not be disturbing. Third, rhythmic tension is heightened by an increase in dynamic power."[9] His last two principles are applicable to our discussion of rock 'n' roll.

Alice English Monsarrat, in her provocative article, "Music — Soothing, Sedative or Savage?" says, "The normal easy meter . . . like that of a waltz is 123, 123, or a fox trot 1234, 1234. But with the advent of the twentieth century, the meters began to gallop brokenly stirrup to stirrup with harmonic dissonance and discord in the melodic line . . . the meter began to appear something like this:

1&2&3 4 1&2&3 4
1 2 3 4 1 2 3 4

"A broken meter in the treble, played over an insistently regular beat in the left hand, with gradually increasing rapidity almost to the point of frenzy . . . is capable of producing the identical disintegrating and almost hysterical effect on an organism; as if a person would try to rush madly in two directions at the same time."

She concludes: "Any psychiatrist knows that it is precisely this two-directional pull of conflicting drives and emotions that is helping to fill our mental hospitals with broken wrecks of humanity "[10]

An authority has stated, "music that is constructive contains always beautiful melody, wonderful rhythm and marvelous harmony; for all constructive sound is comfortable to the feelings, forever producing ecstasy, alertness and peace, energizing the mind and body, facilitating balance and self-control in the listener. 'The purity of music is even more important than the purity of drugs and chemicals,' says James Girard, eminent Boston psychologist."[11]

Dr. Altshuler, in his comments on the structural elements of music, declared that "man is essentially a rhythmical being . . . There is rhythm in respiration, heartbeat, speech, gait, etc. The cerebral hemispheres are in a perpetual state of rhythmical swing day and night."[12]

Alice English Monsarrat correctly points out that it "is precisely at this point that rock 'n' roll and much of the modern music becomes potentially dangerous. This is because, to maintain a sense of well-being and integration, it is essential that man is not subjected too much to any rhythms not in accord with his natural bodily rhythms."[13]

In concluding this chapter it is best to anticipate one question, viz., "but didn't Frank Sinatra do the same thing in his day?" Dr. Howard Hanson in his address before the American Psychiatric Association sets this question to rest once and for all with his comment, "The popularity of Frank Sinatra has caused his name to be mentioned frequently in connection with the deleterious effects of popular music but I can find no evidence to support this claim. Most of the music he sings is sentimental and nostalgic. He sings with sincerity and sensitivity and not infrequently artistry. If young girls are moved to squeal with delight I do not believe any harm has been done."[14]

With teenage mental breakdown[15] at an all-time high[16] and juvenile delinquency nearly destroying our society from within,[17] it is important to note that both are caused in part by emotional instability, which in turn is caused in part by destructive "music" such as rock 'n' roll. Therefore, no matter what one might think about the Beatles, or the Rolling Stones, Dr. Hook, The Mothers of Invention, the Fugs or the Jefferson Airplane, the results are the same — a generation of young people with neurotic tendencies, loose morals and little desire or ability to defend themselves from those who would bury them.

Chapter XV

ROCK AND DEGENERATION

"A larger-than-life portrait of Karl Marx dominated the entrance of a classroom building; a red flag flew from its rooftop. Chains barred the doors of other buildings, and chanting mobs roamed across the campus." Thus begins the description of a revolutionary take-over of Columbia University on April 23, 1968, written by Professor Robert Hessen, a young instructor at the University's Graduate School of Business, and a doctoral candidate in the Department of History.

The revolutionary organization which instigated the seizure of the campus with less than 200 members out of a student body of some 17,800 was the radical, pro-Communist Students for a Democratic Society — euphemistically referred to as the "New Left." According to Professor Hessen, the intellectual heroes of the SDS were Karl Marx and Mao Tse-tung, its action hero was Che Guevara, and, its slogan scrawled across the embattled Columbia campus read, "Lenin won, Castro won, and we will win, too!"[1] It should come as no shock, therefore, for someone to have overheard Gus Hall, General Secretary of the Communist Party, U.S.A., remark, "Fronts are a thing of the past. We don't need them. We've got the W.E.B. DuBois Clubs, the Student Nonviolent Coordinating Committee[2] and Students for a Democratic Society going for us . . . that portion of American youth that realizes society is sick;"[3] or for J. Edgar Hoover to stamp the SDS "subversive."[4]

The SDS clientele quite naturally feed on Marx's *Communist Manifesto*, Lenin's *State and Revolution* and most have consumed Mao's *Quotations* in their quest for the know-how in establishing a Communist society. But beyond this, they also devour their subversive, underground press and that form of rock 'n' roll which not only drowns them in noise but in drugs, promiscuous sex and revolution. And difficult as it may be for some to accept (though the leftist *Christian Century* printed it), the Beatles are "the New Left's favorite cultural heroes."[5]

Jerry Rubin in his scenarios of the revolution entitled *Do It!* has a number of things to say about rock music. His book, published by Simon and Schuster, is supposed to be a Molotov cocktail in the hands of our youth. Says Simon and Schuster, "Jerry Rubin has written *The Communist Manifesto* of our era. *Do It!* is a Declaration of War between the generations — calling on kids to leave their homes, burn down their schools and create a new society upon the ashes of the old."[6] It was this same Rubin who called for the killing of parents as a protest against the establishment.[7]

"Rock 'n' roll marked the beginning of the revolution,"[8] says Rubin. "Hard animal rock energy beat/surged hot through us, the driving rhythm arousing repressed passions."[9] Rock music in turn, he says, caused the sex and drug revolution and these revolutions in turn were channeled into the Communist revolution. "We've combined youth, music, sex, drugs and rebellion with treason — and that's a combination hard to beat,"[10] says Rubin. And again, "sex, rock 'n' roll and dope" are "part of a Communist plot to take over America."[11]

The campus radicals who hypocritically tote the so-called peace symbol while wearing on their lapels a picture of the cold-blooded killer and revolutionist, Che Guevara, and who demand public morality of bankers, generals and U.S. Presidents, while flouting all personal morality, are still singing vigorously the Beatles' classic, "Back in the U.S.S.R." The song was the number one hit in Russia in spite of the fact that the Communist government frowns on rock 'n' roll because of its decadent influence on the young. The Communists found that when they outlawed rock music in the early sixties, they reduced their juvenile delinquency by over 30 per cent in three short years. But Radio Moscow could not resist playing a rendition which contained such "progressive" lyrics as the Beatles' hit number. In fact, Mary Hopkins, who records for the Beatles-owned Apple Records, gave half the plot away when she offhandedly commented, "Now everything connected with Russia is fashionable."[12]

While the uninitiated neophytes are insisting the Beatles are simply having fun, the campus revolutionaries, along with the Communist youth sympathetic to the Soviet Union, are approvingly savoring each meter of,

I'm back in the U.S.S.R.
You don't know how lucky you are, boy
Back in the U.S.S.R.
Been away so long, I hardly knew the place
Gee, it's good to be back home
Leave it till tomorrow to unpack my case
Honey, disconnect the phone
I'm back in the U.S.S.R.
You don't know how lucky you are, boy
Back in the U.S., back in the U.S., back in the U.S.S.R.

Of course, the U.S. radicals in particular also appreciate the Beatles for their subtle and not-so-subtle discs and albums promoting drugs and sexual promiscuity. They know all too well that such ingredients precipitate fuller, riper revolutions.

Jenkin Lloyd Jones, in an editorial entitled, "The Issue Is Degeneracy," observed, "Great civilizations and animal standards of behavior co-exist only for short periods."[13] In the course of his discussion, the two examples cited to illustrate "animal standards" were both related to rock 'n' roll groups. They were the late Jim Morrison of the Doors, and his filthy antics in Miami in March, 1969, which are scarcely printable, and the Fugs. In the album, "The Virgin Fugs," which Jones correctly assesses "is on sale to your child practically anywhere," he finds it not only a purveyor of filth but bears an extravagant admiration for Moscow, Peking and Havana, and says the Fugs sing lustfully that "the Commies are going to take Brooklyn and they will take Nassau, too; the Commies all make good soldiers." Jones recommends the Fugs' miserably played album to "any who still think that the problem, if ignored, will go away."

The Fugs have put in print and on record other material which defies analysis due to its total debauchery. And yet America, which has been somewhat obsessed with water and air pollution, somehow has failed to recognize a form of mental pollution potent enough to rob her of her most priceless natural resource — her youth. Few radio executives have taken the absolutely essential position of Gordon McLendon who found it difficult to believe that American young people were hooked on raw sex, marijuana, and birth control pills. But upon listening to his own

AM and FM radio stations, he was forced to admit that "there were songs that glorified drug addiction, homosexuality and immorality in general." Some he found not only made permissible, but encouraged fornication and "all variety of things that would have been called immoral twenty years ago."[14]

McLendon listened to the lyrics of "I Can't Get No Satisfaction" (I am trying to make some girl), "Sock It To Me Baby," "Let's Spend the Night Together," "Rhapsody in the Rain" (in which a couple makes love in a parked car to the rhythm of the windshield wipers), "Day Tripper" (glorifying a prostitute who plays one-night stands), "Running Around the World" (LSD), "Get Off My Cloud" (marijuana), "Straight Shooter" (heroin), etc., and decided to fulfill his moral obligation to America's youth by dumping the records.

Unfortunately, however, most parents have paid little attention to rock 'n' roll and the harmful effects that it is having on their young people. Peter Udell, a popular song writer in the 1930s recognizes that for the most part it is very hard to understand the lyrics, but "the kids can understand them." He says if you listen to enough rock 'n' roll, your ears tune out the twanging guitars and the lyrics themselves spread like wildfire if there is something there. "Unfortunately," says Udell, "most of the time it is there."[15]

Jazz critic Gene Lees has also noted the harmful effects of rock. He has witnessed the relationship between rock, pot and revolution and the relationship between music and its influence on the state. Lees commented, "If rock music continued as a major influence in entertainment, I felt, the country was in for an era of mounting violence. It is always difficult to document relationships between music and social tendencies. But most people I know who are professionally involved in music believe they exist."[16]

Lees further states, "About three years ago, having caught the reference to drugs — indeed, the exhortation of their use — buried in a lot of rock and folk-rock lyrics, I wrote an article, suggesting that if this continued, the country was in for a wave of drug use that could shake its foundations."[17]

He believes that rock music has given young people a virulent fever and if rock is continually poured into their ears, "you've invented a sure-fire formula for trouble."[18] He also believes, "if you asked me whether rock music has been a symptom or a cause of America's terrible problems with its young people, I would be inclined to say, 'both — but primarily a cause.' Rock music has widened the inevitable and normal gap between generations, turned it from something healthy — and absolutely necessary to forward movement — into something negative, destructive, nihilistic."[19]

According to recent findings, hard rock music is not conducive to digestion, not appropriate for driving in heavy, congested traffic and downright dangerous for cases of hypertension (since it can raise blood pressure to a dangerous point). But, there are also frightening dangers involved for the youth in the physical, moral and spiritual spheres. Although teen-agers at the psychedelic "concerts" tell you they enjoy the beat and the lights, nonetheless, both can be harmful. Sixty-eight flashes per second of the strobe can, for example, freak out the iris and optic nerve centers, and right now there is overwhelming evidence that rock 'n' roll is having a decidedly harmful effect on the hearing of our teens. Many of America's youth could well be deaf by the age of 25 and others with hearing losses of a substantial nature.[20]

Rock 'n' roll, of course, has been banned in some countries (Russia, Spain, Indonesia) and even Saigon was forced to eliminate all twist songs because, "It was not compatible with the country's morality law and anti-Communist struggle."[21] The Beatles personally have been banned in Russia, Indonesia, South Africa, and Israel. These nations were not interested in experiencing the many side effects that necessarily accompany such a rock or Beatle production. In all too many countries, riots and bloodshed resulted, for as John Phillips of the Mamas and the Papas admitted, any pop performers, "by carefully controlling the sequence of rhythms," can create audience hysteria. "We know how to do it," he said. "Anybody knows how to do it."[22] The *Saturday Evening Post* further reports that the Mamas and the Papas instigated a riot in Phoenix mainly to test their theory that it could be done scientifically. They had a riot! Is it any wonder that beat music, which has caused so much havoc, has been labeled by Dimitri Tiomkin as "a return to savagery," by Dr. Frances

Braceland, psychiatrist at Hartford's Institute of Living, "cannibalistic" and even, surprisingly, by David Susskind as "garbage!"

When the Beatles began their trek into hard rock, the *New York Times* reported "fighting all over Britain." "Rarely a night passes," stated the *Times*, without an outbreak in some town or other. Sometimes it is a mere skirmish involving a few hundred policemen, but most often there is a battle with broken legs, cracked ribs and bloody noses."[23] The *Times* also mentions that the words the Beatles shouted at their audiences, "tend not to be of the sort reproducible in newspapers."[24] Because of such antics even the Beatles' press officer, Derek Taylor, stated that the Beatles were rude, profane and vulgar, and when their vulgarity was printed in John Lennon's blasphemous and filthy *A Spaniard in the Works* (which even newsmen agreed could not be printed in a family newspaper), *Parade* magazine wrote, "Parents who believe the Beatles are a quartet of fine, wholesome, uplifting musicians who hold womanhood in highlight and respect, might do well to peruse Lennon's second work for an insight into at least one literate Beatle's morality and mentality."[25] Subsequent chapters will note part of his depraved morality and misdirected mentality!

Yet few have fully understood the impact of rock 'n' roll or the Beatles. Rock music according to *Cavalier*, "is the revolution." It is not only subversive, says *Cavalier*, it is also giving the rebelling teen-ager his first victory in the initial revolutionary struggle for independence and detachment from an increasingly restricting bourgeoisie."[26] Not unexpectedly, *Cavalier's* article concludes with a quote from Chairman Mao, "The sounds of a thousand musical freaks are news bulletins of a youth revolution. It is the voice of change. As Mao once said . . . 'Now the cock crows, dawn breaks over the world, And from a thousand places arises the swelling music. Never were poets so inspired!' "[27]

The hard fact is that in this present revolutionary era, heavy beat music has become the catalyst for the young radicals in their announced plans not only to destroy Western culture, but to dethrone God. And few can really deny that the Beatles, Rolling Stones, etc., have and are playing a strategic and crucial role in the spiritual and cultural demise of the West and in the proposed destruction of Christianity throughout the world. T.S. Eliot once remarked, "The world is trying the experiment of attempting to form a civilized but non-Christian mentality." A look at the critical situation only calls in doubt his use of the word "civilized."

Chapter XVI

ROCK, DRUGS AND THE BEATLES

Rock 'n' roll has become to the drug pusher what the hand is to the glove. "Drug-taking is nothing new to the music business," admitted one music industry spokesman, "but it has always been a secretive thing. No one went around boasting about it, but now it is really getting out of hand."[1] The music reviewer for *Holiday* magazine concurs. When he pondered the question, "Is it possible that the record producers have been fooled by the jargon of the song — have put out such discs not knowing what they mean?" He demurs by stating, "It is unlikely because it is impossible to be in the music business long without seeing pot smoked. The terminology of narcotics is widely known and understood in the industry, both by artists, recorders and producers . . . In songs meant for children of twelve and even younger, they proclaim that it is wise, hip and inside to dissolve your responsibilities and problems of a difficult world into the mists of marijuana, LSD, or heroin."[2] Those on the inside of the music industry know how advantageous it is to deal in pot and naturally the rock groups themselves, in the main, have no qualms over the usage of drugs. *Time* magazine, September 26, 1969, for example, reports that "Rock musicians use drugs frequently and openly, and their compositions are riddled with references to drugs, from the Beatles' 'I Get High With A Little Help From My Friends' to the Jefferson Airplane's *White Rabbit* . . ." *Cavalier*, too, admits that "handfuls of rock groups have been liberated by acid (LSD)."[3] In fact, Grace Slick of the Jefferson Airplane told *Cavalier* in June of 1968, "we all use drugs and we condone the judicious use of drugs by every one. Kids are going to blow their minds somehow, and this is a better way to do it than racking up their car against the wall. Let them groove, do their thing, ball on the grass in the open. I dig watching people make love." And, Frank Zappa of the Mothers of Invention told *Life* that society's major hang-ups could be cured by a drug and sexual openness.[4] Dr. Hook's *Sloppy Seconds* disced by Columbia reeks with similar sentiment.

In speaking with a friend who spent six years playing hard rock (of which the last half were spent in smoking marijuana), he made it quite clear that every rock 'n' roll group he knew considered the playing of rock merely a prelude to the events of the evening which inevitably were concluded by smoking pot and illicit sexual affairs. In fact, their philosophy was to use beat music to "turn on the chicks," and then "smoke pot and bed down." Few would consider this a normal, healthy pastime or a "desire to prove one's manhood."

With such lyrics as "Swallow-that-cube-and-fly-around Now-move-to-the-center-with-a-rolling-sound; Then-speed-to-the-farthest-edge-of-space; See-Purple-Paisley-everywhere," inviting our youth to take a trip on LSD, or others such as "Running Around the World," "Get Off My Cloud," (pot or marijuana) and "Straightshooter" (heroin),[5] there is plenty of reason for grave concern. Yet this is only the beginning! Literally hundreds of drug-pushing discs are available and for our teen-agers' consumption: "Acapulco Gold," "A Day in the Life," "A Little Help From My Friends," "Along Came Mary," "Bend Me, Shape Me," "Blue Cheer," "Buy For Me The Rain," "Colored Rain," "Connection," "Don't Bogart Me," "Express To Your Head," "Faster Than the Speed of Life," "Fixing a Hole," "Full Measure," "Get Out and Up," "Glass Onion," "I Had Too Much To Dream," "Journey to the Center of the Mind," "Jumping Jack Flash," "Lucy in the Sky with Diamonds," "Magic Carpet Ride," "Magical Mystery Tour," "Mainline Prosperity Blues," "Mary Jane," "Merry-Go-Round," "Mr. Farmer," "Mr. Tambourine Man," "Norwegian Wood," "Penny Lane," "Rainy Day Woman," "Rose Colored Glasses," "Rolling Machine," "She's a Rainbow," "Strawberry Fields Forever," "The Pusher Man," "The Wichita Falls," "Two Thousand Light Years From Here," "Voyage Into Golden Scream," "White Rabbit," "Willy and the Rubber Band," "Yellow Balloon," "Yellow Submarine," "You Turn Me On," "You've Got Me High," etc., etc., *ad infinitum ad nauseam.* One has only to check any music center to see the quantity of "underground rock" or "underground music" (now termed "progressive rock") and realize that by definition these records are to be listened to under the influence of drugs. Even newspapers now carry items telling teen-agers when they can listen to underground music on the radio. For example, "Doc Nemo . . . plays underground music every day on WZAK from 2:00 to 4:00 a.m."[6]

Some albums are so obvious that no code sheet is necessary. For example, the Amboy Dukes' "Journey to the Center of the Mind" carries on the front cover of the jacket every piece of drug smoking equipment imaginable. And, who could miss what the Jefferson Airplane were trying to impart in "White Rabbit," with such lyrics as, "One pill makes you larger, and one pill makes you smaller, and the one that mother gives you, don't do anything at all. Go ask Alice when she's ten feet tall, and if you go chasing rabbits, and you know you are going to fall, tell them a hooka — smoking caterpillar has given you the call . . . feed your head, feed your head." Then, too, "Acapulco Gold" reflects the fact that the best marijuana comes from the state of Guerrero in Mexico — the hinterland of Acapulco. Grand Funk Railroad's *High on a Horse* and Dr. Hook's *Freaker's Ball* and *Get My Rocks Off* are also drug saturated.

The *New York Times* reported that lyrics of songs have pushed way beyond the tame rhymes of the past, and have moved into the world of pills, marijuana, and LSD.[7] *Time* magazine wrote that "Rainy Day Woman" by Bob Dylan was taken off the air by many radio stations because of its drug implications. It turned out that "Rainy Day Woman" in junky lingo was a marijuana cigarette.[8] "Better than half of all pop music is inspired by LSD experience," contends Mrs. Judith Kuch. She says "the Monkees' number, 'I'm a Believer,' is ostensibly a love song, but we all know it refers to drugs. So do many of the songs the Beatles sing, like, 'Tomorrow Never Know,' which ends like a page of advice from a psychedelic manual."[9]

On the other hand there are a few like George Marek, head of RCA Victor, who personally feels anyone playing around with the concept of LSD is bad news. Says Marek, "I feel these songs are wrong for the youth, even if they are by Bob Dylan, who is a very good artist. The danger is that the taking of drugs will be made more and more the smart thing to do."[10]

As if to reinforce Marek's observations, *Confidential*, one of the lesser slicks unraveled its mentality by running a three-page spread on a do-it-yourself kit of making a form of the hallucinatory drug, LSD. And then sanctimoniously concluded, "*Confidential* staffers can't quite recommend the finished product because: (1) It's illegal to make LSD, (2) a mistake in mixture or improper dosage could be fatal."[11]

All Narcotics Are Dangerous

Narcotics, of course, are dangerous even when administered under the care of a physician. Both heroin and marijuana are exceedingly dangerous. Heroin is the strongest and most addictive opium derivative and is either sniffed into the nasal passages through the nose or mixed in water and heated to form a solution and injected intravenously with a hypodermic directly into the bloodstream. Marijuana is a derivative from the hemp weed, which affects the nervous system and the brain of the user, causing mental unbalance for varying periods of time and in which a sufficient dose of the active substance — Tetrahydrocannabianol — is capable of producing all the hallucinatory and psychotic effects relative to LSD (which is conceded to be one of the most powerful drugs known).

Repeated use of heroin produces psychological and physical dependence in which the user has an overwhelming compulsion to continue using the drug. Under heroin the body develops a tolerance for it in the bloodstream and virtually all bodily functions are attuned to that presence. Of course, once the victim has the habit, he stops at nothing to satisfy it, and since heroin is considered incurably addictive, when the narcotic is no longer in the body, death can result even during the withdrawal process.

Marijuana, on the other hand, is no less to be desired. Edward R. Cass, Bureau of Narcotics and Dangerous Drugs, in an address before the National Conference School Medical Society, said, "I recently had the privilege of spending several days with Dr. I.C. Chopra, Director of Government Research at New Delhi, India. Dr. Chopra and his father have gained worldwide scientific acclaim for their marijuana research and have written numerous books and reports on the subject. The doctor told me that his country has had 2,000 years of experience in all forms of marijuana, and until 1959 the drug was legal and socially accepted throughout India. In 1959 the India Government finally decided that the use of marijuana had caused such severe social and economic problems that it could no longer be tolerated, and laws were passed which prohibit sale, importation and possession."[12]

Dr. Robert W. Baird, in testimony before the House Select Committee on Crime, bluntly stated, "Anyone who smokes marijuana, whether it be a doctor or lawyer, nun or priest, already has a mental problem. They are taking it to escape reality, to get high, to relax. I do not care what euphemism you want to employ, they are mentally ill."[13]

In his testimony Dr. Baird pointed out 25 important facts about marijuana that should be considered before anyone calls for the legalization of the drug. It distorts time, perception, concentration and emotions. In fact, he testified that one of his patient's mother had died with a coronary and when he brought the youngster to the office and announced to him that his mother had died, the kid, being high on "grass," started to break out in uncontrollable laughter.

Furthermore, as one of Dr. Baird's patients pointed out, you will always find in a group smoking marijuana at least one who will suggest going on to stronger materials and since the powers of concentration and rationalization have been altered by marijuana, it takes little prompting from them to push the rest to stronger drugs.

Two medical men, Dr. Harold Kolansky (Child Analysis Division, Philadelphia Association for Psychoanalysis) and Dr. William T. Moore (Hahnemann Medical College of Philadelphia), studied thirty-eight individuals from 13 to 24 years of age, all of whom smoked marijuana two or more times weekly between 1965 and 1970. All showed adverse psychological effects. Some showed neurological signs and symptoms. Eight developed psychoses and four attempted suicide. Included in these cases were 13 unmarried female patients who became sexually promiscuous while using marijuana and seven became pregnant. According to the doctors' findings, "These patients consistently showed very poor social judgment, poor attention span, poor concentration, confusion, anxiety, depression, apathy, passivity, indifference, and often, slowed and slurred speech."[14] Further the doctors reported, "There was marked interference with personal cleanliness, grooming, dressing, and study habits or work or both,"[15] and again, "The decline in academic performance was in direct proportion to the frequency and amount of smoking."[16] The two men concluded, "Clearly, there is, in our patients, a demonstration of an interruption of normal psychological adolescent growth processes following the use of marijuana; as a consequence, the adolescent may reach chronological adulthood without achieving adult mental functioning or emotional responsiveness."[17]

In a subsequent study found in the October 2, 1972, issue of the *Journal of the American Medical Association*, Moore and Kolansky observe that there is a "specific pathological organic response in the central nervous system (CNS) to cannabis products."

Dr. Gabriel G. Nahos of Columbia University's College of Physicians and Surgeons in his book *Marihuana — Deceptive Weed* likewise admits that marijuana intoxication can lead to permanent brain damage. By studying two different groups of Berbers in Morocco (one group smoking marijuana and one group abstaining) Nahos found that marijuana not only has a deleterious effect on the population, but increases the problem of tuberculosis.

Not only is further research pointing up the harmful effects of marijuana in relationship to the brain, but now according to the *Medical Tribune* of April 11, 1973, marijuana users are showing breaks in their chromosome structure. At first such breaks were attributed to LSD, but further research is laying the breakage to marijuana and not LSD.

Unfortunately, a semantical argument has developed over the usage of the words "addictive" and "dependent." Some argue the drug is not addictive, but rather the user only becomes dependent on it. Others, e.g., Dr. Hardin Jones, of the Donner Laboratory at the University of California (Berkeley), maintain that marijuana is habit-forming and with continued use it is addictive. Naturally, the argument makes little difference since (1) few are so sophisticated as to see any difference between "addictive" and "dependent" and (2) since it takes the user away from reality and removes his normal inhibitions, marijuana is harmful apart from either word. Smith, Kline & French Laboratories, in a special report prepared primarily for educators, found marijuana not only impairing the user's ability to drive an automobile, but producing such physical effects as dizziness, dry mouth, dilated pupils and burning eyes, urinary frequency, diarrhea, nausea and vomiting.[18]

Dr. Hardin Jones in his research found marijuana not only habit-forming and addictive with continued use, but also reported (1) that although it does not lead to the use of harder narcotics through chemical addiction, it promotes a curiosity about the harder drugs; (2) that its effect is cumulative, witness that a neophyte needs several joints to "turn on," whereas a professional can get high on one; (3) that it interferes with normal perceptions; (4) that its cumulative impact brings repeated hallucinations that disturb the reference memory, causing (5) wholesale abandonment of goals and ambitions.

Jones goes on to say that marijuana and other drugs are in a very real sense sexual stimulants. Marijuana is a mild aphrodisiac. "It enhances sensitivity and makes a person more receptive to sensual stimuli," he says, "but this condition only lasts a short period of time and chronic marijuana users find that sex activities without the drug are difficult and confusing."[19]

And one world-famous authority on marijuana, Dr. Constandinos J. Miras, of the University of Athens, who has been studying man and marijuana for over twenty-five years, found marijuana users to have abnormal brain wave readings and marked behavioral changes. Longtime users, for example, revealed chronic lethargy and loss of inhibitions for two years after their usage. Many of his subjects were slipping into less demanding jobs as the habit got a firmer grip on them and were variously depressed and exalted, not always sure when they were having hallucinations. Others went through a rapid succession of physical changes — crying, laughing, sluggishness, hunger for sugar, hallucinating. The idea of the so-called harmless use of marijuana is either ignorance or deception. And one State official in Maryland remarked that marijuana not only induces a lethargy in most people, but a dangerous attitude toward the community.

The hallucinogens which are popularly known as psychedelics

(since they produce sensations distorting time, space, sound and color) include LSD, STP and DMT. All hallucinogens create hallucinations which lessen the user's ability to discriminate between fact and fancy, and studies indicate that LSD may cause chromosome damage which could result in mental deficiencies and blood diseases in children born to users. One of the foremost authorities in the United States on LSD is Dr. J. Thomas Ungerleider. He states that, "LSD has been called a conscious-expanding drug. In fact, it is quite the reverse. It decreases one's ability to select and pay attention. Therefore, it decreases conscious functions. Sensations do become intensified. Perception, however, is not enhanced, and visual and auditory acuteness are not revolutionized, but rather are distorted." Since LSD dulls the user's objective judgment, which is replaced by purely subjective values, Dr. Ungerleider says, "LSD seems to affect a person's value system."[20]

Then, too, both the amphetamines and barbiturates are dangerous drugs. Amphetamines, often called pep pills, produce a feeling of excitation which usually manifests itself in appetite loss with an increasing ability to go without sleep for long periods of time. The most common amphetamines are Benzedrine (called Bennies), Dexedrine (called Dexies) and Methadrine (referred to as crystal or speed). The danger, of course, with amphetamines as well as barbiturates is the psychological desire to continue using the drugs. The most common barbiturates are Amytal (referred to as Blue Heavens), Nembutal (or Yellow Jackets) and Seconal (called Red Devils or Red Birds). In the jargon of drug addicts, barbiturates in general are referred to as "goof-balls" and affect the central nervous system and the brain by slowly depressing the mental and physical functions of the body. A person under the influence of a barbiturate will be disoriented to time, place and person and may experience delusions and hallucinations.

Pushing Drugs

Obviously, such drugs cannot be equated with apple pie and vanilla ice cream. And any drug — marijuana, for example, which at one moment makes a person feel so tiny he is not able to step off an eight-inch curb, and yet an hour later makes him feel so huge he could step off a ten-story building — is dangerous. Any individual, who under the influence of marijuana can barrel down the highway at 80 mph and assume he is only traveling 20 mph, or drive through a red light which appears to be green and smash into a row of cars which appeared to be a mile away, is dangerous. And, any drug — LSD, for example, which makes a person feel he can fly like a bird and so takes off from a four-story building only to discover he is flying to his death — is not safe. And, any record company or rock 'n' roll group that lends respectability to such drugs is not only immoral but criminal. And yet, the single greatest offenders (because of their vast popularity) are the Beatles — the missionaries of the drug culture!

The University of Wisconsin student newspaper, *The Daily Cardinal*, stated that the Beatles have "proselytized the use of drugs so subtly that words and conceptions once only common to drug users are found in sentences of teenyboppers and statesmen alike."[21] Such a charge, of course, will doubtless be met with incredulity by many parents whose teens are caught up in the Beatles' orbit. And many teenagers who religiously worship the quartet will vigorously protest such an accusation. Still, in the Beatles' own authorized biography by Hunter Davies the world is informed that they "have used drug slang in their songs."[22] And Davies' only comment was he found it passing strange that several deliberate slang obscenities went unnoticed. For example, he notes that the Beatles were well aware of the sexual implications of the fireman in "Penny Lane," "keeping his engine clean" and that the "finger pie" referred to is, "an old Liverpool obscenity used by Liverpool lads about Liverpool lasses."

When *Time* reported that "Sgt. Pepper's Lonely Hearts' Club Band" album was "drenched in drugs,"[23] Beatle enthusiasts immediately protested. Yet Davies acknowledges that the one album which "showed many traces of their interest in drugs" was the "Sgt. Pepper" album.[24] *Time* further states the Beatles' flirtation with drugs and the drop-out attitude behind such songs like "A Day in the Life," (which was removed from BBC because of its drug implications[25]), disturbs many fans and worried parents. In the "Sgt. Pepper" album, Ringo Starr quiveringly says, "I get high with a little help from my friends." According to *Time*, "Lucy in the Sky With Diamonds" invokes a drug-induced hallucination, and even the initials of the title spell out LSD, though the Beatles plead sheer innocence. Most, however, do not take the Beatles seriously since "Lucy in the Sky With Diamonds" was advertised on posters with the letters, LSD, underlined. *Time* further says that the overall theme of drugs is no coincidence, since all four Beatles have admitted taking LSD occasionally. And concludes, "the fact remains that when the Beatles talk — about drugs, the war in Vietnam, religion — millions listen, and this is the new situation in the pop music world."[26]

In an article entitled, "The New Far-Out Beatles," *Life* magazine quoted Paul McCartney to the effect that LSD was a universal cure-all. McCartney says, "After I took it, it opened my eyes. We only use 1/10 of our brain. Just think what we could accomplish if we could only tap that hidden part! It could mean a whole new world. If politicians would take LSD, there wouldn't be any more war or poverty or famine."[27] In the Beatles' biography, Jane Asher acknowledges McCartney was on LSD; in fact the house "was full of the stuff." And Paul himself agrees although he insists he was the last of the four to try pot and LSD.[28]

According to the official accounting, the Beatles' introduction to drugs began in Hamburg, Germany, where they vulgarly entertained the Germans by shouting in English "Nazis" and told them "to ---- off."[29] John says, "We learned from the Germans that you could stay awake by eating slimming pills, so we did that." Although the pills were supposed to be pretty harmless, they moved on to others like Black Bombers and Purple Hearts.[30] From this the four began to take marijuana and Ringo confessed that the only fun part of their tours were "the hotels in the evening, smoking pot and that."[31] The "that" will be taken up in the next chapter! John, of course, being the more bizarre of the quartet hid his marijuana in a tool box since he had decided to bury it in his garden in case the police came. But as Davies reports, he had it in the box but he "never really got around to digging a hole for it."[32] By July, 1967, the Beatles, throwing caution to the wind, signed a full-page advertisement in the *London Times* calling for the legalization of marijuana in Britain.[33] Then, too, it was while under the influence of marijuana that not only the "Sgt. Pepper" album, but "Magical Mystery Tour," rolled off the assembly line. Davies reports in his biography that the Beatles arrived at the EMI Studios at 7:30 one evening to record "Magical Mystery Tour," but only had the title and a few bars of the music. Paul played the opening bars on the piano, showing the others how it would go. Davies says that Paul, "gestured a lot with his hands and shouted flash, flash, flash, saying it would be like a commercial . . . (John) opened the sporran and took out some pot, which he lit, then passed it around. They all had a drag."[34]

From marijuana the four turned to LSD. Lennon frankly states that LSD was the drug which really pointed the way. He says, "I was suddenly struck by great visions when I first took acid. But you have got to be looking for it before you possibly find it."[35] Davies notes that it was through drugs that they found out about themselves,[36] and also records that their most creative year was 1967 — "the year of LSD, and Maharishi."[37] But he adds, "by August, 1967, they had given up drugs."[38] The *New York Times* explains that it was during the weekend with the guru that they were sure that drugs were of no use.[39] But, few accept this with any permanent degree of validity. In November, 1968, John Lennon was convicted for the possession of marijuana and fined $360. Scotland Yard's dogs sniffed out the drug when they raided John and his Japanese mistress's apartment. They found traces of marijuana in a cigarette rolling machine, in an empty film tin, 219 grains in an envelope and in a binocular's case. Undoubtedly, Lennon was kicking himself for not having dug that hole in the garden!

And by April, 1969, Scotland Yard again pressed into service a three-year-old Labrador, especially trained to sniff out marijuana, and found George Harrison and his wife, Patty, with enough pot for 120 cigarettes. Both pleaded guilty and were fined $600 apiece.[40]

But the most telling testimony that the Beatles are still sanctioning drugs is found in their December, 1968, album, *The Beatles*, which contains the song, "Glass Onion." The lyrics read,

"I told you about strawberry field [referring to "Strawberry Fields Forever," a previous piece written during their "creative-drug-year-of-1967," which the radicals and hippies enjoy listening to under the influence of pot], You know the place where nothin is real, Well here is another place you can go, Where everything flows." Then, too, it should be noted that "Revolution 9," also contained in the same album, is basically comprehensible only under the influence of drugs. Few sane persons could enjoy listening to eight minutes and fifteen seconds of such weird sounds. But, as one college, drug-taking hippie remarked, "It's groovy."

Though inexplicable, "Revolution 9" is presently being used as a background music for communion services at Drake University's Wesley Foundation. The liturgy entitled, "A Celebration Thing Appropriating the Music of the Beatles," is divided into four parts — each consisting of Beatle music and a focal prayer from Malcolm Boyd's *Are You Running With Me Jesus?* According to the press, the students sing along with the Beatle songs and listen reverently to the instrumental records, since Beatle music "seemed to speak of today and of their own lives."[41] If "Revolution 9" seriously speaks to our generation the United States is already in a cultural depression far more serious than most would care to imagine.

Unfortunately, the Beatles' "Yellow Submarine" has recently submerged our young people in a sea of green. Not only the *Detroit Free Press* declares that "Yellow Submarine" smacks of drug talk — particularly with lyrics like "Sky of Blue, Sea of Green, We all live in a Yellow Submarine,"[42] but *Commonweal* charges the Beatles' recording with drug implications.[43] *Time* also reports a Chicago college student, who smokes marijuana regularly, as saying, "You take it when friends get together or when you're going to see *Yellow Submarine.* It's not to solve problems, just to giggle."[44] In drug jargon, of course, submarine-shaped barbiturates (Nembutal) are called "Yellow Jackets" and are used to submerge the user. Hippies call them "downers," and under their influence the user can experience delusions and hallucinations. Obviously, the drug world of the Beatles progresses unrelentingly. John can emerge from his pad and tell our youth to "turn off your mind, relax and float downstream." And *Cavalier* confesses that sound engineers are still trying to reproduce the "Sgt. Pepper" effects for pot smoking.[45]

This is why Art Linkletter referred to the Beatles as the "leading missionaries of the acid society."[46] Testifying before the House Select Committee on Crime, Mr. Linkletter said that the Beatles, rock music and drug culturalist Timothy Leary were strong contributors to the drug crisis facing America today. He said, "Today in the top 40 pop records played by rock groups, I would say at least half of them are a constant secret message to the whole teenage world to drop out, to turn on, to groove with chemicals."[47]

Even the United Nations *Bulletin on Narcotics* pointed out that the successful Beatle album *Sgt. Pepper's Lonely Hearts Club Band* was the "green light" which began the present avalanche of songs exploiting the drug experience. Says the *Bulletin*, "After *Sgt. Pepper* drug-usage themes in rock and roll visibly increased, and there was progressively less outcry against them, presumably because there were scores of such songs now."[48]

Referring to the Beatles' *Yellow Submarine* album, the *Bulletin* reported, "A yellow submarine is not a banana, but is in British slang, a small yellow capsule containing amphetamines or any other drug. One swallows down a capsule and hence it becomes a 'submarine.' "[49] The *Bulletin* concludes its excellent seven page analysis entitled "Approbation of Drug Usage in Rock and Roll Music" by stating, "The end result of it all perhaps, is that when, sooner or later, an urban child — who lives in the ordinary world, not in the pop world where a drug conviction can be shrugged off — is offered a marijuana cigarette or a dose of LSD, he will remember them not as something his health and hygiene teacher spoke warningly about, but as something Mick Jagger, or John Lennon, or Paul McCartney has used and enjoyed."[50]

Since the Beatles are gods to millions of our teenagers today, if drugs are "in" (or considered "in") by the Beatles, they will be considered "in" by the teenagers. For like it or not, whatever the teenagers' gods sanction — the teens have a tendency to sanction. No wonder America is experiencing a drug epidemic! And even if the Beatles were to swear off all drugs tomorrow, their drug records would still continue to circulate. In fact, when the Beatles did say they were temporarily through with drugs, the "Sgt. Pepper" album still continued to circulate the drug message to our youth. If and when the Beatles seriously kick the drug habit, the only concrete evidence worth recording will be their desire to take their drug records off the stands.

Until such time, a word of warning should be sounded to our youth concerning the harmful effects of drugs both individually and nationally. No nation can long survive with her future citizens wallowing in the mire of sin and degradation because their moral inhibitions were destroyed by deconditioning drugs. The Japanese, for example, did not have to put armies in the field with tanks, guns, planes, bullets and bombs when they conquered Manchuria. Instead, as D.C. Parks notes, "Their shock troopers were dope pushers and peddlers. Their guns were syringes; their bayonets were needles; their ammunition was pills, capsules, powders and solutions."[51] Likewise some have argued that the great Chinese civilization of the Nineteenth Century crumbled when 40 per cent of the people became addicted to opium. Yet tragically, *Time* already concedes that marijuana is changing our culture and one California psychopharmacologist, Dr. Leo Hollister, confesses, "For the first time pot is entrenched in our society, with untold millions using the drug. We have passed the point of no return."[52]

And it must be remembered that under the influence of marijuana, one's will to resist is completely compromised and no one knows this better than Israel when she defeated the Arab nations in six days in June, 1967. Part of the Arab problem according to the Israelis — too many Arab soldiers smoke pot.[53]

Chapter XVII

ROCK AND MORALS

"Great civilizations and animal standards of behavior coexist only for short periods." In seeking to diagnose what has happened to our national standards, a newspaper editor assembled the following: (a) an educator speaks out in favor of free love, (b) a man of God condones sexual excursions by unmarried adults, (c) movies sell sex as a commercial commodity, (d) bookstores and cigar stands peddle pornography, (e) a high court labels yesterday's smut as today's literature, (f) record shops feature albums displaying nudes and near nudes, (g) nightclubs stage shows that would have shocked a smoker audience a generation ago, (h) TV shows and TV commercials pour out a flood of sick, sadistic and suggestive sex situations, (i) a campaign is launched to bring acceptance to homosexuality, (j) radio broadcasts present discussions for and against promiscuity, (k) magazines and newspapers publish articles that flagrantly violate the bounds of good taste, (l) four-letter words once heard only in barroom brawls now appear in publications of general distribution.[1]

We have forgotten Santayana's quip, "Those who refuse to learn from history are condemned to repeat it!"

The nations of record in the Old Testament went to their demise primarily because of their animalistic morals. The Canaanites, for example, wallowed in phallic (sexual) worship practices ending in complete debauchery. Israel and Judah both fell because they were enticed to participate in sex worship practice of their pagan neighbors. Babylon, Egypt, Greece and Rome decayed from within with immorality a necessary condition toward national destruction.

Today, of course, the concept of new morality (i.e., "Thou shalt not commit adultery — ordinarily) covers a multitude of sins. Historically speaking, it is neither new nor moral, and most accurately defined by the Biblical writer, "Every man did that which was right in his own eyes." (Judges 21:25) The Scriptures, of course, both Old and New Testament, are very plain in regard to God's will concerning love, sex and morality. And contrary to Eric Burdon of The Animals who states, "The Christian Church says that sex is wrong,"[2] the historic Christian teaching[3] has always held that "marriage is honorable in all, and the bed undefiled but whoremongers and adulterers God will judge." (Hebrews 13:4) The Scriptural teachings regarding love and sex are presented as beautiful and meaningful concepts and the love between a man and a woman is a reflection of the love between Christ and His Church. (Ephesians 5) Sex in Scripture is never considered dirty or sinful as some would have our youth believe, but adultery, fornication and homosexuality[4] are solidly condemned.[5] God knew, of course, and history concurs, that mankind slides from the risque, ribald or bawdy to the pornographic; from the pornographic to the promiscuous and on to total degeneracy.

New morality is simply a throwback to what mankind has experienced in the past, and at the heart is the "sexual revolution"; presently defined as "everyone getting in bed with everyone else." No home, of course, could long endure under such a moral philosophy, much less the Church or the State. And, it would seem quite obvious, at least to this writer, that no one knows this better than the enemies of our Republic. And, again, few have been more effective in bringing about this sexual revolution among our young people than the progenitors and performers of rock 'n' roll. Indeed, present day rock is having a holiday ridiculing religion and morality while at the same time glorifying drugs, sexual promiscuity and revolution — and all the time claiming to do so under the guise or disguise of art! With identical reasoning, consistency would demand that Jack the Ripper be appointed dorm mother under the guise of fair and equal employment.

Many have insisted that rock 'n' roll is a necessary ingredient of the sex revolution. The Rolling Stones' manager frankly stated, "Pop music is sex and you have to hit them [the teenagers] in the face with it."[6] And Sara Davidson is quoted as saying, "The language, the argot of rock is grounded in sexuality."[7] "The stage is our bed and the audience is our broad," say the Jefferson Airplane. "We're not entertaining, we're making love."[8] In fact, the very name itself, "rock 'n' roll," has sexual overtones, and when the music was so christened by Alan Freed, many Negroes smiled in disbelief since to them the two expressions were sexually descriptive.[9] Not only the lyrics but the beat (now christened "erotic rhythms") have become catalysts for the sex rebellion. And, sometimes even the public performance of the actors adds to the degeneracy. The late Jim Morrison of The Doors, appearing in Miami before some 12,000 young people, put on an indecent and immoral exhibition and was ultimately issued six warrants — "two counts of indecent exposure, two for profanity, one of public drunkenness — all misdemeanors — and one felony count of lewd and lascivious behavior in public by exposing his private parts and by -----." Morrison was quoted as saying, "Man, I'd like to see a little nakedness around here. Grab your friend and love him. There are no laws. There are no rules." The performance was so bad that the head of the Greater Miami Crime Commission, Circuit Court Judge, Arthur E. Huttoe, called the performance, "a conspiracy to corrupt the morals of our youth."[10] And this was not the first time that Morrison has been in trouble. Earlier he faced arrest at New Haven, Connecticut, for indecent and immoral behavior, breach of peace, and resisting a police officer.[11] It was also Morrison and The Doors who started a riot in Phoenix, Arizona, in a similar performance when the group sang their top selling immoral number, "Light My Fire." Morrison's philosophy: "I feel spiritual up there [referring to his performing]. Think of us as erotic politicians. I am interested in anything about revolt, disorder, chaos, especially activity that has no meaning."[12]

Jimi Hendrix, who died from a drug overdose, was no better. According to Arnold Shaw, "he sometimes threw himself supine and, holding the instrument on his belly like an upright phallus, pumped it as he lay on his back. And after that, as a clincher, he played the instrument behind his back, shoved it forward between his legs, strummed on it violently, and then propelled it from his groin, as if it were coming climactically out of his fly."[13]

Most rock lyric writers, of course, try to cover their filth with either double entendre meanings or loud sound to bypass "non-progressive" disc jockeys and/or radio station owners. The Beatles, for example, in their biography, confess that in "Penny

Lane," they were well aware of the phallic (sexual) implications of the fireman "keeping his engine clean." "Finger Pie" referred to an old Liverpool obscenity.[14] Also, according to *Commonweal*, the Beatles' "I'm Only Sleeping," and "Baby You Can Drive My Car," both have indecent sexual overtones.[15]

Bob Dylan in his Columbia release, "I'll Be Your Baby Tonight," (sung by Burl Ives) is bad, but pales into insignificance when compared to "Let's Spend the Night Together," "I Can't Get No Satisfaction," "Rhapsody in the Rain," "Wet Dream Over You," "Group Grope," etc.

In the Rolling Stones' "Let's Spend the Night Together," the young lassies are told that the laddie is plenty high and dry, but he will try, try, try, so let's spend the night together. The male paramour will satisfy her every need, and he is sure she will satisfy him. Likewise in the Rolling Stones' "I Can't Get No Satisfaction," (which *Time* reports sold 4.5 million copies[16]) Mick Jagger wails, "I am trying to make some girl." According to *Time*, however, Jagger insists the public didn't understand the dirtiest line. "That is the one where the girl pleads 'baby, come back later next week' cause you see I'm on a losing streak." Says Jagger, "It's just life. That's what really happens to girls. Why shouldn't people write about it?"[17] Instead of disavowing such materials one record promoter actually comments, "The kids with the clean songs are having a hard time coming up with hit songs."[18]

"Rhapsody in the Rain" was banned by many radio stations because, as Gene Taylor of WLS in Chicago noted, "there was no question about what the lyrics and the beat implied, sexual intercourse in a car, making love to the rhythm of the windshield wipers."[19] And the Beatles have a suggestive number that lasts for a minute and forty-two seconds with only three lines, "Why don't we do it in the road? No one will be watching. Why don't we do it in the road?" And, of course, the situation is no better today with such numbers as "Rock 'n' Roll Children," "Flash," "Freaker's Ball," "T.N.U.C.," "Woman From Tokyo," "Rat Bat Blue," etc.

Pop Music and Sex

Dr. Ronald Sprangler, Chief School Medical Officer,

Nottingham, England, charged that teenaged pop music was probably to blame for the mounting obsession with sex.[20] He was doubtless referring to the beat of the music rather than the lyrics, since in 1964 and 1965 the far out suggestive lyrics were pretty well kept in check. But, few who have studied the matter would deny that the hard beat in rock 'n' roll has genuine sexual implications. Dr. Masterson, head of the adolescent out-patient clinic at the Payne-Whitney Psychiatric Clinic, says, "The music is in a way . . . a kind of sexual expression. The beat has genuine sexual implications."[21] Dr. Granby Blaine acknowledges an element of sexuality in the primitive rhythm.[22] And, Dr. Barnard Saibel, Supervisor of the State Community Services in the state of Washington and who attended one of the early Beatle concerts at Seattle, reports, "The music is loud, primitive, insistent, strongly rhythmic and releases in an undisguised way the all-too tenuously controlled, newly acquired physical impulses of the teenager. Mix this up with the phenomenon of mass hypnosis, contagious hysteria and the blissful feeling of being mixed up in an all-embracing, orgiastic experience, and every kid can become 'Lord of the Flies' or the Beatles."[23]

In the Beatles' authorized biography, Davies recognizes that Beatlemania consisted primarily of young ladies who were emotionally, mentally, or sexually excited who either foamed at the mouth or burst into tears, or simply hurled themselves in the direction of the Beatles.[24] The exact scientific reason for hard rock arousing sexual instincts to the dangerous level is not exactly clear. Rock players openly confess, however, that they can "turn on the chicks" at will. But what happens within the teenager is not exactly easy to explain. It has been known, of course, for centuries that music can soothe and incite, and Dr. Howard Hanson in the American Journal of Psychiatry once commented, "music is a curiously subtle art with innumerable, varying emotional connotations. It is made up of many ingredients, and, according to the proportions of those components, it can be soothing or invigorating, ennobling or vulgarizing, philosophical or orgiastic. It has powers for evil as well as for good."[25]

Former rock player, Bob Larson, in conjunction with a physician, offers some light on the relationship between hard rock and promiscuous sex. He contends that the low frequency vibrations of the bass guitar, coupled with the driving beat of the drum, have a decided effect upon the cerebrospinal fluid. The fluid in turn affects the pituitary gland which directs the secretion of hormones, resulting in an abnormal balance of primarily the sex and adrenalin hormones. Instead of their normal regulatory function in the body, these hormones secreted under such conditions produce radical changes in the blood sugar and calcium of the body. Since the brain is nourished exclusively by blood sugar, it ceases to function properly, causing moral inhibitions to either drop to a dangerous low or be wiped out altogether.[26]

Under marijuana, of course, one's moral inhibitions are also destroyed and this is what Frank Zappa of the Mothers of Invention was referring to when he said that via new morality, a teenager can get the same effect from music that he can from dope.[27] And, it is what Timothy Leary was referring to when he charged that rock 'n' roll is as much a deconditioner as psychedelic drugs. Leary contends that rock 'n' roll is "designed to blow your mind and expand your conditioned reflexes," and "listening to a Beatles album is an hour of deconditioning."[28] Vance Packard put it like this, "The youngsters in darkened audiences can let go all inhibitions in a quiet, primitive sense when the Beatles cut loose. They can retreat from rationality and individuality. Mob pathology takes over, and they are momentarily freed of all civilization's restraints."[29] Packard also agrees that the Beatles have become particularly adept at giving girls this relief which synchronizes with Richard St. Ives' argument that the Beatles have become a kind of modern-day primitive religion — in fact, a fertility cult. Sara Davidson said it like this, "there is some of the groupie in almost every girl who watches a rock singer in leather pants and metal hardware, snapping his body and making a sound so loud it is very near pain."[30]

If they are miniature Molech priests, few will argue with their backlog of experience; from Paul, who mated at the age of fifteen,[31] to John and his escapades with Yoko Ono. When Ringo reported that the only fun part of touring was "the hotel in the evening, smoking pot and that," there is no doubt what was involved in the "that." In the "sacred" biography all are informed, "we got drunk a lot. You couldn't help it. They would send us drinks all the time so we naturally drank too much. We had a lot of girls. We soon realized that they were easy to get. Girls are girls, fellows are fellows. Everything improved 100%. We had been meek and mild musicians at first, now we became a powerhouse."[32]

Of course, among rock musicians this is standard operating procedure. Few would be shocked at George for stating, "I was trying to --- Johnny Guitar's little sister at the time."[33] But for parents who somehow have been forced to believe the Beatles "are a quartet of fine, wholesome, uplifting musicians, who hold young womanhood in highlight and respect," the facts, unfortunately, speak otherwise. When the Beatles were in this country in 1964, all four could have been arrested in Las Vegas, Nevada, for statutory rape. They were involved with two 14-year-old girls in their bedroom all night.[34]

And, for an encore, George vulgarly, after first admiring John's line about "dropping one's knickers" in "I Am the Walrus," announces that the Beatles will be using one particular four-letter word in future compositions. After repeating it six times, he comments, "See, it doesn't mean a thing, so why can't you use it in a song? We will eventually. We haven't started yet."[35] In truth, the whole authorized biography is replete with this and similar four-letter expressions to such an extent that no serious reviewer of the book could recommend it for family reading. George's particular four-letter word finally made its appearance in Lennon's "Working Class Hero."

The love, sex and nonmoral philosophy of the Beatles was summarized by Jane Asher (Paul McCartney's former girl friend) who frankly told the press, "I certainly don't object to people having children when they are not married, and I think it is quite sensible to live together before you are married."[36] True to conviction, Paul and Jane did just that for a number of years, according to their biography. In fact, Paul first read about his M.B.E. award while returning to England from a vacation abroad with Miss Asher.

John, however, has to be the winner when it comes to flaunting morality. "All you've got to do to prove your manhood," says John, "is --- a woman."[37] Although he was forced into his first marriage with Cynthia in a nonscandalous affair, his immoral antics with his Japanese girl friend, Yoko Ono, (now his wife) have reached world-wide proportions. No wonder John wrote "Woman is the Nigger of the World." His own actions have forced his women at least to be less than human. When he says "we leave her flat" he was or should have been thinking of his own Cynthia.

Ono, who has been described as an avant-garde psychedelic artist from Japan who once made a film entirely composed of 365 shots of naked bottoms, was still married to an American film-maker when she announced that she was expecting a baby via Mr. Lennon. Lennon's only comment — "Babies make the world happier, and that's our scene!" To add moral insult to moral insult, however, John and his Japanese mistress contrived to have their pictures taken in the absolute raw and placed on their album mistakenly labeled, "The Two Virgins." The album cover was so offensive that initially only Sweden permitted it into the country. Now, however, even though ruled obscene by the New Jersey Supreme Court Judge, Nelson X. Mintz, it has been released in the United States through Tetragrammaton, Inc., Los Angeles, and promptly one of its renditions, "The Ballad of John and Ono," went to the top of the hit list. "If people can't face up to the fact of other people being naked or smoking pot," reasons John, "then we're never going to get anywhere."[38]

When John made the understatement of the year, "The world thinks we are an ugly couple," he wasn't, unfortunately, referring to the despicable album, but to his honeymoon in which he and Yoko Ono spent their entire seven days in a public bed in Amsterdam, "as a protest against violence everywhere." From the public marriage bed, avant-garde Ono remarked, "Take your trousers off before you start being violent."[39] Even Mrs. Mimi Smith (who raised Lennon) admits that when she saw him in the bed scene on television, she went weak at the knees. She said she raised him with a certain standard, and that "John knows better, but he has been influenced by his new wife."[40]

Whether he knows or not is academic since actions speak louder than words, and his open display of sexual promiscuity can hardly be considered ideal standards either for Christian teenagers or the teenagers of the world. Fred Sparks did not miss the situation by far when he said, "After three months researching rock, I'm convinced the stars have the morals of a rabbit hutch. Compared to the private lives of the Beatles and the Rolling Stones, members of the Jet Set are so many Victorian tea-party pushers."[41]

Chapter XVIII

ROCK AND REVOLUTION

David Triesman, a twenty-year-old radical recently expelled from Essex University in England, was asked by the *London Sunday Times* why the left-liberal and permissive institutions such as Essex, Sussex, Cambridge, Oxford and the London School of Economics in England had experienced violent student rebellions while the strictly disciplined vocational and technical education colleges had not. Triesman replied, "The new sexual permissiveness, [and] the liberal policies at places like Essex and Sussex were precisely what sparked off the student protest movement. You will see, Dr. Sloman and other vice chancellors will be the Kerenskys in our Red Revolution. When they are swept away, we shall properly remodel our society."[1]

Alice Widener, authority on the Communist New Left, observes that the former President of Columbia, Grayson Kirk, was indeed a Kerensky-type who was swept away in a Students for a Democratic Society Red Revolution, April, 1968. Harvard SDS'ers, brazeningly displaying their Communist symbol (the large red clenched fist on the back of their T-shirts[2]), were also calling for Pusey's demise. The National Secretary of the SDS, Michael Klonsky, acknowledged on May 30, 1969, that the SDS's primary task is to "build a Marxist-Leninist revolutionary movement."[3] Klonsky is a son of a one-time official of the Communist Party, U.S.A. and describes himself as a "revolutionary communist."[4]

With such revolutionary rapport between American and British leftists, it is no accident that the Beatles are the "cultural heroes" to both sides of the Atlantic. According to the *Christian Century*, not only are the Beatles the New Left's favorite cultural heroes,[5] but the *Saturday Evening Post* reports, "To British intellectuals, the Beatles are carrying the banner of the British beat generation, and their success represents a breakthrough for the social rebellion the Beatles represent."[6]

What does the "revolution" or "social rebellion" entail which solidifies the Atlantic Union and makes the Beatles so strategic?

What have the Beatles said or done to so ingratiate themselves with those who eat, drink and think revolution? To come by these answers is to penetrate to the heart of the revolution itself. And as one approaches the center, it soon becomes evident that students are merely the cannon fodder for the planners and real instigators.

"Students," explained Ernest Mandel, editor of the Belgian *La Gauche* (The Left) and a key organizer behind the Communist riots and strikes in France that nearly toppled de Gaulle, "are the detonators in the formula for triggering off a social explosion creating a revolutionary situation."[7] Mandel, who has spent considerable time in Cuba, has been banned by the French Government for his role in seeking to overthrow, with Marxist-Leninist principles, the French Government. The program he instituted in France was "to put forth, through mass strikes and mass movements, concrete demands and goals which are unacceptable to the capitalist system and cannot be granted within the capitalist system."[8] Mandel insisted in an address before the Fourth Annual Conference of Socialist Scholars, held at Rutgers University, that the same technique can work to bring down the government of the United States!

It was at the Second Annual Conference of Socialist Scholars that a paper, written by a professor at the University of California (San Diego) who could not be present because he was attending a Communist conference in Prague, was read. His paper said, "The Marxian idea of socialism is not radical enough; we must develop the moral, sexual rebellion of our youth."[9] The professor, Herbert Marcuse, considered "gospel" by the New Left along with Marx, Lenin and Mao, considers himself a Freudian-Marxist. In his work, *Eros and Civilization*, he postulates the proposition that civilization will crumble if its energy can be dissipated by free love and an open sexual revolution. Man, he reasons, has only so much energy; by funneling it into a multitude of sex practices, little will be left to build a productive and prosperous society, thus precipitating a Marxist revolution.

Drugs and Sex

This general philosophy, of course, is not new. In a basic

anti-Christian.[23] George Bernard Shaw, for example, could say, "If Jesus had been indicted in a modern court, he would have been examined by two doctors, found to be obsessed by a delusion, declared incapable of pleading and sent to an asylum." And not inconsistently it was this same Shaw who referred to Lenin as the greatest Fabian of them all,[24] and felt "execution" was fitting punishment for those who resisted his particular brand of socialism.[25]

The Beatles' public pronouncements, in the main, could not please this Socialist-Communist coterie more and, therefore, although the Beatles might not fully understand all the ramifications of their usefulness, they have been considered more than acceptable by the Left.

Hence, rock 'n' roll in general and the Beatles in particular have a special significance to the disrupters of society for their promotion of drugs, avant-garde sex and atheism. The revolution, though sometimes veiled, is fundamentally against Christianity and Christianity's moral concepts. Karl Marx sought to dethrone God before he set out to destroy capitalism and private property.

Indeed, John Lennon uses the same approach of first dethroning God before destroying property in his telling piece, "Imagine." Note the order in which he destroys the concepts of heaven, hell, religion, national sovereignty and private property.

Imagine there's no heaven
It's easy if you try
No hell below us
Above us only sky.
Imagine all the people
living for today. . . .

Imagine there's no countries
It isn't hard to do
Nothing to kill or die for
And no religion, too.
Imagine all the people
living life in peace. . . .

Imagine no possessions
I wonder if you can.
No need for greed or hunger
a brotherhood of man
Imagine all the people
Sharing all the world.

You may say I'm a dreamer
But I'm not the only one
I hope someday you'll join us
And the world will be as one.

Since the rebellion or revolution not only sustains, but feeds on the sexual revolution, it is quite natural that the revolutionaries are against morality and Biblical Christianity which impedes the sexual revolution. If morality, particularly the sexual mores of a society, is under fire, then Christianity is necessarily under attack, for Christianity supplies social ethics its metaphysical underpins. There is good reason, therefore, why the Red revolutionists who are dedicated to attacking Christianity and the morals of Christianity look to the Beatles as their "cultural heroes." Of course, to the naive and uninitiated, the Beatles simply appear as four fine, wholesome, uplifting musicians, but to those who peer at the clenched fisted, radical revolutionists on our college campuses (and their useful idiots), the Beatles take on a vastly different hue and tone.

Many people realized for the first time the Beatles' potential anti-Christian stance when Lennon struck with his statement that the quartet was "more popular than Jesus."

In the Beatles' biography John, George and Paul are actively portrayed as hating Cliff Richard — not because he was popular, but primarily as John explains because of "Cliff's sort of Christian image."[26] George, too, also confessed that he used to laugh reading "about Cliff Richard being a Christian."[27] Lennon being the artist, however, went in for more direct assaults on Christianity and turned out anti-religious cartoons including one with Christ on the cross wearing a pair of bedroom slippers.[28]

When the Beatles initially came to the United States back in

1964 their press officer, Derek Taylor, tried to describe them. "It's incredible, absolutely incredible," said Taylor. "Here are these four boys from Liverpool. They're rude, they're profane, they're vulgar, and they've taken over the world. It's as if they had founded a new religion. They're completely anti-Christ. I mean, I am anti-Christ as well, but they're so anti-Christ, they shock me, which isn't an easy thing."[29]

In an interview with *Playboy* magazine, Paul McCartney, in response to a *Playboy* observation regarding the Beatles' irreverent attitude, commented, "We probably seem to be antireligious because of the fact that none of us believe in God."[30] John said they weren't quite sure what they were "but I know that we're more agnostic than atheistic." Ringo, after hearing Paul remark, "But, believe it or not, we are not anti-Christ," stated, "Just anti-Pope and anti-Christian."[31] Paul closed the subject by pondering, "In America, they're fanatical about God. I know somebody over there who said he was an atheist. The papers nearly refused to print it because it was so shocking that somebody could actually be an atheist."

John Lennon, the spokesman for the Beatles, published his rude, profane and vulgar, *A Spaniard in the Works,* in the summer of 1965. Our Lord was sacrilegiously attacked in a sleazy account of not-so-subtle secondary meanings. Lennon portrayed Christ under the guise of a character called Jesus El Pifco, and described Him as, "a garlic eating, stinking, little yellow greasy fascist bastard Catholic Spaniard."[32]

Writing in double and triple meanings, Lennon played on such words as "thirsty year ago," meaning "thirty years ago," "Laird," meaning "Lord," "can you heffer forgive me Jesus," meaning "can you ever forgive me Jesus," "Her eldest sod," meaning "her eldest son," "some bad Jews," meaning "some bad news" and other expressions like "stable," "mother," "Catholic," "bastard," "Spanish" and "foreigner."

Referring to Jesus' imagined love life, Lennon comments that, "whistling a quaint Spanish refrain Jesus was dreaming of his loved wombs back home in their little white fascist bastard huts." One reviewer of the book commented, "To the budding author's credit, the book is better than his first — and unquestionably dirtier ... At such an early date after publication some older teenagers can be heard quoting from the book. Usually, of course, the passages that cannot be printed in the family newspaper." The reviewer stated that Lennon "shows possible irreverence for fatherhood, religion, etc.," but, "is not likely to affect many outsiders' immediate acquaintances."[33]

The far left publication, *Realities*, grants the book is "pretty dirty." But the reviewer feels that such dirt is a social virtue and strongly recommends it. In commenting on Lennon's chapter, "We Must Not Forget the General E------," he says, "We try to, we hope to, we pretend we have. So, we make its manifestations costly; exorbitant legal costs for adultery and abortion ... expensive, dangerous and poorly administered brothels, and expensive pornography which is also hard to get." *Realities* concluded its review by stating that the book is "sort of like *Playboy*, actually for voyeurs, but slick enough to keep next to New Republic."[34]

Parade, however, a family magazine, reviewed the book and warned, "Parents who believe the Beatles are a quartet of fine, wholesome, uplifting musicians who hold young womanhood in high light and respect, might do well to peruse Lennon's second work [A Spaniard in the Works] for an insight into at least one literate Beatle's morality and mentality."[35]

In the final chapter, "I Believe, Boot," the dialogue proceeds, "Hello, you Rev boy. Well Mr. Wabooba, may I call you Wog? What is the basic problem you are facing?" Answer — "You white trash Christian boy." Instead of Father, Son and Holy Spirit, Lennon writes "Fahter, Sock, and Mickey Most." Instead of God, it's Griff. "In Griff's eye, we are all a bunch of bananas, swinging in the breeze — waiting as it were Wabooba to be peeled."[36]

By Christian standards and certainly by most Western standards, the Beatles symbolize a distinct and unmistakable form of degeneracy. By their own admissions and actions or the statements of their press officer, they are rude, profane, vulgar, irreverent, pornographic, uncouth, smutty, antichrist and immoral.

Yet it was to this list of qualities that John Lennon dropped his literary bombshell with two initial published statements,

"Christianity will go" and "We're more popular than Jesus now."[37] Nearly a month passed before the statement was further expanded to "Christianity will go. It will vanish and shrink. I needn't argue about that, I'm right, and I will be proved right. We're more popular than Jesus now."[38]

In commenting on this much of the Lennon statement, the liberal commentator, Charles McCabe of the *San Francisco Chronicle,* remarked, "I don't think the young fellow is mad or anything. He is a victim of belief which often erodes intelligence. It is a belief often common to those who reap the strange rewards the theatrical life can yield. He thinks he's God. Naturally, he's a bit jealous of those notices his Son has been getting all through these centuries. Since he's a nice kid, I hope he gets over his delusion before it begins to hurt him. But there it is; the light weights who don't want to play Hamlet, want to play God."[39]

By August, 1966, the full quote was finally printed in this country. "Christianity will go," says Lennon, "It will vanish and shrink. I needn't argue about that; I'm right and I will be proven right. We're more popular than Jesus now; I don't know which will go first — rock 'n' roll or Christianity. Jesus was all right, but His disciples were thick and ordinary. It's them twisting it that ruins it for me."[40]

Although some young people became highly indignant and even some rock stations ceased playing Beatle records, most Beatle fan clubs came to the rescue of Lennon with some going so far as to shout, "John, not Jesus, John, not Jesus."[41] In the official biography John confesses that he gave a "slight retraction,"[42] although Davies ironically reports that the "concerts in the Bible belt were the best of all."[43] Nevertheless, when Lennon and his quartet saw the tour stand in financial jeopardy because of his statement, his "slight retraction" comment consisted of, "I am not anti-God, anti-Christ, or anti-religion. I was not knocking it. I was not saying that we are greater or better."[44] And George seconded it by noting, "I know him. He believes in Christianity, but I do agree with him that Christianity is on the wane."[45]

However, since the world is also on the wane, Harrison's statement does lose its punch. And, it is only fair to speculate whether the decline of the one might not somehow or other be related to the decline of the other. But as all Christians know, Christ Himself was never in any popularity contest, and even in His own day, few were willing to take up the cross and follow Him. The disparity between our Lord and the quartet is almost complete, for Christ Himself had nothing of material value, much less millions of dollars from shrieking before teenagers. Christ lived a life of poverty and selflessness while John and his troupe can hardly be considered poverty stricken. Of course, for Christians the great contrast comes in those who love Christ not as a popular figure, but as Lord and Saviour. Few are laying their dead away in the name of John Lennon. But those who have laid their dead away in the name of Christ have received a hope that can never be received by either the example or the message of Beatle Lennon.

Lennon more truthfully told the *Washington Post* that he was bored with the Church of England and went into atheism. He is now influenced by Hugh Schonfield's *The Passover Plot*, which contends the Scriptural account of Jesus is a hoax.[46]

And Harrison is presently leaning toward Hinduism, believing "much more in the religions of India" than anything he ever learned from Christianity.[47] Hence, Paul perhaps summarizes the four best. He describes them as "four iconoclastic, brass-hard, post-Christian, pragmatic realists."[48]

Therefore, most Christians were irate when the British Broadcasting Company (BBC) asked John Lennon to play the role of Jesus Christ in a television series costing nearly $780,000. The producer, Peter G. Scott, who is to make the new series, stated that he knew he would be upsetting some by his choice of Lennon, but said, "I think he would be ideal as Jesus. Lennon is to preach the Sermon on the Mount, take part in the feeding of the multitude, and act out the agonies of the crucifixion," and according to Scott, "We shall show him physically as a man who didn't wash too often, never shaved, didn't have many changes of clothes and spoke to primitive people in a language they could understand."[49] In other words, Christ is to be portrayed as a beatnik (i.e., one who sometimes bathes) which will immediately please the "dirt" crowd and revolutionists who already have posters published declaring Jesus Christ a beatnik revolutionist, wanted for sedition.

Needless to say, the Beatles' revolution against Christianity, if Lennon accepts the role, takes on even greater significance and a new twist since the antichrist is now to play Christ. With this accomplishment under his belt, few can compete with Lennon as king of the bizarre and profane.

Of course, if the Beatles were only the vanguard of the destruction and/or vilification of Christianity and Biblical morality, the Red revolutionists would be pleased, for at the heart of Marxism, as previously stated, is the dethronement of God. Karl Marx was not only a bitter atheist but actively sought to obliterate Christianity and its accompanying morality. *Pravda*, therefore, has not overlooked the favor. In a dispatch datelined Moscow, UPI wired, "The Soviet Communist Party newspaper, *Pravda*, praised Beatle George Harrison today for telling a news conference in New York that American troops should not be in Vietnam. It also gave Beatle John Lennon, who stirred up a storm in the United States by saying the mop-haired quartet was more popular than Jesus, a pat on the back because 'He likes the Soviet Union very much.' *Pravda* said such statements by popular teenaged idols like the Beatles have an important impact on youth."[50]

Communists Enjoy Beatles

Israel G. Young, columnist for the pro-Communist *Sing Out!* publication,[51] pointed out back in 1964 that "the Beatles have gone further than all the contemporary folk song writers in that they are not so obvious in their philosophy."[52] The Beatles, however, are not totally incognito. For example, on the front cover of their drenched-in-drugs album, "Sgt. Peppers' Lonely Hearts Club Band," the Beatles selected a montage of familiar faces crowding about themselves. Ringo frankly admits, "We just thought we would like to put together a lot of people we like and admire."[53] *Time* magazine acknowledges that appearing on the photo montage, among others, is Karl Marx.[54]

Christians seemingly should have been alerted to the British foursome in August, 1964, when Derek Taylor admitted they were antichrist. But, certainly all Americans should have been forewarned that something was wrong in March, 1964. In a UPI dispatch from Carnegie Hall, New York, Americans were informed that the Communist newspaper, *The Worker*, was celebrating its 40th anniversary, and that over 1,000 persons who attended were asked to give forty $1 bills — one for each year — inside an envelope as a contribution to the paper. The article reports that before the speeches began, David Landsman, "a young beatnik folksinger," sang "We Shall Overcome," (Pete Seeger's composition[55]) and dedicated it to the Soviet-executed spies, Julius and Ethel Rosenberg. The UPI dispatch concluded, "Landsman noted that it was on the same Carnegie Hall stage that the British rock 'n' roll singers, the Beatles, made their American debut several weeks ago. He said the Beatles marched in a ban-the-bomb protest march two years ago and lauded him as 'one of us.' Everybody cheered the Beatles."[56]

One year later *Insurgent* magazine, the official voice of the W.E.B. DuBois Clubs of America (which J. Edgar Hoover in his *Law Enforcement Bulletin*, October, 1964, mentioned was spawned by the Communist Party, U.S.A.), in its very first issue paid homage to the Beatles with an article by the editor, "The Beatles — Those Lucky Lads From Liverpool." The article contends that "the social consciousness of the Beatles has gotten little play in the American press, but it becomes evident to the followers of the group who are tuned into such things."[57]

Nothing, however, has so excited the followers of the group to "tune in" as the Beatles' $10 album, "The Beatles," in which the Communist *Daily World* noted "cuts of brilliance." The paper praised George Harrison's little ditty, "Piggies," for its characterization of bourgeoisie society in terms of different classes of pigs.

> 'Have you seen the little piggies — crawling in the dirt — and for all the little piggies — life is getting worse — always having dirt to play around in. Have you seen the bigger piggies — in their starched shirts — you will find the bigger piggies — stirring up the dirt — always have clean shirts to play around — In their eyes,

there is something lacking — what they need is a damn good whacking. Everywhere there is lots of piggies — living piggy lives — you can see them out for dinner — with their piggy wives — clutching forks and knives to eat their bacon.'

The *Daily World* also felt that the lyrics of "Why Don't We Do It in the Road," were rare since, "It is hard to imagine a better put-down of the excesses of the white blues singers."[58] The *Daily World* also briefly mentioned "Revolution 9," an eight minute and fifteen second piece which, if listened to under the right ingredients of drugs, could spell revolution with a capital R. But, stranger than fiction, the Communist newspaper never uttered a word about the first number on the album, "Back in the U.S.S.R.," which is currently the top hit in the Soviet Union. Obviously the lyrics have left even the Reds speechless; particularly the line, "You don't know how lucky you are boy, Back in the U.S. Back in the U.S. Back in the U.S.S.R."

Rolling Stones Get Into Act

Sharing the Communist *Daily World's* review sheet, which incidentally the *World* gathered from the Liberation News Service/Mayday wire service, not unexpectedly was the Rolling Stones' new album, "Beggar's Banquet." Mick Jagger, head of the Rolling Stones, is one of the few Beatle friends, or as their biography records, "Apart from Mick Jagger, of the Rolling Stones, the Beatles have picked up no friends from the pop music world."[59] Jagger, like the Beatles, has been both drug-oriented (having received a three-month sentence for possession of narcotics[60]) and a participant in the sexual revolution. At one point Jagger said he was happy about becoming a father when he got a particular young lady in trouble, but "says he doesn't plan to marry."[6+] Jagger has also been a student at the Fabian Socialist London School of Economics,[62] where in January, 1969, the slogan of the students was "Kill the Bourgeoisie." The London School of Economics, of course, was established by the pro-Communist Fabian Socialists of Great Britain under the leadership of Sidney Webb, whose monumental volume entitled,

Soviet Communism — A New Civilization, later turned out to be written not by Webb, but by the Soviet Foreign Office in praise of the U.S.S.R. and Joseph Stalin.[63]

According to *Time* magazine, the Rolling Stones' album, "Beggar's Banquet," was held up in its distribution because of its offensive album cover which consisted of a lavatory wall scrawled in what is politely called graffiti but more realistically termed, filth on bathroom walls. The photo also contained an unpleasant-looking toilet with a caption, "God Rolls His Own." *Time* further says that one of the songs on the album entitled, "Street Fighting Man" was released earlier on a single to be played during the Democratic National Convention, but was promptly boycotted by most Chicago radio stations.[64] Part of the lyrics said,

> Everywhere I hear the sound of marching, charging feet, boy — the sound of fear and the time is ripe for rising in the streets, boy. Cause, what can a poor boy do — except sing a rock 'n' roll band — cause sleepy London town — is no place for a street fighting man. The time is right for violent revolution.

Needless to say, the Rolling Stones are definitely considered "in" by the Red revolutionists on our campuses along with the Beatles. And, according to the Communist *Daily World*, "the Stones may not be sure where their heads are, but their hearts are out in the street ... the question is where will the Stones (and their audience) go from here? My guess would be to the streets."[65]

The objectionable Rolling Stones' album cover, however, was not a first. In June, 1966, Capitol Records had released 500,000 copies of a Beatle album which it had to recall at a cost of $250,000 because disc jockeys refused to handle it. On this album cover, the Beatles were dressed in butcher smocks, amid chunks of raw meat and bones, and the decapitated heads of dolls. Although the Beatles pleaded "pop art" others saw it as sick, bestial and even sadistic. Few thought it healthy and uplifting for America's teenagers! But then whoever believed that America's enemies really wanted American teenagers to feast on healthy, uplifting materials!

Early in December, 1963, the *New York Times* portrayed the Beatles as "spokesmen for the new, noisy anti-establishment generation," and part of the strong reaction against England's southern middle class.[66] The *Los Angeles Times* characterized them as "the epitome of the successful rebel rebelling at many of the middle class values."[67] The truth of the matter is that the Beatles economically were, in fact, middle class, and even John Lennon's maternal aunt, Mrs. Mimi Smith, admitted, "John didn't grow up in a slum. He just likes for people to think that. I brought all the furniture in this room with me from the other house which he did grow up in. I get terribly annoyed when he is billed as a street-corner boy. We had a very comfortable home and a good area overlooking the golf links with five parks nearby and the Welch Mountains in the distance, and John had the whole of the top floor of the house to do as he liked."[68]

But ideologically speaking, because of their basic anti-Christian philosophy, the Beatles have not chosen to align themselves with the forces of freedom in the struggle that is presently going on in the world today between communism (which is essentially atheism) and freedom. John Lennon and Paul McCartney, for example, were among 125, including Jean Paul Sartre and Gunnar Myrdal, who called for the immediate American withdrawal in Vietnam.[69] Naturally such action on their part endears them even more to the Red revolutionists on campuses who are pulling for the victory of North Vietnam. Then, too, Harrison has stated that the American military draft is "diabolical" and that we could do without it, although he doesn't point out that England itself has abolished the draft and is not faring well. Harrison told *Holiday* magazine, "You have got to get them hip to all this government bull, all the governments, all the religions, and all that bull that has been going on and on, and it will just keep going on and on unless we hip the people."[70] John frankly confesses, "I have seen England and the USA, and I don't care for either of their governments. They're all the same. Look what they are doing here. They stopped Radio Caroline and tried to put the Stones away while they are spending billions on nuclear armaments and the place is full of United States' bases that no one knows about. They are all over North Wales."[71]

The potential effect the Beatles can have on a nation has been adequately illustrated by the *Saturday Evening Post.* "The British Empire has all but vanished," states the *Post* "and . . . the whole structure of English life has had to be broken and reformed, and in this difficult surgical operation, which might have cruelly disturbed the psyche of a nation, the Beatles have acted as antic anestheists (burlesque druggers)."[72] The article further states, "There is an inescapable sense of holiday in England — a springy, frothy sense of release. In many ways it is deplorable. In many ways it is sad. For myself, I would rather have a power back with the headaches, but there is no denying that it is fun. The Beatles have been the minstrels of this emancipation."[73] Although it is incredible to suppose that the demise of an empire is an emancipation, nonetheless, the potential power of the Beatles cannot be underestimated. Of course, some saw the decline and fall of the British Empire in 1964, when the British Government presented the Beatles with the Members of the Order of the British Empire Awards [MBE]. *The London Daily Mail* ran a caption reading, "One a.m. picture: Beatles, Paul home early from a holiday in Portugal with girl friend, Jane Asher, saw the MBE announced in the early edition of the *Daily Mail.*" One American publisher noted that nothing could better describe the fall of the British Empire in its present sad state than the fact that the Queen announced the Beatles as Members of the Order of the British Empire on her birthday. In days gone by such honors came to men and women who had accomplished a great deal in the field of arts, letters, business, science and medicine, i.e., men and women who had spent a lifetime working to make something of themselves and to contribute to the welfare and knowledge of their fellowmen. But now, for some reason, she finds a reason to give it to, "four absurd characters."[74] Medals, of course, from all over the world poured back to the Queen in protest, and one, a Lt.,Col. Frederick Wagg, returned all 12 of his medals in protest over the Beatles' receiving the MBE award. Wagg had won all his awards in WW I, WW II, and the Afghan Campaign. He also wrote the Prime Minister of the Labor Party in protest and followed it through by taking the Labor Party out of his will.[75]

Lennon Confesses

For those finding the above material too harsh on the Beatles, we would conclude this chapter by suggesting a reading of the confessions of John Lennon which appeared in *Rolling Stone* magazine.[76] Lennon begins by admitting, "There is a better book on the Beatles [i.e., better than Hunter Davies' *The Beatles*] by Michael Brown, *Love Me Do.* That was a true book. He wrote how we were, which was b-------. You can't be anything else in a pressurized situation . . . those things are left out by Davies, about being b-------. F------ big b------, that's what the Beatles were. You have to be a b------ to make it, that's a fact, and the Beatles are the biggest b------- on Earth."[77]

When Yoko Ono, his wife, asked him how the Beatles managed to keep such a clean image, John Lennon replied, "Everybody wants the image to carry on. You want to carry on. The press around, too, because they want the free drinks and the free w----- and the fun."[78]

Lennon in his confessions says that he has been on pills since he was 17 and soon after turned to pot. He then says, "I have always needed a drug to survive. The others, too, but I always had more, more pills, more of everything because I am more crazy probably."[79]

When the interviewer commented, "There are a lot of obvious LSD things you did in the music," John replies, "Yes."[80]

As we just mentioned, Lennon castigates Davies' book because, "There was nothing about the orgies and the ---- that happened on tour." He says that the "Beatles tours were like the Fellini film Satyricon. We had that image. Man, our tours were like something else, if you could get on our tours, you were in. They were Satyricon, all right. Wherever we went, there was always a whole scene going, we had our four separate bedrooms. We tried to keep them out of our rooms. Derek's and Neil's rooms were always full of junk and w----- and who - the ----- knows what, and policemen with it."[81]

"When we hit a town, we hit it. There was no - - - - - - - about. There's photographs of me crawling about in Amsterdam on my knees coming out of w- - - - houses and things like that. The police escorted me to the places, because they never wanted a big scandal, you see."[82]

Regarding revolution, Lennon confesses, "I resent the implication that the Stones [Rolling Stones] are like revolutionaries and that the Beatles weren't. If the Stones were or are, the Beatles really were too."[83] He further says, "I wanted to say my piece about revolution. I wanted to tell you, or whoever listens, to communicate, to say 'What do you say?' this is what I say."[84]

"On one version I said 'Count me in' about violence, in or out, because I wasn't sure. But the version we put out said 'Count me out' because I don't fancy a violent revolution happening all over. I don't want to die; but I begin to think what else can happen, you know, it seems inevitable."[85]

"*Revolution 9* was an unconscious picture of what I actually think will happen when it happens; that was just like a drawing of revolution."[86]

When asked about violent revolution being the end of the world, he replies, "Not necessarily. They say that everytime, but, I don't really believe it, you see. If it is, ok, I'm back to where I was when I was 17 and at 17 I used to wish a - - - - - earthquake or revolution would happen so that I could go out and steal and do what the blacks are doing now. If I was black, I'd be all for it; if I were 17, I'd be all for it, too. What have you got to lose? Now, I've got something to lose. I don't want to die, and I don't want to be hurt physically, but if they blow the world up - - - - it, we're all out of our pain then, forget it, no more problems!"[87]

Lennon further says, "I am wearing a Chairman Mao badge. I'm just beginning to think he is doing a good job. I would never know until I went to China. I'm not going to be like that, I was just always interested enough to sing about him, I just wondered what the kids who were actually Maoists were doing."[88]

When asked about the Beatles' "Give Peace A Chance?" Lennon replies, "in my secret heart I wanted to write something that would take over 'We Shall Overcome.' " However, he now thinks his new song, "Working Class Hero," is the revolutionary song. "It is really just revolutionary. I think its concept is revolutionary and I hope it's for workers and not for tarts and fags . . . I think it's for the people like me who are the working class — whatever, upper or lower — who are supposed to be processed into the middle classes, through the machinery, that's all . . . I'm saying it is a revolutionary song; not the song itself but that it's a song for the revolution."[89]

Part of "Working Class Hero" reads, "As soon as you are born they make you feel small; By giving you no time instead of it all; Till the pain is so big you feel nothing at all; A working class hero is something to be, A working class hero is something to be.

"Keep you doped with religion and sex and T.V.; And you think you are so clever and classless and free; But you're still f------ peasants as far as I can see; A working class hero is something to be, A working class hero is something to be."

Lennon concludes, "Yes, a working class hero is something to be. If you want to be a hero well just follow me; If you want to be a hero well just follow me."

"Working Class Hero" is found on John Lennon's record, "Plastic Ono Band," which also includes his atheistic philosophy summarized in his work entitled, "God." He says, "God is a concept by which we measure our pain. I'll say it again, God is a concept by which we measure our pain." He goes on, "I don't believe in the Bible, I don't believe in Jesus, I don't believe in the Beatles, I just believe in me; Yoko and me and that's reality."

Incidentally, "Yoko and me" were in New York not too long ago (July, 1971) at Max's Kansas City, a New York restaurant frequented by underground newspaper and movie people. On this particular occasion, however, Lennon and Yoko had as their guests Abbie Hoffman and Jerry Rubin (two of the Chicago Seven and fund raisers for a variety of way-out groups, including the Mayday Tribe which tried to close down the government in Washington recently).

Fred Sparks reported, "Over drinks, Lennon gave Hoffman and Rubin an envelope containing fifty $100 bills — $5,000 — for 'the cause.' According to my sources, Lennon, the most radical Beatle, said he hoped some of the money would assist members of the SDS [Students for a Democratic Society] who are being sought for several bomb outrages."[90]

Such, then, is a brief examination of the "social rebellion" the Beatles represent. Although not as obvious as Ed Sanders of the Fugs who stated, "Our role is to influence them with socially radical views,"[91] the Beatles have not been exactly wallflowers either. And even Yoko Ono now confesses that her and John's goal is to press for a world of "no money, no police, no government."[92] There is ample reason why the radicals on college campuses regard the Beatles with the same admiration they hold for Che Guevara, and it isn't only because Lennon enjoys Russell, Tillich and Allen Ginsberg.[93] The Beatles have, over the past years, lent themselves more and more to the far-out crowd, and although part of this can be attributed to the very nature of rock 'n' roll itself, which *Cavalier* labels subversive and revolutionary,[94] this is not the whole answer. Drugs, promiscuous sex, and the Beatles' consistent anti-Christian stance account for the basic reasons for the New Left's honeymoon with the English teddy boys.

Chapter XIX

A BETTER WAY

"The Word in current pop music is Revolution."[1] So writes Mary Swindell of the *Cleveland Press* as she ponders the question, "Rock as a revolutionary tool?" Difficult for some parents to believe perhaps, but for teenagers who listen to "I pledge allegiance against the flag and all for which it stands,"[2] the subject is not all that foreign. Swindell rightly notes that current rock is replete with references to drugs and sex and quotes Martin Perlich, vice president of Disc Records (and who himself plays "a lot of underground rock and folk music" on WCLV), to the effect that rock music has "radicalized" the young. "It radicalizes them, estranges them from the traditional virtues which they no longer see as relevant,"[3] says Perlich.

The hidden dangers of rock 'n' roll should be apparent to all who take a second look. There are emotional, psychological, spiritual, moral and, last but not least, national dangers. The idea of rock 'n' roll serving as a conditioner of violence and revolution cannot be hastily set aside. One has only to observe what rock has done to cause our young people to riot and participate in social rebellion, chaos and bedlam, to understand how significantly music fits into any revolutionary era. And Jacques Barzun's work, *Darwin, Marx, Wagner*, should quickly dispel from our minds any slighting we might give to the importance of music when it comes to culturally preparing the way for ideas — including revolutionary ideas.

Wagner, of course, was a life-long socialist and boasted, "My task is this: to bring revolution wherever I go."[4] Barzun's thesis is that it was no accident that during the "Wagner era," the ideas of Darwin and Marx swept Europe and England. Wagner set the cultural matrix for the speedy acceptance of such ideas. Similarly, it is now being argued that hard rock 'n' roll is setting the cultural matrix for the acceptance of drugs, promiscuous sex and revolution. And this is doubtless what Martin Perlich meant when he said, "Wagner was happy to describe his music as tribal and revolutionary, and this is exactly what current rock music is."[5]

When rock 'n' roll hit Britain in 1954, even the Beatles' biography admitted, "cinema seats started to be ripped up."[6] And this has been basically and consistently the history of this form of music since "Blackboard Jungle" moved on to center stage. This or that rock group "wound up the crowd so tight they snapped" has been the lament of scores of law enforcement officers who have been called in to quell the miniature and some not so miniature riots that have occurred across America. In fact, over 1,000 frenzied young people wrecked the former Brian Epstein's theatre alone.[7] And now a survey reveals that 87 per cent of the teenagers listen to rock 'n' roll; with 83 per cent purchasing discs within a year's time; and according to one source, over one billion dollars was spent for this form of music in 1969 and 1970.[8]

Although some authorities argue that rock 'n' roll is a good way to wear off energy, the truth of the matter is just the reverse. But even if true, the cure would still be worse than the disease. Rock 'n' roll winds up the individual. It doesn't wind him down! Even disc jockeys admit to playing a few soft numbers after "hard" rock to "cool down" the kids. At the Baltimore decency rally where hard rock was constantly beat at the young people, the rally ended in disaster. The answer to the antics of a morally and spiritually sick Jim Morrison is not more hard rock 'n' roll from a clean rock group (if there is one), but at the very minimum music, to quote Hansen, that is "soothing, ennobling, philosophical."

Music professor Frank Garlock commented that "almost daily the newspapers report on neurotic behavior which has accompanied or followed a rock 'n' roll session. Social disrupters have used rock 'n' roll and its performers to promote revolution. "Rock 'n' roll," he says, "often acts as an accompaniment for teenage wars, riots and sex orgies." Professor Garlock, in analyzing music in general and rock 'n' roll in particular, states that "the manner in which music affects the listener varies according to the proportion of tension and relaxation in the music. Good music has a balance of these two elements. The more exciting the piece of music, the more elements of tension will be found in it, but no good music ever uses one to the exclusion of the other." He lists certain elements of rock, viz, constant repetition of pitches, almost no melody, slightly under true pitch, overuse of high pitches, unnatural accents, breaking up of rhythms, etc. It is, therefore, "no wonder," he says, "that the kids scream, faint, gyrate and go into ecstatic convulsions."[9]

Since parents have a sacred responsibility toward their young people in raising them in the nurture and admonition of the Lord (Ephesians 6:4), it is obvious that such a charge includes the music they listen to as well as the food they eat. It is obvious that something has to be done about the mental pollution that is inundating our young people. The Scriptures state that the children of this age are in their generation wiser than the children of light (Luke 16:8), and nothing would seem to better illustrate this than the fact that many Christian young people are seriously "hooked" on hard rock and experiencing many of its deleterious side effects. Composer Andre Previn notes that there is an easy way to upgrade pop music to what it was at one time. Says Previn, "The disc jockeys could play good music. I think anything heard a lot becomes popular. If they played excerpts from Wozzeck a lot, the kids would whistle it on the way to the ball game. I think it is appalling the closer the songs are to the idiot level, the more they play them, and the better they sell."[10]

One Way Out!

David Gornston, nationally known music publisher, educator, author and lecturer, feels that every professional musician should be alerted in every corner of the country so that he as an individual can vocally and violently object to every manifestation of poor musical taste. Gornston insists that as soon as a professional musician hears a radio or TV program featuring musical "garbage," he should object directly to the station, sending his protest directly to the advertiser sponsoring the program, and urging his friends and neighbors to express their distaste for the cheap and the shoddy. He says all people with discriminating musical tastes should be urged to complain in restaurants, schools, college cafeterias, etc., whenever the juke box is stocked with "sound monstrosities" which purport to be music.

Gornston then makes an interesting observation: "Discriminating musicians must realize that a handful of characters help to perpetuate poor taste in music by controlling the commercially contrived system of record selection known as 'the Top 40.' Those things which are referred to as being 'in the market' are really only the records, selected by the Top 40 D.J.'s and the radio stations, which are produced in quantity by record performers who want to 'get into the Top 40 market.' Thus, a vicious cycle is established so that not only are 'good music singles' not released, but are actually automatically eliminated if they are produced and distributed. A concerted effort to knock out this commercial record cancer might be accomplished by having the union, in conjunction with the professional dancing instructors and serious school educators, release and espouse a 'good music Top 100' music list of their own. This list would represent a broad cross section of artists and big bands which reveal musical competence and taste."[11]

One unusual standard of musical competence and taste might well turn out to be the family plant. In a series of experiments in which potted plants were exposed to everything from Bach and Beethoven to hard rock groups the results were predictable. "What acid rock did to the petunias shouldn't happen to our teenagers,"[12] was the conclusion!

The article entitled, "Music that Kills Plants" begins, "For nearly two years now, Mrs. Dorothy Retallack of Denver has been killing off assorted potted plants by making them listen to rock music."[13]

In her series of experiments, Mrs. Retallack discovered that just three hours of acid rock a day shrivels young squash plants and flattens philodendron and crumbles corn in less than a month. Wonders Mrs. Retallack: If the sound of rock does that to plants, what is it doing to our human teenagers? "Could the discordant sounds we hear these days," states Mrs. Retallack, "be the reason humanity is growing neurotic?"[14]

Of course, we have maintained this for some time, but never really thought about plants supplying us with nature's answer to atonal music. In one potent picture of two plants dying the cut line reads, "Two Cherokee bean plants, one dying from acid rock sound, the other tilting from atonal music." It might as well have read, "Two teen-age beanies, one dying from acid rock sound, the other tilting from atonal music."

In contrast, another cut line under a healthy group of plants reads, "Bach organ music was soothing to these plants: they grew relatively straight and healthy in controlled environment."

Mrs. Retallack's professor of biology (Temple Buell College), Francis F. Broman, makes it clear that the undertaking was scientific. Says Broman, "I should point out that Dorothy worked under strict scientific controls from the first, and we did everything possible to insure accurate, unbiased results."[15]

The experiment went something like this — several groups of assorted plants, usually five different plants to a group, would be placed in controlled-environment chambers (big closed cabinets on wheels in which light, temperature and air were regulated automatically). At one side of each cabinet, a loud-speaker was placed to introduce sound, usually from a tape recorder.

Mrs. Retallack once piped music from two Denver radio stations to her plants. One group was exposed to a Denver station KIMN (a rock station) and another group to KLIR (a semi-classical station). The results: "The petunias listening to KIMN refused to bloom. Those on KLIR developed six beautiful blooms. By the end of the second week, the KIMN petunias were leaning away from the radio and showing very erratic growth. The petunia blooms hearing KLIR were all leaning toward the sound. Within a month all plants exposed to rock music died."[16]

Mrs. Retallack summarized, "If rock music has an adverse effect on plants, is the rock music listened to so long and so often by the younger generation partly responsible for their erratic, chaotic behavior?"[17]

In a three-week experiment Mrs. Retallack played the recordings of Led Zeppelin and the Vanilla Fudge to a group of beans, squash, corn, morning glory and coleus. To another group with the same plants she played contemporary *avant-garde* music and to a third group she played nothing (as a control).

Result: At the end of the first 10 days, the plants exposed to the rock were all leaning away from the speaker. At the end of three weeks the plants were dying. The squash had almost fallen over. The morning glory, instead of crawling up as is natural, had sagged and was stretched over four pots, in the direction away from the music. Corn stalks sagged in the middle. The beans were stunted and tilted far away from the speaker. All the plants showed browning leaves except the crimson coleus.

The beans listening to the contemporary atonal music leaned 15 degrees from the speaker and had middle-sized roots.

The controlled group grew the highest and had long, bushy roots. But, and not too surprising, Mrs. Retallack found that plants listening to calm devotional music measured two inches higher than those even grown in silence. And besides, the plants instead of turning away from the speaker "leaned into it."

Channeling Youth's Energy

Dr. George W. Crane tells the story of a Welsh lad, John Thompson, who at 12 years of age got up at 5:00 a.m., walked two miles to a coal mine in England, carrying his lunch pail. There he checked in at 6:00 a.m. and worked a twelve-hour day, six days per week, quitting at 6:00 p.m. to walk the two miles back home.

The superintendent, however, noted that the little twelve-year-old was particularly bright, and he urged him to attend night school after the 6:00 quitting whistle had blown.

John still left home at 5:00 a.m., worked from 6:00 in the morning until 6:00 at night and then attended night classes, following which he walked the two miles back to his widowed mother. Yet, he made top grades and won a scholarship to Oxford, from which he graduated and entered the ministry. He came over to Canada and later moved to Illinois only to be instrumental in erecting the tallest church in the world in the Chicago Loop — The Chicago Temple — where incidentally Dr. Crane himself has taught the Dixon Bible Class for 33 years.

Doubtless the energies of John Thompson were constructively channeled in the proper direction, and it would seem that our Christian young people could likewise use their tremendous energy to further the Body of Christ and make their world a brighter place to live. Great cries have gone up over the fact that American slums and ghetto areas have all but wiped out the hope of a large number of Americans. Who could object to the channeling of the energy of youth to such areas and to the places that need a cleaning and rebuilding? Structures which need to be eliminated but are not because of excessive cost could be torn down by volunteer teenagers who wish to expend their energy on behalf of others. Streets and alleys that need attention and vacant yards that need renovation could be reclaimed with the help of energetic youth. In truth, there must be 101 various avenues where our young people could serve in their own area; areas that would speak to the energies of Christian youth.

There is also a spiritual issue that cannot be overlooked in any discussion of music and particularly rock 'n' roll. For those teenagers who have bowed their knee to the Beatles or any rock group, it should be made quite clear that this can only be corrected when the heart of the young person is made anew by a personal confrontation with the real Lord and Saviour of the Universe — Jesus Christ. As humans we are only too prone to worship the creature more than the Creator. The love of God is still the highest and most powerful motive known to man, and even the Nineteenth Century British historian, Lecky, though an unbeliever, had to admit that "it may be truly said that the simple record of [Christ's] three short years of active life has done more to regenerate and soften mankind than all the disquisitions of philosophers, and than all the exhortations of moralists. This has been the wellspring of whatever is best and purest in the Christian life." Then, too, the atheist, H.G. Wells, confessed that even to this day "this Galilean is too much for our small hearts." Christ, Himself, has indeed filled the hearts of men, women and teenagers with an impassioned love which has shown itself capable of acting on all ages, nations, temperaments and conditions. "This is His commandment, that we should believe on the name of His Son Jesus Christ, and love one another." (I John 3:23)

Teenagers, not only in this country but throughout the world, who are looking for an answer to their spiritual and moral dilemmas can find just such an answer in the person of Jesus Christ. According to the Bible, Christ came to earth to seek and to save that which was lost (and few teenagers today need convincing that they stand in need of a cleansing from their sins). Christ lovingly went to the cross to bear our sins and iniquities,[18] for it was through the instrumentality of the cross that the penalty of sin (eternal death) was paid in full. And now Christ lives evermore to assure us of our living, eternal hope — eternal life.

Through resurrection, Christ has taken away the one fear that has bound all human beings for centuries — death.[19] And by acknowledging this resurrected Lord as our personal Saviour,[20] teenagers can fearlessly stand up to the threats of today, realizing that their lives are hid with Christ in God.

Music that is basically un-Christian, that lures us from first principles, washes our minds in cheap filth, evokes riotous feelings, incites to rebellion will be rejected out of hand when our lives are truly "led by the Spirit."[21] Our discrimination between good music, which uplifts and builds, and bad music, which debases and destroys, will be sharpened when our standard of judgment is Christian instead of "earthly."

At this moment there is indeed a vast amount of spiritual and moral energy concentrated around the person of Jesus Christ. He, for a fact, is the divinely attractive power, acting mightily in the spiritual and moral world. Christ, Himself, is personally calling those with excessive energy to do His work in His vineyard and to constructively use what each has (be it physical, spiritual or moral energy) for the glory of the King of Kings and Lord of Lords.

This material, of course, is not being written with any spirit of hate or malice. Truth is to be spoken and written in love. Christians are to love their enemies. Christ from the cross said, "Father, forgive them for they know not what they do," and this best summarizes our feelings toward the four contemporary British pagans; Father forgive them — they know not what they are doing! In fact, when one considers the influence the Beatles have on our youth (even the four and five-year-olds are being subjected to a one-half hour Beatle cartoon series every Saturday morning) one wishes, along with St. Paul, that he were accursed from Christ that their souls might be saved. Few in history have had the privilege to manifest such influence for good or for evil; unfortunately, the Beatles have chosen the broad way — taking legions with them.

Speaking the truth in love, however, does not entail banking the truth. The ministry of warning is an unpleasant but necessary

God-ordained ministry and for Christians a word of warning concerning those who would destroy their offsprings' souls should be sufficient. Unfortunately, for those still outside the grace of God, harder lessons are usually required before the dangers of rock 'n' roll are recognized; young lives destroyed in the drug epidemic, the sexual revolution,[22] or caught up in the Red revolution on campus.

The challenge facing all Christians and patriotic Americans is indeed herculean, but we all must stand firm in the face of an increasing perversion of our culture (music, art and literature) remembering, "He who learns nothing from history is condemned to repeat it."

PART FOUR

COMMUNIST USE OF FOLK MUSIC

"I knew a very wise man who believed that if a man were permitted to make all the ballads, he need not care who should make the laws of a nation. And we find that most of the ancient legislators thought they could not well reform the manners of any city without the help of a lyric and sometimes of a dramatic poet."

— Andrew Fletcher, Scot patriot,
writer, orator and one time
member of the Scotland
parliament, *Stevenson's Book
of Quotations* (New York:
Dodd-Mead, 1958), p. 123

Chapter XX

PEOPLE'S SONGS

We have noted two types of music: rhythmic, and its effects on our children; beat, and its effects on our adolescents.

For college and university students, the subverters have made use of a third type, viz., folk music.

One of the clearest and most recent presentations of this truth is R. Serge Denisoff's *Great Day Coming – Folk Music and the American Left*. Denisoff, too, examines the use of folk music by the Communist Party and the Party's ability to use "folk material as a weapon to achieve particular socio-political ends."[1] Denisoff admits that one need only read the *Daily Worker*, *New Masses*, or *People's Songs Bulletin* to observe "a great deal of objective evidence of the Communists' relationship to folk music."[2] Although Denisoff doesn't approve of this author's reliance on Government reports he does acknowledge that "views expressed in Communist publications can be assumed to reflect political policy and implicit support."[3]

Therefore, any reader who finds the following materials unintelligible or unbelievable might wish to consult Denisoff's work. In fact, Denisoff states in his very first chapter that the teachings and example of Lenin and the Bolsheviks pointed the American Communists in the direction of folk material.

The Proletarian Musicians Association, meeting in Moscow in 1929, made it explicitly clear that classical music was "bourgeois" whereas folk music was "the music of the toilers, the exploited, and the oppressed classes" and a type of music usable for "the ultimate victory of the proletariat builders of Communist society."[4]

In 1945-46 the Communists not only established Young People's Records but also formed a specific corporation dealing with folk music — People's Songs, Inc.

This corporation is to the college and university students what Young People's Records is to children in kindergarten and the early grades.

According to one report, "People's Songs was an organization . . . composed of a number of persons on the board of directors who have been called before this committee or identified by this committee as members of the Communist Party, and the purpose of which, from information made available to the committee, was to extend services to the Communist Party in its entertainment projects."[5]

The California Senate Factfinding Subcommittee on Un-American Activities released a study with the following information concerning People's Songs: "It has injected itself into Communist fronts, and Communist schools, and leftwing trade union and political activity . . . People's Songs, Inc. is now writing songs and plays, promoting choruses and schools for Communist fronts . . . [it] staged a benefit for the Communist Party in New York City on November 30, 1946. Advertisements and press notices for its activities are to be found in the *Daily Worker* . . . People's Songs have sent delegated representatives to the Prague conference of the Communist World Youth Festival." In conclusion the Senate Committee found, "People's Songs . . . a vital Communist front in the conduct of the strategy and tactics of the Communist Anti-Imperialist War technique of the Seventh Period of Communist strategy in America and one which spawned a horde of lesser fronts in the fields of music, stage, entertainment, choral singing, folk dancing, radio transcriptions and similar fields. It especially is important to Communist proselyting and propaganda work because of its emphasis on appeal to youth and because of its organization and technique to provide entertainment for organizations and groups as a smooth opening wedge for Marxist-Leninist-Stalinist propaganda."[6]

The Marxist interpretation of this organization openly admits, "People's Songs sponsored their own big sings and concerts, or as they were named in the Almanac days, Hootenannies. But with the turn to the Truman Doctrine, to the cold war and domestic red-baiting, it slowly became clear that organized labor with some important exceptions, was going to ride on the anti-Communist bandwagon."[7]

Both People's Songs and Young People's Records worked together at school workshops cited subversive by the Attorney

General of the United States[8] and both have had interlocking personalities on each other's board.[9] In fact, so important have the songs produced by People's Songs, Inc. become in Red ranks "that the Communist schools in Hollywood ... People's Educational Center ... and the Jefferson School in New York have inaugurated classes in the science of agitational song writing."[10]

People's Songs was incorporated January 31, 1946, in New York City. Among the directors and incorporators were Pete Seeger, Herbert Haufrect, Lee Hays, Daniel Lapidus and Robert Claiborne. Joseph Brodsky was the attorney for the corporation.

The board of directors included the following: B.A. Bodkin, Tom Glazer,[11] Horace Grenell, Woody Guthrie, Herbert Haufrect, Paul Kent, John Hammond, Jr.,[12] Millard Lampell, Bess Hawes,[13] Bob Russell, Waldemar Hille,[14] Earl Robinson,[15] Kenneth Spencer, Alec Wilder, Palmer Weber and Walter Lowenfels.[16]

And the Board of Sponsors included Sam Barlow, Leonard Bernstein,[17] Norman Corwin, Lincoln Kerstein, Larry Adler, C.B. Baldwin, Carl Carmer, Oscar Hammerstein II, E.Y. Harburg, Judy Holliday, Lena Horne, John Houseman, David Capp, Alain Locke, Dorothy Parker, Herman Sobel, Aaron Copeland,[18] Louis Untermeyer, Sam Wanamaker, Paul Robeson,[19] Josh White, Moe Asch[20] and Lila B. Pitts.[21]

Chapter XXI

PETE SEEGER AND WOODY GUTHRIE

Reprints of the People's Songs *Bulletin* make it obvious that Pete Seeger, People's Songs Executive Secretary, was the motivating and driving force behind the organization. Seeger admits, "We called our organization People's Songs to distinguish it from the scholarly folklore societies, and started a bulletin. I wanted it to be a weekly; others persuaded me to be more conservative and make it monthly."[1]

He readily acknowledges the role of People's Songs in bringing about a revival of interest in folk music and even explains how folk music – Seeger style – grew in popularity among our university and college students. He says, "Because the young people in summer camps and schools grew up and went to college."[2] It takes little ingenuity to grasp the significance of this statement and the nature of the camps and schools, e.g., the Jefferson School of Social Science or the Metropolitan Music School, Inc., referred to in his admission.

Seeger also admits that the magazine *Sing Out!* carried on where People's Songs left off.[3] The People's Songs *Bulletin* ceased publication in 1949. One year later *Sing Out!* was born assuring continuance of the *Bulletin's* basic philosophy and over the years has increased its circulation to 25,000.[4]

Mr. Seeger has been very busy over the past two decades performing for Communists, pro-Communists and left-wing organizations and causes. *Life* magazine described him as "A Minstrel with a Mission,"[5] but failed to inform its readers of his long-range mission. Seeger's songs, books, and articles in *Sing Out!* magazine would seem to clearly define his stand in the struggle between Communism and Freedom – the struggle which George Meany, President of the AFL-CIO, says is "the problem of our time . . . overshadowing all other problems." In Seeger's book, *American Favorite Ballads,* we are told point blank, "Workingmen of all tongues unite – you have NOTHING TO LOSE but your chains – you have a world to win. Vive La Revolution Sociale."[6]

Marx said nearly the same thing in the closing lines of the *Communist Manifesto.*

Through the pages of *Sing Out!*, Seeger and his associates have consistently defended the Spanish Communists of the Lincoln Brigade as well as the Communist take over of Cuba.[7] They continuously derogate the House Committee on Un-American Activities (now the House Committee on Internal Security), going so far as to call Herbert A. Philbrick and Louis Budenz "stool pigeons."[8] And naturally they proceed to foment class hatred between white and black.[9] In the Sept./Oct. 1970 issue Seeger copyrighted on behalf of the Black Panther Party the following ditty:

Cause there ain't enough pigs [police]
In the whole wide world
To stop the Black Panther Party
From serving the people

Poor Black Power
Gun totin' power
Pig killing power
It's growing by the hour.

A two-year Harvard man, Pete Seeger has been identified under oath by an FBI undercover agent as having been a member of the Communist Party.[10] His actions over the years would hardly disprove the charge. The Attorney General of the United States has declared subversive the following organizations with which Pete Seeger has affiliated himself: (1) American Committee for Protection of Foreign Born, (2) American Committee for Yugoslav Relief, (3) American Youth Congress, (4) American Youth for Democracy, (5) Civil Rights Congress, (6) Committee for a Democratic Far Eastern Policy, (7) Committee for the Negro Arts, (8) Communist Party, (9) Council on African Affairs, (10) Jefferson School of Social Science, (11) National Council of the Arts, Sciences and Professions, (12) Nature Friends of America, (13) New Masses, (14) Voice of Freedom Committee and (15) Win-the-Peace Conference.

Seeger's Activities

His biography over the past few decades reads like a Who's Who in Communist Activity. *News and Views* for July, 1965,[11] listed over ninety Communist fronts and activities of Pete Seeger, but even this is a partial listing of his hundreds of pro-Communist activities over the past thirty years. He was billed as the entertainer, according to the *Daily Worker* of March 29, 1946, at a supper given for Peter V. Cachione, Chairman of the Brooklyn Communist Party.

He provided the entertainment, according to the *Daily Worker* of June 20, 1947, for the Allerton Section of the Communist Party's housewarming.

He entertained the Southern California Chapter of the subversive American Committee for Yugoslav Relief, according to the *People's World* of October 22, 1947, at one of their picnics.

Seeger provided the entertainment, according to the *Daily Worker* of April 30, 1948, for the Essex County Communist Party's May Day Rally.

He entertained the Cultural Division of the Communist Party of New York at a May Day show, according to the *Daily Worker* of May 4, 1949. This same *Worker* identified Seeger as a member of the Music Section of the Cultural Division of the Communist Party along with two other members of The Weavers' singing group.

Seeger was the entertainer, according to the *Daily Worker* of June 1, 1949, at the Testimonial Dinner of the twelve U.S. Communist Party leaders at St. Nick's Arena.

Pete marched in the Communist Party of New York May Day parade in 1950. He also marched in the May Day parade in 1952.

Seeger lectured at the subversive Jefferson School of Social Science, according to the *Daily Worker* of February 15, 1954.

He was a sponsor, as shown by letterhead stationery of July 10, 1955, of the subversive New York Committee for Protection of the Foreign Born.

He entertained at the rallies of the subversive National Council of American-Soviet Friendship in 1958, 1960 and 1962.

Seeger, a major fund-raiser for the subversive National Council to Abolish the House Un-American Activities Committee, entertained the organization's meeting in 1960, 1961, and 1962, according to *The Worker* of October 16, 1960, April 21, 1961, and January 28, 1962.

According to *The Worker* of March 4, 1962, Pete Seeger provided the entertainment for a rally of the Veterans of the Abraham Lincoln Brigade cited as subversive by several Congressional committees.

Seeger provided the entertainment for the Youth Against the House Un-American Activities Committee. One government report stated, "One rally of the group held on January 31, 1960, featured Clark Foreman, executive director of a cited Communist-front, the Emergency Civil Liberties Committee, as master of ceremonies. At that rally he lavishly praised Harvey O'Connor, an identified Communist. Pete Seeger, another identified Communist, provided the entertainment."[12]

"The case of Pete Seeger, the folk singer," according to another government report, "offers another example of the type of assistance the U.S. Communist Party receives from abroad. Seeger, as mentioned before, has been identified as a member of the Communist Party and today, as for many years past, is an inveterate promoter of party fronts and the party line."[13]

Further information from government sources regarding Pete Seeger: "On April 24, 1962, *The Worker* (Communist Party newspaper) announced a 'Folk and Jazz Concert' to raise funds for the United States Festival Committee. Identified Communist Party member Pete Seeger was listed among persons scheduled to perform."[14]

And again, "Some demonstrators, on April 15, burned their draft cards and even the American flag in the New York City demonstration. Swastikas were also placed over reproductions of the U.S. flag in order to imply that the U.S.A. is a Nazi-like nation... Identified Communist Party member, Pete Seeger, provided the entertainment for the New York activity."[15]

Mrs. Paul Robeson, in a column in *The Worker*, writes that "Carnegie Hall was put to very fine use the night after Christmas 1964, when Pete Seeger, having collected songs from people all over the world, sang them back to the people."[16] Eslanda Robeson's eulogy of Seeger was so moving that even Jacob

Dworkin of Moscow commented, "I could only wish that such concerts could be organized in every city, bringing to the people a feeling of universal working class brotherhood and arousing the best impulses that are hidden in every honest American for peaceful coexistence and hatred toward those who are planning a new war. I am taking this opportunity to extend my sincere thanks to the singer Pete Seeger, to Eslanda and our great friend, Paul Robeson and their families and naturally to *The Worker* for publishing Eslanda's excellent article."[17]

According to the Communist press, Seeger was to perform at a rally of the Committee for Non-Violent Action in New York City. The purpose of the rally was to propagandize for U.S. surrender in Vietnam.[18]

"American Dialog," the semi-official cultural publication of the Communist Party, has announced the appointment of Pete Seeger to its board of sponsors.[19] The Dialog's editor is Joseph North, writer on the editorial board of the *Worker.* Associate editor is Walter Lowenfels, identified under oath as having been a member of the Communist Party,[20] and more recently editor of the latest Communist collection of poems published by International Publishers under the title,*Poets of Today.* Other sponsors of "American Dialog" include Will Geer,[21] John Howard Lawson,[22] Linus Pauling, Paul Robeson, Bertrand Russell, Rev. Stephen H. Fritchman, Waldo Frank[23] and Shirley Graham DuBois.[24]

Pete Seeger gave his open endorsement and recommendation to the Communists' Ninth World Youth Festival for Peace and Friendship. The festival was to be held in Communist Algeria. Seeger comments, "If you believe in peace on earth and if you can scrape up the money for the trip, it's Algiers; July 28th-August 7th."[25] Since Ben Bella's regime was overthrown, the Festival was held in Helsinki. On June 1, 1965, Pete Seeger and Bernice Reagon were the entertainers at a folk concert in New York to raise money for the World Youth Festival.[26]

The World Youth Festivals are the products of the World Federation of Democratic Youth and the International Union of Students, both formed at the end of World War II under the direction of Moscow. Beginning in Prague, Czechoslovakia, in 1947 and every two years thereafter through 1959, these groups jointly sponsored a World Youth Festival. Then after a first-time lapse of three years, the eighth festival was held in Helsinki, Finland, during the summer of 1962.[27] An American student attending the Eighth World Youth Festival testified, "It was definitely anti-American. The theme of every seminar was 'Hate America'. As Mr. Quinlan said, the cultural activities were all against America, pictures of the Hiroshima Bombing, the puppet shows that were given were against America. There was a farce on religion, things of this nature."[28]

The 1965 Festival was little better. *National Review* reported, "Grand slam for America at Communist-dominated World Peace Congress in Helsinki last week. America fielded the biggest delegation (98 out of a total of 800) and all ten of the reports before the house that were adopted, with the enthusiastic assent of the U.S. delegates, were anti-American' . . ."[29]

Seeger In Moscow

Another Seeger gift to Moscow was his appearance at Moscow University where he sang an anti-U.S. song for his Communist audience. He sang a Vietnam protest ballad, "King Henry," whose "bitterness was aimed at the American military presence in Vietnam."[30] The American Embassy had nothing to do with his appearance, according to the press, but the State Department issued him a visa.

The ironic significance of Seeger's trip to Moscow was that it came only a few months after the once conservative Missouri Lutheran Synod featured him at its International Walther League Convention held at Squaw Valley, California, July 5-9, 1965. The *Newsletter* announcing the folk singer's appearance portrayed him as "a well-known folk singer whose unique ability to analyze and cut to the heart of the problems with music is honored and respected throughout the world." "He is noted," continued the *Newsletter*, "for his sensitivity to the needs of the people and the underdogs of society, never hesitating to speak out for truth and love of those in need. Many young people will know him for the music he has written or co-authored. Among these are: 'Where Have All the Flowers Gone' — 'We Shall Overcome' — 'If I Had a

Hammer' — 'Kisses Sweeter Than Wine.' His Columbia recording 'We Shall Overcome' is considered a classic of the folk singing world. Pete Seeger will offer a message of enslavement and freedom — an honest message from one in the midst of the struggle."[31]

Needless to say, Seeger is not concerned with the truth when it involves Communist Party activities, and for the Walther League to listen to a message on "enslavement and freedom" from one who is constantly defending and playing for those representing the greatest slave tyranny of all history is sheer folly and deceit.

However, to prove Seeger's remarkable ability to deceive even the elect, in a post-convention rally of the Missouri District Walther League held at St. Paul's College in Concordia, Missouri, August 20-22, 1965, the Lutheran young people were actually told, "If only more leaguers, pastors and adults could have been there to hear Mr. Seeger testify to the leaguers with his unforgettable folk music, his humbleness, his interest in keeping our youth strong in devotion to our country as the land we love so well . . . To accuse a man of 'faking' such a tremendous presentation and following discussion would be most un-Christian as were the acts done by so many of our Lutherans who thought this fellow must come off the program. Certain 'disturbed' Lutheran people still will not agree with the 3,200 leaguers, pastors and high-ranking Synod officials that this man was genuine. Mr. Seeger's devotion to the United States of America must not be challenged anymore. Were you there?"[32]

One can be sure that Mr. Seeger did not sing and play his weird rendition of "Aimee McPherson"[33] or give forth with "Working men of all tongues unite, you have nothing to lose but your chains, you have a world to win — vive la Revolution Sociale."[34] And naturally he would not tell these Christian young people that his "We Shall Overcome" was made popular through the efforts of the pro-Communist Highlander Folk School of Monteagle, Tennessee, and just happens to be Fidel Castro's official revolutionary slogan.

It should also be noted that Mr. Seeger was in Moscow in 1964 where he was royally entertained by the "famed" Soviet Army Chorus.[35] According to the *New York Times*, "Mr. Seeger punctuated his informal singing and playing with folksy comments about American folk music, some of its leading figures — including the late Huddie (Leadbelly) Ledbetter and Woody Guthrie — and some outspoken criticism of television."[36] He also led the audience in his "We Shall Overcome."

From this type of activity alone, but certainly in conjunction with scores of other pro-Communist activities, one would expect a Christian organization like the Missouri Walther League to cease sitting at Seeger's socks — singing Seeger's songs.

At least the *Knoxville Journal* tried to expose Seeger and his trip to Moscow. The paper said, "People hereabouts noted in yesterday's Journal, with interest if not surprise, that good old American Folk Singer Pete Seeger had finally made it to the mecca of Communism to give some of his widely known anti-US performances. From Moscow, Reuters reported that Seeger sang a song of protest against American policy in Vietnam for the first time during his three-week tour of the Soviet Union to students of Moscow University. The occasion was the second of three appearances in the Russian capital at the end of a three-week tour of Soviet Central Asian and Trans-Caucasian cities.

"Pete's name is known here because of its close association over several years with the Highlander Folk School at Monteagle, which is now Highlander Center here on Riverside Drive. He is an old buddy of Guy Carawan, another so-called folk singer, who made an appearance in months past at the Presbyterian Center on the University of Tennessee campus. For many years the Communist apparatus throughout the world has methodically urged its people to make use of 'folk songs' to spread Red propaganda and the folk singer has played an important part in this process.

"The reader will recall the Highlander was founded by Myles Horton in company with James Dombrowski, an identified Communist, who until some years ago was included in the Highlander board of directors and now is the head of the Southern Conference Educational Fund, a Communist outfit based in New Orleans. Carl Braden, several of whose so-called civil rights workers have appeared in the police news locally within the past few weeks, is a close associate of Dombrowski, and he and Mrs. Braden are employed by the Southern Conference Educational Fund.

"There is doubtless great rejoicing among Pete Seeger's old time associates that he has had this *triumphal tour of treason* [our emphasis] in a country where most of us wish that all good American Communists would go to take up permanent residence."[37]

Also disturbing at the Missouri League's August meeting was its distribution of *Songs For Today*. It is a compilation of basically good music except for the shocking suggestion, "One of the most intriguing studies of folk song literature is to be found in a pamphlet entitled 'Sing Out' published by Oak Publishing, New York, New York. Some one of you might want to send for it as a resource for understanding this kind of music. Folk singers, such as Joan Baez or Pete Seeger, have produced a large number of records that are rich resources for the history and flavor of these melodies and words."[38] In the book's selected bibliography for further study, *Sing Out!* is again mentioned.[39]

Then, too, in more recent happenings, Concordia Publishing House in a new publication "Spirit Talk" called Seeger, The Beatles, Joan Baez and Bob Dylan "pop prophets" and recommended their music as "songs of social significance and theological importance."[40]

Seeger and His Peace Medal

In 1967 Seeger received partial payment for his pro-Communist activities — he personally accepted the Communist East German peace medal in an East Berlin Hootenanny Club. A member of the Communist East Germany peace council bestowed the award upon Seeger because he is supposed to be a "fighter for freedom" and "against oppression."[41] Nothing was said about the oppressive and freedom-restricting Berlin wall that Seeger went through to obtain his reward for faithful service.

Indeed one year later Seeger was back in the U.S. setting up "coffeehouse" programs outside military bases geared to quicken dissent on Vietnam among GIs leery of going to South Vietnam. Assisting Seeger in the programs were Barbara Dane, Dustin Hoffman, Phil Ochs, David Dellinger, Edward Albee and Rev.

William Coffin, Jr.[42]

Although Seeger refers to himself as "I'm as Communist as the American Indian,"[43] his activities point to a deeper analogy. The Communist *Daily World* provided one when it reported Seeger in Havana, Cuba, dedicating songs to self-admitted Communist Angela Davis and otherwise entertaining Castro's young revolutionaries.[44]

Consistently enough, Seeger, under oath, has declined to answer whether or not he ever was a member of the Communist Party.[45] When he was indicted in 1955 for contempt of Congress, he refused to answer questions concerning his Communist associates and affiliations. Still, it took a jury of twelve Americans only one hour and twenty minutes to find Pete Seeger guilty on all counts. During the trial, Federal Judge Thomas F. Murphy asked the singer once again if he were then, or ever had been a member of the Communist Party. Seeger once again declined to answer.[46]

Consistent with the trend of our time, Seeger's conviction was later overturned by a U.S. Court of Appeals on a minor technicality. (See *Congressional Record*, February 18, 1969, p. E1060.) The courts have become so effective in hampering the prosecution of subversive activities in our nation that even the Attorney General has a difficult time citing any new organization as subversive. "The limitations placed on his office by the courts is having the effect of stopping further citations."[47]

Yet one of the most amazing psychological miracles of our times is the ability of Pete Seeger to maintain a sense of quasi-respectability. Alger Hiss, Owen Lattimore and a whole host of other traitors were never able to maintain such an aura. Who but Seeger could entertain on Sesame Street, the Dinah Shore Program, the Johnny Cash Show and at the same time recommend Gus Hall's work *Ecology: Can We Survive Under Capitalism?* In fact, the Communist *Daily World* for February 19, 1972, quoted Seeger as saying, "If you think you've already heard from the biologists and the lawyers, you better be prepared to hear also from the Marxists. A good place to start would be *Ecology: Can We Survive Under Capitalism?* by Gus Hall, leader of the U.S. Communist Party."

In 1968 he was the honored guest and entertainer of the World Council of Churches meeting in Uppsala, Sweden. According to one report the "delegates from the 'Third World' found Seeger enchanting."[48] But others were bound to find him "enchanting" since there was "a deep current of anti-Americanism [running] beneath assembly deliberations. It seemed to be based on opposition to the war in Vietnam and to America's affluence as well as on a preference for socialism and Communism over capitalism."[49]

Of course, W.C.C. leadership had already declared Pete Seeger, Joan Baez and Phil Ochs as the new hymn writers for the coming new day. It seems our present hymns are too "individualistic." Instead, our new hymns will taste something like the following:

It was on a Friday morning that they took me from the cell
And I saw they had a carpenter to crucify as well
You can blame it onto Pilate, you can blame it on the Jews,
You can blame it on the Devil, It's God I accuse.
It's God they ought to crucify instead of you and me
I said to the carpenter a hanging on the tree.[50]

Seeger, along with Woody Guthrie, Bob Dylan, Ted Bikel, Paul Robeson, Burl Ives, Richard Dyer-Bennett, also received excellent publicity in the Boy Scout magazine *Boy's Life*. In fairness, however, it should be noted that the publisher of *Boy's Life*, Oliver S. Johnson, later retracted the article and said, "We certainly don't intend to mention any more Communists. Editor Robert Hood regrets that the original article wasn't scrapped."[52]

However, in 1970, *Guideposts*,[53] edited by Norman Vincent Peale, not only ran a complimentary article on Seeger (Seeger is now a conservationist — just like Alger Hiss was once described as a bird watcher), but made reprints available to church groups, clubs, friends and relatives. To label Seeger a conservationist is as misleading as labeling Hiss "a State Department employee."

The respectable *Audubon* magazine followed the same format with an article on Seeger entitled "A Man, A Boat, A River, A Dream."[54]

Because of space limitations, further information on Seeger, his background and activities may be found in the February 18, 1969,

Congressional Record, page E1060. Also Denisoff in *Great Day Coming* presents an excellent analysis of Seeger's Communist activities.

Woody Guthrie

One of Mr. Seeger's most loyal compatriots in the Communist subversion of American folk music was Woody Guthrie. Identified under oath as having been a member of the Communist Party, Guthrie's activities on behalf of international Communism are well known. At one time Guthrie said, "The best thing that I did in 1936 was to sign up with the Communist Party . . . I bought and gave away about a dozen of these little blue USSR Constitution books since 1936."[55]

Even John Greenway admitted that Guthrie and Seeger were hammering "folksongs into weapons of subversion."[56] And R. Serge Denisoff acknowledged that Guthrie's political materials were "well accepted, predominantly by urban radicals and Communists in New York and elsewhere."[57] He also noted that the Communists found "their 'Communist Joe Hill' in an 'Okie balladeer,' Woody Guthrie, and in the Almanac Singers."[58] The feeling was that what Marx wrote and Lenin did, Woody sings! One government documentary reported, "Now, Woody Guthrie, a Communist, is a guitar-playing, ballad-singing entertainer, brought to New York by Will Geer, also a Communist, and incidentally the grandson-in-law of Ella May Bloor, known as 'Mother Bloor,' Pennsylvania State Secretary of the Communist Party . . . during the past three or four years Woody Guthrie has become one of the outstanding entertainers in the Communist Party, Communist Party fronts and other left-wing organizations . . . I have heard him on numerous occasions and it is always with this definite Communist Party tinge, and in his singing and in his talk he has never tried to attempt to conceal the fact that he was a columnist for the *Daily Worker* or that he was a member of the Communist Party and represented it as such."[59]

The International Publishers' work on folk music admits that Guthrie was a part of the "radical" movement and "wrote a regular column, 'Woody sez,' in the *Daily Worker*."[60]

Phil Ochs, author of "Draft Dodger Rag," "I Ain't Marching Anymore" and other pro-Communist folksongs, writing in a Communist monthly publication, *Mainstream*[61] stated, "I have run across some people who seem to consider Guthrie solely as a writer of great camp songs. They cannot fathom or don't want to fathom the political significance of a great part of his work."[62]

Perhaps the most frank admission of Guthrie's Communist activities is found in an article by Ernie Marrs printed in the pro-Communist folk publication, *Broadside*. Marrs writes, "Just about every time you turn around these days, it seems like, someone is writing another piece about Woody Guthrie. That wouldn't be so bad, except for one thing, and even then it's a good starting point.

"Here's the trouble — most of them are saying the same things over and over, in slightly different words. You can get the King James text of it from John Greenway's 'American Folksongs of Protest,' which is not a bad book — in fact, I'd call it required reading for any serious student of American folksong. The newspaper and magazine writers add a few frills here and there, change one thing or another, leave out this and that, and the resulting picture becomes more wishy-washy all the time. Judging by what most of them say, Woody wrote 'Grand Coulee Dam,' Dust Bowl songs, kid songs, union songs, 'Philadelphia Lawyer' (Woody's name for that one was 'Reno Blues,' by the way), a book called *Bound For Glory*, and presumably went to Sunday School the rest of the time.

"What about the Woody Guthrie that wrote a book called 'Study Butte,' which even International Publishers found too warm for the times?

"What about the Woody Guthrie that got into political trouble with the Mexican police, while on the way to sing on a radio station down there?

"What about the Woody Guthrie that wrote columns for the *People's World* and the *Daily Worker*, and did he write for them partly because the management of the more capitalistic newspapers thinks you have to have a long string of letters after your name before the people understand your words?

"What about the Woody Guthrie that wrote twelve songs on venereal disease for Uncle Sam's Army?

"What about the Woody Guthrie that drifted into the office of the American League Against War and Fascism back in the late '30's, in Los Angeles, used up a month's supply of their mimeograph stencils running off a songbook to peddle, left the place looking like a lost cyclone hit it, and got out before the boss got back and gave the secretary hell for letting him in? (She helped Woody with the next songbook, too.)

"What about Woodrow Wilson Guthrie, the schoolboy? Where did he go to school? When? How long?

"Perhaps the most invisible Woody Guthrie of all is the uninhibited and often ribald one. He got downright bawdy, gloriously so, and pretty often at that. Of this side of his writing and singing, Oscar Brand once said, 'Woody Guthrie didn't write bawdy songs often. When he did, they were about the filthiest ones ever written.' I am forced to disagree on both counts, for many of them have been preserved in his own writing, and in the least of the ones I've seen, I found more truth and honesty than in ninety percent of Tin Pan Alley's offerings and outpourings. He called them as he saw them; and, personally, I prefer honest 'filth' to nasty-nice lies any day, but tastes differ."[63]

This is the Guthrie that Oklahoma's ex-Senator Fred Harris wanted to make into a folk hero!

Chapter XXII

"SING OUT!", FOLKWAYS RECORDS AND OAK PUBLICATIONS

With the demise of People's Songs in 1949, many of its functions were transferred to People's Artists, Inc. Since Pete Seeger was one of People's Artists' leaders, it made little difference in name except for the fact that California's Factfinding Subcommittee on Un-American Activities had cited People's Songs subversive in 1949.

The official publication of People's Artists, Inc., was called *Sing Out!*. Its first issue was May 1950 and according to International Publishers' folk book, "The first and second people's song books, *People's Song Book* (1948, reprinted 1956) and *Lift Every Voice* (1953), were the bibles of the guitar strummers and *Sing Out!* was that extra special Sunday sermon."[1]

People's Artists was declared subversive by our government in 1951,[2] and the long-time editor of its publication, *Sing Out!*, Mr. Irwin Silber, has been identified under oath as having been a member of the Communist Party,[3] In one Congressional report, Silber was designated as "a Communist propagandist."[4] He was, according to the HCUA hearing, "a Communist while . . . instructing at the Jefferson School of Social Sciences."[5] The Jefferson School has been declared subversive by the Attorney General of the United States. One need only look at *The Vietnam Songbook* compiled and edited by Silber and Barbara Dane to realize whose side he is on. With People's Artists' citation in the government's *Guide to Subversive Organizations and Publications*, Sing Out, Inc. and Oak Publications have, in the main, replaced People's Artists, Inc., although one can still purchase the materials of People's Songs and People's Artists from Sing Out, Inc. and the more recent Oak Publications.

Anyone reading *Sing Out!* magazine over any period of time will have little trouble detecting its pro-Communist bias. One single issue contained the "Ballad of Che Guevara" and the "Ballad of Ho Chi Minh" with the latter containing the punch line,

"Fight for freedom with Uncle Ho." We are further informed that "to kill is often an act of love." Written by Julius Lester, he goes on to say, "and I learned that from a beautiful shy young girl who is a guerrilla in South Vietnam. She's killed 25 G.I.'s and I knew when I met her that she knew about a love that I haven't experienced yet, but I look forward to the day when I will place a person in my rifle sight, squeeze the trigger, hear the explosion, and watch that person fall."[6]

Associate Editors of *Sing Out!* include Pete Seeger, Ed Badeaux, Joanne Grant, Julius Lester and Jerry Silverman.

Julius Lester, also a former contributing editor of *Broadside*, recently attended the 40th Anniversary of the Communist Publishing House, International Publishers, and glowingly related, "A speaker said the books of International Publishers will become standard equipment in the schools. I have news for you, they already are standard equipment in the Freedom School of Mississippi."[7]

Silverman, who has been lauded as "one of the most successful guitar teachers," appears in the most unusual publications. Four Continent Book Corporation is engaged in the Communist propaganda import business. "During the period of 1946 to 1960, Four Continent Book Corporation . . . imported from the Soviet Union printed material valued in excess of $1,000,000."[8] In one of Four Continent's official bulletins, openly displaying "Imported Records of the USSR" on the frontispiece, Jerry Silverman is credited with arranging the guitar chords for forty-four Russian folk songs and popular songs.[9] The bulletin is printed in both Russian and English.

Silverman also compiled a work for Oak Publications entitled *The Panic Is On*. It is advertised as "The panic is on and 62 other songs — outrageous, irreverent, subversive, and far out."[10]

Sing Out!, designated as "The Folk Song Magazine," is published by Oak Publications. Its songs are generally pressed by Folkways Records, Broadside Records, Elektra, Vanguard and sometimes Columbia Records. Broadside is a product of Folkways Records, and Elektra and Folkways work together.[11] In a recent Oak Publications announcement, the public was told, "In conjunction with Folkways Records, Oak Publications has now put out combination sets of its popular folk music instruction manuals with accompanying instruction records." In other announcements, we are openly told, "Books by Oak, Records by Folkways."[12]

Oak is also trying its hand at publishing filth, e.g., *The Erotic Muse*. The advertisement reads, "The Erotic Muse is the most definitive collection of so-called 'dirty' songs ever assembled for publication."[13] The only friendly review of the book that I could find was in the March/April, 1970, issue of *Sing Out!*. Oak and Folkways along with *Sing Out!* have until recently occupied the same address at 165 West 46th Street, New York City, for many years.

According to the *Washington Post*, Oak "is the largest publisher of folk music material in the field ... Oak's two owners, Irwin Silber and Moses Asch, are also the principal owners of *Sing Out!* considered the definitive folk song magazine."[14] Pete Seeger is also mentioned as part owner of the magazine.

The production director of Folkways Records is Moses Asch. He helped Seeger launch People's Songs and served as one of its sponsors.[15] For some time Asch was one of the co-owners and co-publishers of *Sing Out!*.[16] Asch not only wrote editorials for *Sing Out!*[17] but also reviewed books and records for the magazine. In one issue he favorably reviewed Walter Lowenfels' *Poets of Today*, published by the Communist International Publishers.[18] Gus Hall, general secretary of the Communist Party USA, likewise thought a great deal of Lowenfels' book and in a letter to Lowenfels said, "I changed all my family Christmas buying and instead bought 20 copies of *Poets of Today* with a note that I can't think of a better way of starting the New Year than by reading poems from this collection."[19]

Mr. Asch also wrote the foreword to Pete Seeger's work, *American Favorite Ballads.* In it he said, "Folkways Records, Pete Seeger, *Sing Out!* magazine and the host of folk song collectors, folk singers and record companies have made their contribution."

Pete Seeger, in his regular Johnny Appleseed, Jr. column (he's seed planting) in *Sing Out!* says, "Folkways Records stands for all time a unique landmark in the history of the recording companies of the world ... Moe Asch set out twenty-five years ago to document the music and sounds of the world . . . Credit Moe Asch with a second big accomplishment: his example has encouraged the starting of numerous other small recording ventures, in the United States and elsewhere, to continue the huge job of documenting the music and sounds of the world, unarranged, unprettified, unadorned . . . or unsatisfied."[20]

One possible small recording venture is called Paredon Records, Inc. with offices in Brooklyn at Box 889. In its mailing of October, 1971, the reader is treated to some remarks from *Ho Boc* the literature and art magazine of North Vietnam. It seems that *Ho Boc* thought Irwin Silber's *Vietnam Songbook* "a precious book." Of course, from the Communist side of the world it is. It contains such thoughts as, "Things are in a jam down in Vietnam, People down there don't dig Uncle Sam. Rule by the people just can't be wrong, And the people down there are the Viet Cong."

Paredon Records contends that its records "consist of music and speech, poetry andinterviews, documentary or dialogue, which are a part of the people's struggles." Therefore it is pushing Irwin Silber's pro-Communist *Vietnam Songbook* and such records as: "The East is Red," "Vietnam: Songs of Liberation," "Cuba Va!," "Huey Newton Speaks," "Angela Davis Speaks," "History of the Soviet Union in Ballad and Song" and other pro-Red selections.

Folkways Records has "documented" numerous Communist compositions of what it clandestinely terms "songs of struggle and protest."[21] Those records include the songs of the Communist Lincoln Brigade in Spain, the Communist Lumumba in the Congo, the Communist FLN in Algeria, songs composed by Communist Hanns Eisler,[22] anti-Polaris songs from Scotland, songs of Communist Joe Hill and songs of Angola's Communist "freedom" fighters.

In a recent publication, *The Fabric of Terror*, firsthand testimony concerning the Communist "national liberation" fighters in Angola, that Folkways Records considers so necessary to record, is given: "The beasts [Red-inspired savages] made no color discrimination. They slaughtered white, mulatto and Negro alike. They would throw the smaller children high into the air, let them drop on the soil to break their bones and then they . . . would play a brutal game of football with the bodies of those dying children, while the poor mothers screamed like crazy in the hands of the beasts. I didn't believe that anything so evil could exist in the world."[23] In another chilling incident we are told how the followers of Holden Roberto, a disciple of the late Communist Patrice Lumumba, actually cut up their helpless quivering victims through buzz saws — feet first![24]

Needless to say, the Communist *Worker* thinks very highly of Folkways Records,[25] but why the United States Government should subsidize such an obviously pro-Communist recording company is another matter! In a newsletter, Folkways Records proudly admits, "The Federal Government has recently made additional funds available to schools through the expanded National Defense Education Act, which now covers many new areas in addition to Science and Modern Language. Folkways Records are on most lists of approved material for this purpose. Take advantage of this aid by getting the best education recordings available."[26] Folkways Records, like Young People's Records and Children's Record Guild, are also popular in record catalogs for school teachers, especially Lyons *Elementary School Catalog* and *Tools of Teaching Catalog.*[27]

Scholastic Magazines, Inc. mailed an advertisement to high school teachers announcing that it and Folkways Records were practicing "togetherness" and that Folkways Records could now be purchased through Scholastic Magazines, Inc. One piece of material was actually headed, "Scholastic Order Form For Folkways Records." In an accompanying piece of literature one is informed that "*Scholastic* is now the exclusive educational distributor for Folkways Records."[28] The letter concludes with a P.S.: "Folkways Records are eligible for purchase under the provisions of NDEA [National Defense Education Act.]"

The catalog released by Scholastic Magazines contains such folk singers as Pete Seeger, Woody Guthrie, Jerry Silverman, Mike Seeger, Peggy Seeger, The Seeger Family, Lee Hays, Will Geer, Malvina Reynolds, Cisco Houston, Guy Carawan, Langston Hughes, Martin Luther King, Almanac Singers, Frank Hamilton and the New Lost City Ramblers. The catalog offers for high school consumption such records as: Songs of the USSR Revolution, Songs of the Spanish Civil War, Songs of the

[Communist] FLN, Ballads of Sacco and Vanzetti, Angolan [Communist] Freedom Songs, Songs against the House Committee on Un-American Activities, Songs for W.E.B. DuBois and the Songs of Communist Hanns Eisler. In the material accompanying the record, "Songs of Hanns Eisler," Eric Bentley explains that Eisler was the author of the infamous "Comintern" song:

Rise up, fields and workshops! Come out workers, farmers!
To battle, march onward! March onward, world stormers!
Eyes sharp on your guns, red banners unfurled,
Advance, proletarians, to conquer the world!

Oh you who are missing, oh comrades in dungeons
You're with us, you're with us, this day of our vengeance;
No fascist can daunt us, no terror can halt!
All lands will take flame with the fire of revolt!

The Comintern calls you! Raise high Soviet banner!
In steeled ranks to battle! Raise sickle and hammer!
Our answer: red legions! We rise in our might!
Our answer: red storm troops! We lunge to the fight!

From Russia victorious, the workers' October
Comes storming reaction's regime the world over.
We're coming with Lenin for Bolshevik work
From London, Havana, Berlin and New York!

Sing Out! contained an extremely complimentary article on Hanns Eisler by Eric Bentley who began his eulogy with, "Hanns Eisler, 1898-1962, is at last emerging from the relative obscurity imposed upon him by political prejudice."[29]

The Senate Internal Security Subcommittee, in its investigation of the Pugwash Conferences, released the following concerning Eisler:[30] "The *Daily Worker* of December 17, 1947, page 7, announced that Dr. Linus Pauling had signed a petition to Attorney General Tom Clark protesting the deportation proceedings against Hanns Eisler, composer of the international anthem of the Communist International and brother of Gerhart Eisler, official representative of the Communist International in the United States in the 1930's. Hanns Eisler was defended by the American Committee for Protection of Foreign Born which has been cited as subversive by the Attorney General."

The California Factfinding Committee on Un-American Activities pointed out that greetings were extended from the Hanns Eisler Branch of the Communist Party of Los Angeles County to another section of the conspiracy, and concluded, "the fact that a branch of the Communist Party in Los Angeles County was named after Hanns Eisler indicated his extreme importance to the Communist Party."[31]

Scholastic Magazines has not been the only company to be enticed into the Folkways web. Folkways Records has likewise entered into an arrangement with MGM (Metro-Goldwyn-Mayer). MGM and Folkways are discing a new label, Verve-Folkways. The new agreement "came into being as a result of a distribution deal between Moe Asch's Folkways Records and the MGM organization."[32]

According to news reports, "The deal between MGM and Folkways calls for MGM to select 275 albums from the Folkways catalog and to have first refusal on all new Folkways products."[33]

The major reason for the merge was to produce a new type of music, rock 'n' folk. Since Folkways and its sister organizations have folk music cornered through copyright, the rock 'n' roll companies interested in discing rock 'n' folk must come to Folkways for permission to use its folksongs, many of which are Marxist-oriented and even outright Communist.

The press release went on to state, "At the end of the month, Verve-Folkways will release its first single, a folk-rock record with two new English artists." It concluded: "Last week the first V-F program, 12 albums, was released. Two of the releases are with the New Lost City Ramblers (Mike Seeger's group) and Dickens S. Foster, while two are by Peter LaFarge and Dave Van Ronk singing blues. The rest with Lightning Hopkins, Leadbelly, the late Cisco Houston, Woody Guthrie and Pete Seeger, are authentic folk."[34]

This new marriage of beat and folk music is proving a total capitulation on the part of the US record companies to the Red-infested folk field. And since *The Worker* insisted on this exact type of music, labeling it "the 'soul' music of our sidewalks,"[35] it is absolutely consistent to learn from *Newsweek* magazine that Bob Dylan is the father of the new music and Irwin Silber and Moses Asch its major authorities.[36]

Chapter XXIII

BROADSIDE OF NEW YORK CITY

Sing Out! magazine's associate editor, Pete Seeger, helped launch a sister publication which was primarily established to print "radical" materials — "radical" in red linguistics meaning "Communist." This publication, with its genealogy firmly bedded in the tradition of the International Workers of the World's *Little Red Song Book* and People's Songs *Bulletins*, edited by Seeger, is called *Broadside.*[1]

The Communist publishing firm in the United States has printed a paperback edition on folk music entitled *Freedom in the Air.* The author, Josh Dunson, is a contributing editor of *Broadside.* In the book, Dunson reveals, "The American radical tradition and the need to combat commercialism influenced the formation of *Broadside* . . . The need for such a magazine was felt very strongly by Malvina Reynolds, Pete Seeger and Sis Cunningham's family. Sis Cunningham, formerly a singer with the Almanacs, [is] . . . *Broadside's* editor . . ."[2]

When *Sing Out!* changed its policy to printing only songs that were already circulated, a need was presented that merited a publication that would print original "radical" copy. *Broadside* was that publication. Founded in February, 1962, the publication has published steadily over the past years, and in an ad in *Sing Out!* boasted, "*Broadside* was the first to publish such songs as 'Blowin' in the Wind,' 'Little Boxes,' 'Ramblin' Boy.' "[3]

Broadside was also the first to publish "What a Friend We Have in Hoover," sung to the tune, "What a Friend We Have in Jesus." Its author, Tom Paxton, writes:[4]

What a friend we have in Hoover,
Freedom has no truer friend.
Is your thinking left of center?
He will get you in the end.
Does your telephone sound funny?
Is some stranger standing by?
Do not bother your repairman;

Take it to the F.B.I.

Are you now or have you ever
Been a member of a cell,
Are you running short of comrades?
Things aren't going very well?
Is the *Daily Worker* falt'ring
Has your treasury run dry?
Half your comrades know the answer:
Take it to the F.B.I.

The editor of *Broadside*, Sis Cunningham, has an enviable record of leftwing achievements. In the early 1930's she taught at the Commonwealth Labor College, nine miles out of Mena, Arkansas. She admits that the songs sung at the college "were not generally in what might be considered the American folk tradition." She says, "The most popular was the 'Internationale' and there was great interest in Chartist and IWW songs, as well as those in support of the Soviet Union, like 'Bankers and Bosses Hate Soviet Stars' and 'The Song of the Red Air Fleet.' "[5]

Sis Cunningham, wife of Gordon Friesen, then turned to the Almanac Singers, a singing group of the early 1940's which was organized by Pete Seeger and Lee Hays, and officially cited subversive by the United States Government.[6] The original Almanac Singers included Seeger, Hays, Millard Lampell and Woody Guthrie, but passing in and out of the Almanac picture were such varied individuals as Cisco Houston, Josh White, Tom Glazer, Sis Cunningham, Peter and Baldwin Hawes, Bess Lomax, Arthur Stern, Richard Dyer-Bennett, Huddie Ledbetter [Leadbelly], Sonny Terry, Brownie McGhee and Earl Robinson.[7]

Mrs. Friesen in the late 1940's was also part of the leadership of People's Artists, an organization cited subversive in the *Guide to Subversive Organizations and Publications.*[8] In the testimony of Walter S. Steele, Mr. Steele states, "People's Artists, Inc., referred to previously herein, maintains offices with Stage for Action at 11 West Charles Street, New York. It has sections in the Midwest and far West. Its leaders include Paul Bain, Bob Claiborne, Sis Cunningham, Eve Gentry, Cisco Houston, Phil Irving, Jane Martin, Brownie McGhee, Harry B. Ringel, Pete Seeger and Sonny Terry.

Claiborne and Seeger are with People's Songs, Inc. In Los Angeles the outfit is referred to as People's Artists Bureau."[9]

In 1952, Sis Cunningham was identified under oath as having been a member of the Communist apparatus. It seems that she was working at the district office of the Communist Party in Detroit, Michigan, with the title "Literature Director." The government report states, "At the time I knew Sis Cunningham, she was working at the district office of the Communist Party, that would be district 7 . . . Sis Cunningham was married to a newspaper reporter for the *Detroit Times*, I do believe, a fellow by the name of Gordon Friesen."[10] In this same testimony, given by Richard F. O'Hair, a former Military Intelligence agent within the Communist Party, O'Hair says, "Milton Freeman was a member of the Midtown Club of the Communist Party, was the husband of Sis Cunningham, and during his stay in Detroit was employed by the *Detroit Times* as a reporter."[11]

Another early founder of *Broadside* magazine was Malvina Reynolds. Her repast turns Sis Cunningham's into pale pink. Karl Prussion, for many years a member of the Communist Party, knew Mrs. Reynolds well. In his excellent publication *Heads Up*, Mr. Prussion, former counterspy for the F.B.I., states, "She has been part of the Communist conspiracy all her life — she was born into it. Her father was a charter member of the Communist Party, her sister was a Communist organizer, her brother-in-law for years has been a Commie-liner, her uncle was a member of the conspiracy. Malvina's cousin is a member of the Communist front organization, the National Lawyers' Guild.[12] She was first a member of the Young Pioneers (age one to thirteen), then the Young Communist League and finally the Communist Party affiliated to the Communist International. She has been rigorously trained in Red schools and attended the National Training School of the Communist Party and is rigidly disciplined.

" 'Bud' Reynolds, Malvina's husband, attended the International Communist Training School in Moscow, and was a member of the Michigan District Central Committee of the Communist Party. He was a Communist cadre and was expert in the leadership of provocative demonstrations and marches in the midwest area. He has many times attended top level meetings of the Central Committee of the Communist Party, U.S.A.

"Both Malvina and 'Bud' Reynolds visited your writer [Prussion] in the summer of 1956, while he was a counterspy for the FBI, to renew 'comradeship'. During their visit they stressed the importance of using the song-lyric media of reaching the youth of America with Communist doctrine and tactics."[13]

The advisor to *Broadside* is Pete Seeger. His name is carried on the magazine's masthead along with the numerous contributing editors of *Broadside*: Len H. Chandler, Jr., author of "Beans in my Ears," which was banned by many Public Health Departments; Gil Turner, one of the singers in the New World Singers group; Phil Ochs, present day star of both *Sing Out!* and *Broadside*, and author of such flaming Red folksongs as "I Ain't Marching Anymore," "Draft Dodger Rag," "Ringing of Revolution," "Talking Cuban Crisis" and "Ballad of William Worthy." Peter LaFarge, now deceased, but author of the poem, "Vision of a Past Warrior," which merited admission in the International Publishers' volume, *Poets of Today*, edited by Walter Lowenfels; Gordon Friesen, husband of the editor and writer of *Broadside* articles; Josh Dunson, author of the vicious "Talking Vietnam Blues," and Bob Dylan.

Dylan's familiarity with the whole *Broadside* enterprise is apparent from the history of *Broadside* itself. Dylan, according to Josh Dunson, was a regular visitor at the Sis Cunningham home and an early critic of *Broadside's* topical songs.[14] He fit in so well that before too long he was made a contributing editor of the Journal.[15] His own feelings toward the editor of *Broadside* can be judged by a letter he wrote her, "I shall get up to see you one of these days.Just cause I haven't in a while please don't think I'm not with you. I am with you more'n ever. Yours perhaps is the only paper that I am on the side of every single song you print and I am with with with you."[16]

In a *Broadside* article by Josh Dunson entitled "Yevtushenko, Lorca and Bob Dylan," Dylan is compared to the Russian Communist, Yevtushenko, and to the Spanish pro-Communist Garcia Lorca. Referring to Dylan as a "social critic," Dunson says, "Dylan in his songs too calls for the righting of the wrongs in his society, but they are so multitudinous and deeply imbedded what may be necessary is a new society as Woody Guthrie visualizes."[17] Needless to say, Woody Guthrie visualized a new Communist society!

In an interview with Dylan, the Communist publication, *National Guardian,*[18] reported, "Dylan has often been compared with Woody Guthrie, whom he reveres, and with Bertolt Brecht, his favorite poet."[19]

Bert Brecht has long been recognized for his pro-Communist affiliations. Sergi Tretyakov, a leading Soviet writer, in an interview with Brecht in Moscow said, "His play, 'Die Massnahme,' the first of Brecht's plays on a Communist theme is arranged like a court . . ."[20]

Brecht has collaborated with the Communist Hanns Eisler for over twenty years and the House Committee on Un-American Activities summed up his activities, "From an examination of the works Mr. Brecht has written, particularly in collaboration with Mr. Hanns Eisler, he seems to be a person of international importance to the Communist revolutionary movement."[21]

Dylan's feelings toward the United States were in sharp contrast to his attitude toward the Soviet Union. In the *National Guardian* interview he said, "Ain't nobody can say anything honest in the United States. Every place you look is cluttered with phoneys and lies." In referring to Communist Russia he states, "I'd like to visit Russia someday; see what it's like, maybe meet a Russian girl."[22]

Broadside is indeed a monthly folk journal of naked Communist propaganda. And although it hides behind such euphemisms as "protest" and "topical," its true intent is evident by its blatant dragooning of American culture and its consistent support of America's Communist enemies.

Its direct and indirect support of the Vietcong is only exceeded by its hatred toward everything American.

"Talking Vietnam" by Phil Ochs, a contributing editor of *Broadside,* contained the following perversion:

> Sailing over to Vietnam, fighting for the
> flag, fightin for my mom
> Well, training is the word we use, nice word
> to have in case we lose

. . . Training a million Vietnamese . . .
To fight for the American Way.

Well they put me in a barracks house just
across the way from Laos
They said, you're pretty safe when troops
deploy, but don't turn your back on your
houseboy
. . . When they ring the gong . . . Watch out for the
Vietcong.

Well, the sergeant said it's time to train
So I climbed aboard a helicopter plane
We flew above the battle ground
A sniper tried to shoot us down
. . . He must a-forgot we're only trainees . . .
Them commies never fight fair.

Well, the next day we trained some more
Burned some villages down to the floor,
Burned down the jungles far and wide
Made sure those reds had no place left to hide . . .
Threw all the people in relocation camps . . .
Under lock and key . . . Made sure they're free.[23]

Such cynicism is common in the pages of *Broadside.* It is a magazine fanning the flames of discontent and surrender by using every available psychological device to undermine the United States of America. Its support of the Communists in Vietnam is not an exception, but consistent with its character.

Malvina Reynolds, an early founder and almost monthly contributor to *Broadside*, wrote a folk piece, "Peace Isn't Treason."

Peace isn't treason, Peace is good reason
Peace is Heaven's will; Peace on earth is
what He said,
And I believe it still.
Is our country then so weak, that it can only
thrive

By bombing peasant villages
And burning babes alive — burning babes alive?[24]

Julius Lester, another contributing editor of *Broadside,* had the following to say concerning Vietnam in a poem, "Talking Vietnam Blues":

I guess you all heard about the Vietcong
Who sneaked around in Vietnam
Sneak upon Americans in the dead of night
And even if it is war, sneaking ain't right

The Secretary of Defense was mad . . .
Sneak attack . . . What'd he expect . . .
Engraved announcements?

Well, the President sent planes to North Vietnam
Told 'em "Go up there and drop some bombs
"We aren't spreading the war, just retaliatin'
"Everybody knows we're a peace-loving nation."

The more peace the better
Peace for every man
Piece of an arm . . .
Piece of a leg . . .
Six feet apiece . . . for everybody.[25]

In one *Broadside* issue, the late President Johnson is referred to as Hitler for conducting the war against the Communists in Vietnam. "Hitler ain't dead," we're told, "he just talks with a drawl." The song concludes, "Hitler ain't dead, but his time has come."[26] With the release of a Senate Internal Security Subcommittee report, "Murder International, Inc. — Murder and Kidnapping as an Instrument of Soviet Policy," and its findings that "the international murder apparatus of the Russian government continues to operate full blast."[27]

The Communist press sums up the importance of *Broadside*: "Two magazines are essential for an understanding of the topical and freedom song movement, *Sing Out!* and *Broadside*."[28]

Chapter XXIV

COMMUNIST SUBVERSION OF FOLK MUSIC

The influence of these individuals, with their publications and recording companies in the area of folk music, is astounding. It is our studied opinion that the Communists and pro-Communists have an unbelievable influence in the folk realm. They and their ideological comrades continue to receive the major publicity, and the press buildup is nearly as great for them as for the Beatles.[1]

The American Broadcasting Company issued a Hootenanny Song Book in conjunction with its Hootenanny program. The Song Book, containing reprints of *Sing Out!*, was compiled and edited by Irwin Silber with music edited by Jerry Silverman. It openly admits that "the folk music revival" was a movement which grew slowly during the war years and in the postwar age gained momentum with the formation of a group known as People's Songs, Inc., an organization of folk song singers. It was under the auspices of People's Songs that the "first 'Hootenannies' were presented on a large scale."[2]

The ABC-TV Hootenanny Song Book contains the works of Pete Seeger, Woody Guthrie, Mike Seeger, Peggy Seeger, Ewan MacColl, Cisco Houston, Irwin Silber, Jean Ritchie, Leadbelly and Malvina Reynolds. Most of the songs are depressing and obviously designed to stimulate revulsion toward patriotic sentiments. In fact, upon analyzing most of the publications of these individuals, one is struck with the seemingly deliberate attempt to denigrate the United States of America. Even our national anthem has to be splashed in the mud with an introductory remark, "The fact that the tune of this one of America's first revolutionary songs, was an old English drinking song proves that it came from the people and shall forever belong to the people."[3] Across the page from our national anthem is the "United Front" song which contends:

> And just because he's human
> He doesn't like a pistol to his head,
> He wants no servants under him

And no boss over his head.

And just because he's a worker
The job is all his own,
The liberation of the working class
Is the job of the workers alone.

In the *ABC-TV Song Book,* Jesse James no longer is a murderer and thief, but some peculiar type of humanitarian, since he stole from the rich and gave to the poor.[4] Obviously, he stole from the rich since the poor had nothing to be stolen, but whether ol' Jesse gave to the poor has yet to be established. The Virgin Birth of Christ is mocked with "The Cherry Tree Carol."[5] Silverman and Silber write a salty old blues "replete with not-so-secondary double meanings."[6] Morality is flouted with "Blow the Candles Out."[7] In fact, the only uplifting song in the whole production is "Moscow Nights," translated into English by Jerry Silverman and copyrighted by *Sing Out!*. The lyric ends with:[8]

Promise me, my love, as the dawn appears
And the darkness turns to light,
That you'll cherish, dear, through the passing years
This most beautiful Moscow night.
That you'll cherish, dear, through the passing years
This most beautiful Moscow night.

The discography (record) list in the back of the song book contains a who's who of pro-Red writers and singers of folk songs. It offers the Folkways Records' list of artists.

YOUNG FOLK SONG BOOK

Simon and Schuster published a work entitled *Young Folk Song Book.* It is edited by Earl Robinson, a Communist fronter and Fifth Amendment patriot, and dedicated to Woody Guthrie with an introduction by Pete Seeger. It contains the familiar names of Irwin Silber, Alan Lomax, Bob Dylan, Joan Baez, Malvina Reynolds, Mike Seeger and Peggy Seeger.

Joan Baez features Reynolds' "What Have They Done To The

Rain"[9] which was a part of the Communist thermonuclear holocaust fear propaganda concerning atomic fall-out. However, one can be confident that these Marxist minstrels will remain quiet over any Soviet infringement of the Moscow Test Ban Treaty. The State Department admitted "that the Soviet nuclear blast January 15, 1965 ... released radioactive debris in the atmosphere."[10] This is a prima facie violation of the 1963 Test Ban Treaty, even though "Russia ruled out any violation in the Treaty because the amount of radioactivity released was insignificant."

Bob "bola de churre" Dylan, who openly scorns clothes, baths and razors and is portrayed as "sloppy, disheveled, unshaven ... talks angrily and irreverently,"[11] opens his repertoire with "Song To Woody" — — —

> Hey-Hey, Woody Guthrie, I wrote you a song
> About a funny old world that's a-coming along.
> Seems sick and it's hungry, it's tired and it's torn
> It looks like it's dying and it's hardly been born.[12]

Dylan's "Ballad of Hollis Brown" portrays the "exciting" story of one who ends all by shooting his wife, five children and finally himself. In another of his favorites, "Masters of War," we are told he "likes to set up a rhythm, almost monotonous in its simplicity, and then put in front of it a hard driving melody and a powerful story. The song builds and maintains its intensity until, by the end, your head is ready to come off ..."[13]

According to *Life* magazine, his "villains are the people he calls 'Masters of War' who profit from the manufacture of weapons; the hypocrites who claim that 'with God on our side' they can justify whatever evil they want to commit; the professional anti-Communist; the segregationists who caused the death of people ..."[14]

It has perhaps never occurred to Mr. Dylan that World War II was started when Communist Russia signed a non-aggression pact with Adolph Hitler and actually helped the Nazis swallow Poland. It may also have escaped him that the Communists have been on the offensive with their "Wars of National Liberation" all over the world and that the single greatest threat to world peace is atheistic

Communism's intent on total world conquest. He may not be able to stomach "professional anti-Communists," but for reasons known only to him it is quite obvious that he can stomach "professional Communists."

In *Life's* eulogy, bearded bodyguards (Castro-style) protect "unwashen" Bob as he sings:

> Come Mothers and Fathers throughout the land
> And don't criticize what you can't understand
> Your sons and your daughters are beyond your command
> Your old rules are rapidly aging
> Please get out on a new one if you can't lend your hand
> For the times they are a-changing.[15]

Also included in *Young Folk Song Book* is Mike Seeger and his singing group, The New Lost City Ramblers, and Peggy Seeger, half-sister to Pete and sister to Mike Seeger. Peggy Seeger is married to Ewan MacColl and lives in England. Together with her husband she has published a book, *Songs for the Sixties.* Workers Music Association in London printed the book.[16] Until recently her husband has been denied a visa into the United States. His manager, Mr. Harold Leventhal, in a statement, said MacColl "was considered ineligible for a visa due to some regulation regarding his 'alleged' political beliefs."[17] Describing Peggy Seeger's exploits, Irwin Silber said, "In Russia at a World Youth Festival and in Communist China [defying the American State Department ban], Peggy was an American voice, singing the songs of her own heritage . . ."[18] Such are the personnel that make up Simon and Schuster's song book for young people.

Fireside Book of Folk Songs

Fireside Book of Folk Songs, also published by Simon and Schuster, is extremely popular in the classrooms of our public school systems. The work is beautifully bound with excellent style and art reproductions. However, even though obviously printed for children, it contains selections that do not "fill the eyes, the ears and the heart with pleasure," as we are assured on the jacket.

The Russian folk song "Meadowlands" is included in this work. The song is a tribute to the Communist Red Army — the army which William Z. Foster, former head of the Communist Party USA, said would someday assure a Soviet America.[19] "Meadowlands" is also to be found in *The People's Song Book*, originally published by Boni and Gaer, then People's Artists, Inc., then Sing Out, Inc., and now by Oak Publications.[20] The lyrics are totally nonevasive.[21]

In another selection entitled "Moscow," the children are informed that the song is "one of the stirring Red Army Songs that have come to us from the Soviet Union,"[22] and closes with, "We'll always stand together for dear Moscow's land."

"Tachanka" is also included in this volume. It is introduced with the following remarks, "A tachanka is a four-wheeled farm wagon much used in the Ukraine. During the Civil Wars the partisans set up in it any kind of gun they could get hold of and thus improvised a sort of mobile fire-power which for the first time offset the traditional and historical cavalry superiority of the Cossacks and the regular Tsarist army. So it has a sentimental and class significance to the Soviets."[23] Folksongs written during Khrushchev's death purges of the Ukraine[24] are missing!

"Come, Fellow Workers" is a Red Chinese song.[25] "Freiheit" is a tribute to the Communists fighting in Spain and is introduced with the explanation, ". . . the song of the Thaelmann Battalion; the first unit of the International Brigade."[26] "Los Cuatro Generales" also refers to the Spanish Communist forces,[27] and most of these pro-Communist songs are in *The People's Song Book*.

There are a few folksongs included which are obviously in bad taste, e.g., "Careless Love,"[28] but the most brazen pro-Red American folksong included in the *Fireside* book is entitled "Joe Hill." It is prefaced with "Joe Hill, a great labor organizer and poet, was executed in 1915 on a murder charge which union circles have always considered a frame-up."[29]

Apart from the obvious question as to which union circles, the unsuspecting reader is not informed that Joe Hill was an organizer for the old I.W.W., the forerunner of the Communist Party USA, and still on the Attorney General's list of active subversive organizations.[30] The volume, *Songs of Joe Hill*, has been published by People's Artists, Inc., and includes some of his best compositions. "Pie in the Sky," one of his better known, reads - - -

Long-haired preachers come out every night
Try to tell you what's wrong and what's right;
But when asked, how about something to eat,
They will answer with voices so sweet
You will eat, bye and bye
In that glorious land above the sky
Work and pray, live on hay
You'll get pie in the sky when you die (that's a lie).[31]

Some of Joe Hill's other songs make his Red position obvious. For example, in his "Workers of the World Awaken" we are told,

Workers of the world, awaken! Rise in all
your splendid might;
Take the wealth that you are making — it
belongs to you by right.
No one will for bread by crying, we'll have
freedom, love and health,
When the grand red flag is flying in the
Worker's Commonwealth.[32]

In his "Should I ever be a Soldier" he writes,

We're spending billions every year for guns
and ammunition
Our Army and Our Navy dear to keep in
good condition
While millions live in misery and millions
die before us,
Don't sing "My Country 'tis of thee," but
sing this little chorus,
Should I ever be a soldier,
'Neath the Red Flag I would fight;

Should the gun I ever shoulder,
It's to crush the tyrant's might,
Join the army of the toilers, men and
women fall in line
Wage slaves of the world arise
Do your duty for the cause
Land — and liberty.[33]

In a vicious parody on the Gospel hymn, "There is Power in the Blood of the Lamb," Joe Hill wrote, "If you've had 'nuff of the blood of the lamb, then join the Grand Industrial Band; If, for a change, you would have eggs and ham. Then Come! Do your share like a man."[34] His famous "The Rebel Girl" was dedicated to the late Elizabeth Gurley Flynn,[35] a former officer in the Communist Party, USA. Oddly enough, the Amalgamated Clothing Workers of America (AFL–CIO) still persist in singing Earl Robinson's "Joe Hill"[36] and even the Catholic Young Christian Workers Song Book has this song praising Joe Hill.[37]

The importance of Joe Hill can be seen from the fact that a full length motion picture was shown throughout the country entitled "Joe Hill." The title song which reads "I dreamed I saw Joe Hill last night, alive as you or me. Says I, but Joe you're ten years dead. I never died says he," was written by Earl Robinson of Metropolitan Music fame and sung by Joan Baez.

Dr. Jere Real, in an article on folk music, writes: "*Pageant* magazine published another folk masterpiece (March 1964), this one by music writer Nat Hentoff,[38] entitled, 'The Odyssey of Woody Guthrie — The Rebel Who Started the Folk-Song Craze.' That article tells of the glories of a number of persons who've been influential in folk-song propaganda: Guthrie, Millard Lampell, Malvina Reynolds, Louis Gordon, Lee Hays and, of course, Pete Seeger . . . Gordon is a former young Communist Leaguer, while Millard Lampell was identified as a Communist in Allan Sloan's testimony before HCUA.[39] Malvina Reynolds, mentioned by Hentoff, has recently attained a certain fame of her own in the folk fad. She was the author of a musical attack on development housing, entitled 'Little Boxes,' which has been very popular. Miss Reynolds is a Ban-the-Bomber like so many other folksingers. She was also identified as early as 1950 in sworn testimony before the House Committee on Un-American Activities and before the Senate Internal Security Subcommittee in 1963 as a Communist. She was even a columnist for the Communist publication, *People's World*,[40] and was registered as a Communist voter in 1936 and 1942."[41]

Hootenanny Tonight

Fawcett Publication press has produced a paperback book on folk music entitled *Hootenanny Tonight*. Pete Seeger and Woody Guthrie are favorably mentioned on the very first page. On the next page we are told, "However, I feel particularly indebted to Irwin Silber of *Sing Out!* magazine for his cooperation and advice. Over the years, I have found *Sing Out!* to be an extremely valuable source of ideas, information and just plain gossip about the world of folk music. If this sounds like a plug, that's exactly what it's meant to be. I enthusiastically recommend *Sing Out!* to everybody who enjoys this book. (Please write to Sing Out, Inc., 165 West 46th Street, New York 36, N.Y. for more information.)"[42]

One only wonders if Mr. Leisy, compiler of *Hootenanny Tonight*, fully realizes what he is saddling on the backs of innocent and naive readers. Mr. Silber and his potent *Sing Out!*, as mentioned before, are not exactly red, white and blue. In one of Mr. Silber's "Fan The Flames" of discontent editorials, he writes, "I wish there were an article on the songs of the Viet Cong which we could print in *Sing Out!* At the moment, I don't know how else to express the sense of despair and shame that I feel, as an American, at the actions of my government in Vietnam. Who is there who will shame and thereby vindicate the national conscience with a song, a play, a poem, a painting, a story, that will cut through the sham patriotism and pin the guilt of this madness on those who have decided to put American troops into battle 6,000 miles from home, to violate the borders of another land and to drop bombs on another country?"[43]

In a later "Fan The Flames" article, Silber refers to the former Secretary of Defense as "Mack the Knife" for his role in the Vietnam War. In verse form Silber quotes some unnamed agitator:

Who's aggressing?
Who is messing
In another country's life?
Not Hanoi, friend,
It's our boyfriend
McNamara, Mack the Knife.[44]

If Mr. Leisy has trouble understanding *Sing Out!* foreign policy, obviously some of *Sing Out's* readers aren't having the same difficulty. In a letter to the editor, Mr. Paul Perrine of Palm Beach, Florida, wrote, "Your editorial this month (*Sing Out!*, September 1965) is ridiculous. What true lover of the arts would mix it with present foreign policy? Robert Lowell is in the same category as Len Chandler who *uses* folk music to further his own 'causes.' What about my causes, such as being *for* stopping Communism in Vietnam, etc.? I can't see what this has to do with the enjoyment of folk music any more than it has to do with enjoyment of classical music. As long as people like you condone this sort of thing, true folk music, which is the basis for our enjoyment of the art, will suffer.

"It is becoming obvious that your magazine and its editors have no interest in folk music. You are a bunch of con-artists who get people to pay to read crap like your editorial under the guise of its being all about folk music.

"If you actually are a bunch of pro-Communist pacifists, I wouldn't expect this letter to have any effect whatsoever."[45]

In the same issue of *Sing Out!*, Mr. Joe Henderson, Croton-on-Hudson, New York, wrote, "You stuff too much into *Sing Out!* that has nothing to do with folk music. For instance, Irwin Silber's 'Songs from Berkeley' in the May issue, which makes heroes out of some clowns who make the cause for free speech something to laugh at. And 'Fan The Flames' in the same issue. Hoo-hah! 'Songs of the Vietcong,' indeed! Tell me, Mr. Silber, did you, during World War II, collect 'Songs of the Storm Troopers'? Stick to folk music. You're a bomb at politics."[46]

Needless to say, *Sing Out!* gave a warm review to *Hootenanny Tonight.* Written by Oscar Brand, it even referred to Leisy as "the phony gospel preacher who is converted."

According to Brand, "Jim Leisy has been saved."[47]

Although Leisy's work features many innocuous folk songs, it also contains the now famous "Suicide Song," a song apparently so popular that even third graders were "chanting invitation to suicide" in a California grade school.[48] The lyrics of the song are sick:

> Oh, come with me to the kitchen, to the kitchen,
> to the kitchen,
> Oh, come with me to the kitchen, and there a date
> with death we both will keep.
> Turn on the gas in the oven, in the oven, in the oven
> Turn on the gas in the oven and it will gently lull
> us both to sleep.
> Chorus: Listen to the his-sing sounds, listen to the
> his-sing sounds
> They're calling, gently calling, you and me.
> Listen to the his-sing sounds, listen to the
> his-sing sounds
> We'll say goodbye and die in ecstasy.[49]

The words were written by James Leisy and Pat Blanke and to be sung to the tune of "Listen to the Mockingbird." According to Leisy, it was written "one gloomy Sunday afternoon. It had a certain appeal in the high days of sick humor and I performed it occasionally and included it in the sick-song section of *Songs for Swingin' Housemothers.* I never really thought much of it, despite audience enthusiasm, until I began hearing it back from others in remote corners of the country. Pat and I were pleased to become a poor folks' Tom Lehrer — particularly when we heard he'd bought the book."[50]

However, it can hardly be considered "innocent fun" when one considers the following: "Child suicides are increasing at an alarming rate, according to the National Education Association, and now approach two a day. According to one official, there were probably between 369 and 738 suicide attempts in New Jersey in the four years 1960-1963, with at least 41 of them successful. The danger signs can appear as early as the first few months of kindergarten."[51] The article further states, "Five million Americans have tried at some time in their lives to commit suicide, and one million of them will eventually succeed. Tragic as these acts may be — especially to the surviving families and friends — the heartbreak is doubled when a child takes his life, or attempts to do so. Parents, teachers, classmates, all feel, too late, they could have done something."[52]

Hootenanny Tonight also contains the following fear verse, sung to a popular folk song:

> The atom bomb fell just the other day,
> The H bomb fell in the very same way.
> Russia went — England went — and the USA.
> The human race was finished without a
> chance to pray.[53]

Pete Seeger, Woody Guthrie, Peggy Seeger, Ewan MacColl, Jean Ritchie and *Sing Out!* are found throughout the book. But, of course, the bait is swallowed if the book does nothing more than persuade its readers to write Sing Out, Inc.

Longines' Symphonette

The Longines' Symphonette Recording Society distributed an album entitled "Legendary Folk Songs." The list of performers reads like a who's who of *Sing Out!* magazine. Pete Seeger, Woody Guthrie, Joan Baez, Mike Seeger, Phil Ochs, Cisco Houston, Jean Ritchie, Oscar Brand, Leadbelly, Sonny Terry, Leon Bibb, Ed McCurdy, Erik Darling, the New Lost City Ramblers and The Weavers are among those who Longines claims are the fifty greatest folk singers. Mishel Piastro chose the record selections with the comment, "Folk music is also an ideal way to gain the flavor of history and social studies during our nation's development."[54] Longines doesn't inform its many friends that sitting at Seeger's socks studying the social sciences would be comparable to taking an academic bath in Brezhnev's Baltic Sea.

A *Reader's Digest* article entitled "Behind the Folk Song

Frenzy"[55] continues to bolster the prestige of Guthrie, Leadbelly, Dylan and Reynolds. One can rest assured that the six million Americans now strumming guitars will inevitably find themselves served *Sing Out!* material if they follow the sympathies of the *Digest* article. "Newport Folk Festival" and "coffeehouses" are glibly thrown about without the slightest word of warning to the uninitiated.

Paul Nelson, former managing editor of *Sing Out!* and now a screenwriter, gave a glowing report of the Newport Folk Festival 1964, and the part played in that festival by Pete Seeger, Malvina Reynolds, Joan Baez, Judy Collins, Bob Dylan, Peter, Paul and Mary,[56] Doc Watson and other *Sing Out!* favorites.

The "coffeehouses" innocently mentioned in the *Digest's* article are not ordinary coffeehouses! For example, *Sing Out!* proudly announced, "The only Right Wing Coffeehouse on the West Coast [the Rally Right Political Folk-Singing Club] folded after three weeks."[57] There seems to be a list of "coffeehouses" available that specialize in "topical songs," i.e., songs of immorality, against the HCUA, against the South, songs for communism and revolution. These "coffeehouses" are geared to the folknik-beatnik set and must be quite popular, for *Sing Out!* has joyously announced a new full-length film entitled *Once Upon A Coffee House*[58]. Oscar Brand, radio folk-jockey, author of *The Ballad Mongers*[59] and sometime writer for *Sing Out!*, stars in the film. The story naturally portrays a young conservative millionaire falling in love with an attractive folksinger on a visit to a coffeehouse.

The *Digest* article admits that folksongs are a weapon, but concludes, "the folk frenzy is a matter for rejoicing" since it is making activists out of our college students. When one fully comprehends the "active-togetherness" experienced by the folksingers and Communists at Berkeley, one wonders whose side the *Digest's* writer is on?

The article's most obvious inconsistency is the writer's approval of *Time's* analysis of folk music, i.e., "rootless root seekers discern in folk songs the fine basic values of American life," along with his approval of *Variety's* analysis of folksinger Bob Dylan,

"Complaints against warmongers, poverty, injustice, atom fall-out, hard-hearted sweethearts and the selling and buying of soap. Nowhere was there one word of hope or remedy." The truth of the matter is that *Sing Out!* and its approved list of songs and singers are not about to sing America's finer qualities. A study of *Sing Out!* publications makes this obvious. For example, *Sing Out!* in one volume extols:(1) the gallows, p. 4; (2) death, p. 5; (3) seduction and hanging, p. 6; (4) child's loss of father, p. 8; (5) unjust and imperialistic Mexican War, p. 10; (6) misplaced love, p. 13; (7) poaching, p. 16; (8) ban the bomb, p. 17; (9) revolution, p. 18; (10) murder, p. 19; (11) desertion, p. 24; (12) illicit love, p. 26; (13) suicide, p. 29; (14) illicit love, p. 31; (15) murder, p. 33; (16) the bomb at Hiroshima, p. 39; (17)illicit love, p. 40; (18) death, p. 43; (19) parody on Korean veterans, p. 44; (20) wife-stealing, p. 45; (21) illicit love, p. 46; (22) parental disobedience, p. 47; (23) blood, p. 48; (24) chain gang, p. 51; (25) funeral mockery, p. 53; (26) death, p. 55; (27) laughter when children die, p. 57; (28) gallows, p. 59; (29) betrayal by false-hearted woman.[60] The other volumes in the reprint series are similar and some even worse. But then, one cannot "Fan The Flames" of discontent and revolution with fine qualities.

In contrast to *Sing Out!* procedure, Randy Sparks, formerly of the Christy Minstrels, says, "I have always tried to promote the happy, upbeat things in America."[61]

"Folk music is the idiom of the individual, seeking, rebelling," says *McCall's* magazine. Little, however, in the article, "Sight & Sound," would sound a warning to the American public that the rebelling, to a great extent, is Communist-inspired. The article favorably mentions Joan Baez, stating "Joan Baez was an empathy-stirrer in the Berkeley student-faculty clash,"[62] but failed to point out that J. Edgar Hoover publicly informed Congress that "students and faculty members with subversive backgrounds took part in recent demonstrations at both the University of California and the University of Wisconsin."[63]

The *McCall's* article concludes that Beatle music is waning in favor of the folk music of Pete Seeger, Bob Dylan, Joan Baez, Ted Bikel and Peter, Paul and Mary. It seems that Sid Bernstein, "pop impresario who brought the Beatles to Carnegie Hall last year

(1964), will stage the first New York Folk Festival, also at Carnegie Hall." The artists that Bernstein will bring to New York are, in the main, *Sing Out!* favorites. Trading Beatle music for this type of folk music is, as we have been seeking to portray, only a jump into another Red-infested area.

The Book-of-the-Month Club's recording division, The Classic Record Library, has offered to the American public a release entitled "American Folk Singers and Balladeers." Not satisfied with having thrust Children's Record Guild upon the American people, the Book-of-the-Month Club, in cooperation with Vanguard Recording Society, is now pushing Pete Seeger, Mike Seeger, Joan Baez, Erik Darling, The Weavers, Doc Watson, Jean Ritchie and other *Sing Out!* favorites.

The Book-of-the-Month Club would seem to stand in need of a thorough cleansing. According to the Veritas Foundation, "over 30% of the authors of the selections and dividend books of the Book-of-the-Month Club from 1926 through 1957 had Communist front affiliations. Since there is no equivalent listing of persons affiliated to purely socialist fronts, we can only speculate that of the remaining 70% a considerable proportion were of socialist origin. Such poisonous socialist and Communist propaganda items as Bernard Shaw's *Intelligent Woman's Guide to Socialism* and the official Soviet text of *New Russia's Primer* were distributed by the hundreds of thousands due to the impetus given to them by the Book-of-the-Month Club operation."[64]

In selling the four-record album one is informed that there "are two infanticides: Joan Baez's elfin voice makes pathos of *Mary Hamilton*; Ian and Sylvia somehow get a 20th-Century tension into the cruel mother's deed in the ancient *Greenwood Side.* Murders are harder to count. One is twice told the killing of Billy de Lyon by Stagolee, or Stack O'Lee, sung by the Rooftop Singers with drive, and by Mississippi John Hurt in what must be close to the original levee style . . . There are two murders and a suicide in *The Brown Girl,* which Hedy West learned from her grandmother in Georgia. The song, plainly, long antedates Grandmother and Georgia as well, since the bridegroom performs the second slaying with a sword which was part of his wedding attire — very long ago, very far away.

"But 'here and now' are represented, too. *Woke Up This Morning* evolved during an all-night singing contest between white and Negro freedom riders detained in a Mississippi jail. It, too, has the stamp of agelessness on it. You can sense it. These songs, old and new, are vitally and unmistakably, all of them, expressions of reality, which is the most gripping of all dramas . . . They strike direct from human nature; they say what they mean. Here you have them by the people who know them best, love them best and sing them best."[65]

Columbia Records

No sooner, however, does one attempt to set aside Book-of-the-Month Club's folksters,, than Columbia Records and its selections of folk entertainers appear. The names, advertised by Columbia, reveal the simple but monotonous fact that things haven't really changed much. Pete Seeger, Joan Baez, Len Chandler and Bob Dylan are all presently being disced and/or distributed by Columbia Records and its Record Club.

Josh Dunson, in his *Freedom in the Air*, published by the official Communist publishing house in the United States, International Publishers,[66] relates some interesting background material regarding the marriage of Bob Dylan and Columbia Records.

Dunson writes, "Bob Dylan, who is by far the best of all the topical song writers, found himself in a position of having recorded his songs for Columbia and not having them released. Only two songs out of the twelve on his first record were written by himself, and neither of them could be considered political in nature . . .

"However, his popularity grew even greater when he started to sing songs dealing with integration, war and the anti-shelter campaign. Finally, realizing their commercial potential, Columbia released his topical songs on *Freewheelin'*.

"When Columbia took this step, they gave their Artist and Repertoire man, John Hammond, a big green light. An extensive advertising campaign was initiated months before the actual release of the album, *Freewheelin'* containing the lyrical 'Blowin' in the Wind' and the highly poetic 'Hard Rains A-gonna Fall.' Alongside the clever and light 'It's All Right' there was the heated address to those whose wealth was based on war in the song, 'Masters of War.'

"In this song, Dylan expressed a bitterness that thousands of young people felt toward the generals and war manufacturers who rule a world ready to destroy itself . . . there is some truth to the statement that Dylan is the 'spokesman for our generation.' Perhaps it is more exact to say that Dylan has the talent to picture in his songs what people his age are feeling and thinking.

". . . Dylan had forced his songs and his contemporaries into the mass media. Within a year, 'Blowin' in the Wind' was leading the hit parade, and Dylan was to appear in a feature story in *Life* and as a performer on the Steve Allen Show."

And it is Dunson's considered opinion that Freewheelin' "spread more radical ideas to more people in a few short months than all the northern protest meetings and marches since 1960."[67]

Chapter XXV discusses more fully Columbia Records and its discing of the Communists' official revolutionary folksong sung by Pete Seeger.

When Pete Seeger made the comment that "the guitar could be mightier than the bomb,"[68] he wasn't engaging in wishful thinking. The truth is that these Marxist folksingers are achieving their nefarious objectives. Singing their Marxist ditties and making their listeners feel nauseated at living in America is proving extremely effective; and their scientific modus operandi is described thus by Dr. William J. Bryan, Jr.: "Sometimes a well-known folksong's tempo will be changed to the same beat as the normal pulse beat which makes it more effective for induction."[69] This is identically the same technique used by Young People's Records for children.

"Right now," according to Seeger, "many of the song traditions of the 1930's are seeing new life as never before — in the freedom songs of the South and in the topical singers of many a campus."[70] The following analysis in these two areas more than confirms Seeger's admission.

Chapter XXV

FOLK MUSIC AND THE NEGRO REVOLUTION

The revolutionary folksong of the Communists in this country is Pete Seeger's famous "We Shall Overcome." In fact, as Dr. Fernando Penabaz has pointed out, Fidel Castro's official slogan for the Communist regime in Cuba is precisely "Venceremos," i.e., "We Shall Overcome."[1] Fidel Castro closes every public speech with, "Patria o muerte, venceremos" (Fatherland or death, we shall overcome), and his captive mobs dutifully chant, "Venceremos."

Seeger was assisted with the words and music by Zilphia Horton, who was reported to be "more pro-Communist than her husband,"[2] Frank Hamilton, a member of The Weavers (formerly called the Almanac Singers), and Guy Carawan, of Red China fame.[3] Oak Publications, publishers of *Sing Out!*, has produced a volume of folksongs entitled *We Shall Overcome.* The volume was compiled by Guy and Candie Carawan for the Student Non-violent Coordinating Committee. In the preface, Guy Carawan states, "I came to the South about a year before the Sit-Ins began and made my home base at Highlander Folk School."

The "togetherness" of communism, folk music, Highlander Folk School (now known as the Highlander Center), SNCC, *Sing Out!*, Pete Seeger, Oak Publications and "We Shall Overcome" is important.

The folksong, "We Shall Overcome," was introduced into the Communist-planned Negro revolution through the Highlander Folk School in Monteagle, Tennessee. According to Carawan, "This modern adaptation of the old Negro church song, *I'll Overcome Someday*, has become the unofficial theme song for the freedom struggle in the South. The old words were: I'll be all right . . I'll be like Him . . . I'll wear the crown . . . I will overcome.

"Negro Food and Tobacco Union workers in Charleston, South Carolina, adapted the song for picket line use during their strike in 1945, and later brought it to Highlander Folk School. It soon became the school's theme song and associated with Zilphia

Horton's singing of it. She introduced it to union gatherings all across the South. On one of her trips to New York, Pete Seeger learned it from her and in the next few years he spread it across the North. Pete, Zilphia and others added verses appropriate to labor, peace and integration sentiments: We will end Jim Crow . . . We shall live in Peace . . . We shall organize . . . The whole wide world around . . . etc.

"In 1959, a few years after Zilphia died, I went to live and work at Highlander, hoping to learn something about folk music and life in the South and to help carry on some of Highlander's musical work in Zilphia's spirit. I had no idea at that time that the historic student demonstrations would be starting in the next few years and that I would be in a position to pass on this song and many others to students and adults involved in this new upsurge for freedom."[4]

Josh Dunson in his *Freedom in the Air* says much the same: " 'We Shall Overcome,' ' the central song of today's freedom movement, can be traced to Mrs. Horton's activity among the tobacco workers on strike in the 1940's. They had adopted the old Baptist hymn 'I'll Be All Right,' changing it to 'We Will Overcome' for their strike. It was collected by Mrs. Horton and became part of the Highlander song books.

"Zilphia Horton slowed down the tempo of the song and accompanied herself with an accordion in the white-mountain hymn-style. She taught it to Pete Seeger, who played it for a number of years in the North, adding verses and using a tremulo-banjo background. When Guy Carawan came to Highlander in 1959, he put the pulse or beat back into the song but kept Mrs. Horton's slower pace. At the April 1960 sit-in workshops, a number of other verses were added, including Myles Horton's 'The truth shall make us free,' when Carawan taught over 80 sit-in leaders the song for the first time. The last significant addition was made by the Albany Movement, which added the phrase 'I know that I do believe' before the final 'We shall overcome some day.' "[5]

The Highlander Folk School was organized by Don West and Myles Horton. West was identified under oath as having been a district director of the Communist Party in North Carolina.[6] Myles Horton was identified by John P. Frey, president of the Metal Trades Department of the AFL, as one of the persons who "attended a secret convention in North Carolina, at which time plans were made for spreading the revolutionary theories throughout the South."[7] When asked to become a member of the Communist Party, Horton replied, "I am doing you just as much good now as I would if I were a member of the Communist Party."[8]

Also closely associated with West and Horton was Dr. James Dombrowski, a protege of identified Communist Dr. Harry F. Ward[9] and himself identified as having been a high-ranking member of the Communist Party.[10] Significant also is the fact that all three, West, Horton and Dombrowski, were graduates of Union Theological Seminary, New York, and disciples of Harry F. Ward. Also of interest is the fact that the counsel for Dr. Dombrowski when he appeared before the Senate Internal Security Subcommittee was Benjamin E. Smith, a member of the subversive National Lawyers Guild[11] and at present registered under the Foreign Agents Registration Act as an agent for Fidel Castro.[12]

Benjamin E. Smith along with Kinoy and Kunstler were three who helped guide the legal affairs of the Mississippi Freedom Party. Interestingly enough, the law firm Kunstler, Kunstler and Kinoy, Smith's comrades in practice, represented Jack Ruby, who killed Lee Harvey Oswald, President Kennedy's assassin and former member of the Fair Play for Cuba Committee.[13] Kunstler was called as legal counsel for two Chicago individuals who were brought before the House Committee on Un-American Activities to testify concerning their Communist activity,[14] and in more recent times, of course, Kunstler was the attorney for the Chicago Seven Conspirators.[15]

Paul Crouch, an honorary commander of the Red Army and organizer for the Communist Party, formerly on the editorial staff of the *Daily Worker*, testified before the Senate Internal Security Subcommittee that "the Highlander Folk School is a school operated at Monteagle, Tennessee, ostensibly as an independent labor school, but actually working in close cooperation with the

Communist Party."[16]

Out of the loins of this little Red schoolhouse issued forth a student and close friend of the school: the late Martin Luther King. It was King who ultimately made the Reds' Revolutionary Folk Song national in scope. The American Broadcasting Company's song book explains it for posterity: "A number of years ago, members of the CIO Food and Tobacco Workers Union introduced the song (We Shall Overcome) at the Highlander Folk School in Monteagle, Tennessee. At the height of the successful Montgomery (Alabama) bus boycott led by Rev. Martin Luther King, a few years back, it was sung by Negroes in the face of a hostile mob — and television cameras caught the simple, moving dignity of the song and the people who sang it for the entire nation to see and hear."[17]

Martin Luther King, Jr.

Martin Luther King, Jr., referred to as a "troublemaker and rabble rouser" by the late President Harry Truman,[18] and as "the most notorious liar in the country" by the late FBI Director J. Edgar Hoover,[19] was not only a student of the Highlander Folk School of Monteagle, Tennessee,[20] but also openly welded his Southern Christian Leadership Conference to the Highlander Folk School.[21] *Freedom in the Air* revealed the fact that the Atlanta "Sing for Freedom" held May 7-10, 1964, was initiated by King's SCLC, SNCC and the Highlander Folk School.[22] In fact, when the Highlander Folk School changed its name and location to Highlander Center of Knoxville, Tennessee, Martin Luther King, Jr. was on the board of sponsors of the new organization.[23]

It was Martin Luther King, Jr., singing "We Shall Overcome," who led the nondescript marchers from Selma to Montgomery. Although the march contained some of good will,[24] there were many instances of gross immorality in public between Negro and white.[25] One minister stated that there "was evidence of much fornication ... and young women were returning to their respective homes apparently as unwed expectant mothers."[26] Rev. King, the perfect wolf in sheep's clothing, charged that the marchers were of a "higher moral tone than most."[27]

Representative William L. Dickinson, in a speech before the House of Representatives on March 30, 1965, stated that the marchers were promised "$10 per day, free room and board and all the sex they would want from opposite members of either race . . . Negro and white freedom marchers invaded a Negro church in Montgomery and engaged in an all-night session of debauchery within the church itself."[28] Morrie Ryskind, a columnist for the *Los Angeles Herald-Tribune*, nauseated by the vile acts of the marchers in Alabama, cried out, "But was the Cause really helped when 75 of those picketing Gov. George Wallace demonstrated by rising at a given signal and urinating in the streets?"[29]

But speaking before the capitol in Montgomery or participating prominently in the march and demonstrations were such notorious and identified Communists as Carl Braden[30] and Abner Berry, a member of the Central Committee of the Communist Party as well as a fellow student with King at the Highlander Folk School.[31]

Dr. Martin Luther King, Jr., who was associated with self-avowed Communists, e.g., Hunter Pitts O'Dell[32] and who was himself linked (mainly via finances) with "over sixty Communist fronts, individuals, and/or organizations, which give aid to or espouse Communist causes,"[33] also spoke at the capitol. Representative Dickinson, in his speech before the House of Representatives, said that Martin Luther King, Jr. "has been virtually surrounded by Communists or Communist fronts since 1955."[34]

Thus Dr. Martin Luther King, Jr., trained in part with Communists at the Highlander Folk School and an active participant in numerous Communist fronts, e.g., the National Committee to Abolish the House Un-American Activities Committee,[35] has time and again given aid to the Communist revolution in the United States.

Frank S. Meyer, former member of the Communist Party and now an able columnist for the *National Review* as well as author of the excellent book *Moulding of a Communist*, states the following concerning King: "As I read Dr. King, I wondered where I had previously heard those accents combining surface virtues with threatening ultimatum. Suddenly I remembered. It was in the writing of Friedrich Engels, denying that the Marxist revolutionaries of his day espoused violence. No, he said, we shall not institute violence; all we shall do is make the maintenance of existing civil order impossible and then its defenders will have either to use violence or to surrender."[36] He concludes, "This is the meaning of Dr. King's nonviolence: it is more convenient in the mobilization of force against constitutional order to bring it about that the first overt act of violence proceeds from others. It is a tactic, and it is hypocrisy on a grand scale."

The truth of the matter is that King agreed completely with Meyer. In a *Saturday Review* article he admitted his four-fold plan: (1) Nonviolent demonstrators go into the streets to exercise their constitutional rights. (2) Racists resist by unleashing violence against them. (3) Americans demand Federal intervention and legislation. (4) The Administration, under mass pressure, initiates measures of immediate intervention and remedial legislation.[37]

It was King who announced his coming visit with President Johnson and upon being received was assured a "voter-rights bill" would soon be ready. It was — straight out of the Communist "Lincoln Project" drawn up in 1957.[38] The bill affects the six southern states that the Communists hope to turn into a Negro-Soviet America.[39]

On March 10, 1965, identified Communist Harry Bridges in a speech at San Francisco called for "A boycott against the State of Alabama."[40] Eighteen days later, on March 28, 1965, Martin Luther King, Jr. "called on America and the world . . . to engage in a massive economic boycott against Alabama."[41] No wonder *The Worker* declared, "Those who forecast or hoped for a decline in the Freedom Fight after the passage of the Civil Rights law, including President Johnson, failed to understand the nature and the goals of the Civil Rights Revolution. That Revolution was never stronger and never more widely supported than it is now . . ."[42]. *Political Affairs*, monthly Communist publication, made it explicitly clear that the Civil Rights Revolution would "lay an indispensable basis for the socialist and Communist future" of the United States.[43]

King consistently followed the Communist Party line, e.g., in his attitude against America's only friend in the Congo, Moise Tshombe,[44] in the position against rescuing the hostages (including missionaries) the Communists were slaughtering in the Congo,[45] and his insistence that we pull out of South Vietnam and allow it to go Red.[46] When Los Angeles was burned by Red-inspired goons and lackeys,[47] King arrived on schedule to denounce the police as brutal (a Communist tactic for decades) and to demand the firing of one of America's greatest chiefs of police, the late William H. Parker. Mayor Samuel W. Yorty of Los Angeles had the following to say concerning King's so-called charge of police brutality, "Eleven out of every one hundred Los Angeles policemen were assaulted last year. When you hear talk of police brutality, remember that brutality against the police is a tremendous problem. Communists and their sympathizers have bandied about police brutality charges for three decades as part of a big lie technique."[48]

Following his Los Angeles debacle, King turned his attention toward the international arena and demanded U.S. recognition of Communist China. Allen and Scott admitted, however, that King slowed down on this demand since there was a possibility of breaking some type of law. However, since King publicly announced his intention of breaking every law he felt unjust, this law might well have entered his category of unjust laws.

Although it is considered improper now to criticize the late Dr. King (liberal clergymen refer to him as the "voice of God"), still the record must speak. The Johns Legislative Investigating Committee of the State of Florida declared, "Dr. Martin Luther King, Jr. and unruly whites were to blame for last summer's racial trouble in St. Augustine." The 147-page report stated that King deliberately selected St. Augustine as the most economically vulnerable target in Florida. The Committee also charged that major TV news organizations made contributions to both factions in the racial conflict for the purpose of obtaining sensational action shots which "presented a distorted view of conditions in St. Augustine."[49]

Senator Mark Hatfield criticized civil rights leaders — including Dr. Martin Luther King — who break laws under the general doctrine of civil disobedience. In a commencement address Hatfield declared, "I say to you that in a nation founded upon a constitutional form of government, which has processes by which we can change laws with which we disagree, we do not have the right to deliberately violate laws, no matter what our rank of life."[50]

SNCC

John Lewis, one time national chairman of the Student Nonviolent Coordinating Committee and an active participant not only in the Selma march but also in the Harlem rally, which called for the removal of our troops from Saigon to Selma,[51] returned from a tour in Africa where he and ten other SNCC workers were the honored guests of the Guinea Government. Lewis also toured Liberia, Ghana, Zambia, Egypt and Kenya and, according to *The Worker*, called for the cementing of relationships "between the African Liberation Movements and the Civil Rights Movement in America."[52] African liberation movements or "national wars of liberation," as they are called, are Communist-controlled and manipulated!

However, it was Lewis' organization, the Student Nonviolent Coordinating Committee, for whom the Highlander Carawan compiled his work, *We Shall Overcome.* Perhaps this accounts for a University of Pittsburgh chaplain, Rabbi Richard L. Rubenstein, admitting that the leaders of SNCC were a group of "activists and revolutionaries." He said they "wanted dead bodies, our bodies."[53] During the Montgomery demonstrations, SNCC leaders "went into a high school and asked young children to leave their classes and join the demonstration . . . SNCC leaders did the same thing at a grammar school . . . that was both immoral and illegal."[54]

This, of course, is not surprising to the readers of the *New Republic*, who were told in August 1964, by Christopher Jencks, that the Student Nonviolent Coordinating Committee "represents a new generation of Negroes . . . rebellious and radical," and that these young radicals were not looking for a chance to "make it" in white America, but "a chance to remake America along more egalitarian and proletarian lines." Jencks says, "SNCC workers are fascinated by Mississippi because to their minds it comes closer to being a 'pre-revolutionary situation' than any other in America."[55]

Christian Crusade's *Weekly Crusader* published a lengthy article on the SNCC organization. One section entitled "SNCC Attitude Toward Communists" read:

"During April 1965, a celebration in honor of Paul Robeson's 66th birthday was held in the Americana Hotel in New York. Paul Robeson is a Negro singer who has long been active in Communist causes and who, in 1949 at a Soviet-controlled 'peace' conference in Paris, claimed that American Negroes would not fight for the United States against Soviet Russia in case of all-out military conflict. Robeson has also been identified as a Communist by witnesses before Congressional committees. This tribute to Paul Robeson on his 66th birthday was reported in an article in *The Worker* of May 2, 1965. *The Worker* claimed that '2,000 friends and admirers' were present.

"This article in *The Worker* identified John Lewis, chairman of the Student Nonviolent Coordinating Committee, as one of the 'young torch bearers' who was there to help honor Paul Robeson. According to *The Worker,* Lewis 'was there to tell how Robeson, "an All-American football star and Phi Beta Kappa graduate, internationally famous actor and singer . . . represented the entire Negro people of this country." . . .'

"This article in the May 2 issue of *The Worker* went on to report that Lewis tied his SNCC into Paul Robeson's philosophy (which is the Communist philosophy) as follows: 'We of SNCC are Paul Robeson's spiritual children. We too have rejected gradualism and moderation. We are also being accused of radicalism, of Communist infiltration.' Of course, it would be hard to name a person who is more notorious in this country for activity in behalf of Communist causes than is Paul Robeson.

"The 'liberal' *Atlanta Constitution* of February 2, 1964, reported that the Student Nonviolent Coordinating Committee included 'at least two faculty members of Atlanta Negro Colleges who have been identified by an FBI undercover agent in public hearings before the House Committee on Un-American Activities as Communist Party members' and that 'several other SNCC workers have been involved in Communist Party-related activities.'

"The *Atlanta Constitution* article identified the two college faculty members as Mrs. Isobel Cerney, a teacher of public speaking and English at Morris Brown College, and Dr. Harry C. Steinmetz, whom the *Constitution* identified as a 'professor of psychology.'

"Another 'liberal' source which recognized the SNCC's tolerant attitude toward Communist conspirators was *Newsweek* magazine in its April 12, 1965, issue. *Newsweek* reported: 'SNCC's attitude about Communist participation in its activities is decidedly laissez-faire. It makes no effort to screen its 250 field workers for Communist sympathies, and has no regulation barring Communists from leadership posts . . .' *Newsweek* went on to quote an SNCC official in Los Angeles as saying, 'We're more revolutionary than the Communists.'

"Liberal Mississippi editor Hodding Carter III found out from personal experience the SNCC attitude toward Communist conspirators, reported in the April 12, 1965, issue of *Newsweek* as follows: '. . . when moderate Mississippi editor Hodding Carter III — whose *Greenville Delta Democrat-Times* had been giving sympathetic coverage to SNCC activities — took some visiting journalists to the local headquarters in January, he was dismayed to find piles of Communist literature on display.'[56]

"Another goal of the Student Nonviolent Coordinating Committee which may throw further light on the reason the Communist conspirators were so interested in the election of an SNCC official to the Georgia House of Representatives relates to undermining the FBI. An article in *The Worker* of December 6, 1964, reported on this SNCC objective as follows: '*The Student Voice*, weekly publication of the Student Nonviolent Coordinating Committee, in an editorial last week characterized the FBI under J. Edgar Hoover as a "police state to Southern Negroes" and declared "It is now time to end the Hoover version of the FBI." . . .'

"Still another important Communist conspiracy goal which is pushed by the Student Nonviolent Coordinating Committee is the drive to force the United States to cease resistance to Communist aggression in Vietnam. SNCC was one of the cooperating organizations in the Easter, 1965, 'peace' march on Washington. The April 20, 1965, issue of the Communist conspiracy's newspaper, *The Worker*, reported that ' "Snick" not only endorsed the march but . . . did quite a job mobilizing for it . . .'

'Apparently the Student Nonviolent Coordinating Committee has tax-exempt status for promotion of its harmful objectives. The news story in the February 2, 1964, issue of the *Atlanta Constitution*, from which we quoted earlier, referred to SNCC as a tax-exempt organization."

In concluding its analysis of SNCC, the *Weekly Crusader* stated, "A false and harmful theory in regard to our nation's race problems is the theory which insists that once the demands of organizations such as SNCC are met, our race problems will vanish. This is an absurd theory that has been disproved over and over again. The activities of these 'civil rights' organizations show that this is just not true. The fallacy of this theory was noted by UPI writer Lyle Wilson in an article which appeared in *The Tulsa Tribune* of July 30, 1964. Mr. Wilson wrote: "The comforting Northern theory that the problem of race relations would solve itself once Negro citizens won the right to vote has been shot full of holes by the New York City race riots. Negroes vote freely in New York . . .' Actually, current history is proving that the situation will grow worse as more and more demands of these radical Negro racists and their white sympathizers and dupes are met. Anyone who will dig into the facts of the Communist involvement in the 'civil rights' strife will come to the conclusion that these forces have no stopping point short of complete destruction of the American way of life. Once this important fact of life can penetrate the minds of a substantial proportion of the American people, a move back toward a sensible analysis of the problem by government officials can be started. Of course, it is a tough proposition as long as politicians are being put into office and perpetuated in office by following this fallacious line of reasoning concerning our nation's race problems. It will take a widespread awakening of the people to bring about the type of political pressure which will stop this current trend toward national disaster."[57]

The official folksingers for SNCC, according to Josh Dunson in his *Freedom in the Air*, are Chuck Neblett, Rutha Harris, Bertha Gober, Bernice and Cordell Reagon. They have formed a singing group known as "The Freedom Singers" and Dunson says, "The

Freedom Singers were the major group responsible for spreading freedom songs over the nation."[58] He also very convincingly connects or marries this singing group to SNCC with his comment, "The group was formed with the aim of raising money and spreading the ideas of SNCC. All the singers were SNCC field secretaries."[59] Although the group started slowly, according to Dunson, they "were finally able to command high fees for engagements. These fees were turned over to SNCC and netted between $45,000 and $50,000. The successful concert tour managed by Toshi Seeger, Pete's wife, acquainted tens of thousands of college students and adults with the work of SNCC and the significance of the movement."[60]

SNCC and its singers have been involved in numerous activities in the South. In the Atlanta "Sing for Freedom," as it was called, SNCC joined forces with Martin Luther King's Southern Christian Leadership Conference (SCLC) and the Highlander crowd. The folk festivities were held on the old campus of the Gammon Theological Seminary and the "Sing" was planned by Bernice and Cordell Reagon, Ruby D. Robinson, Dorothy Cotten, the Rev. Young and Guy Carawan. Participating in the "Sing for Freedom" were such personalities as Phil Ochs, Len Chandler, Tom Paxton, Ernie Marrs, Bud Foote and Ted Bikel (described by Dunson as one who "has had a long and close association with the Southern student movement"[61]).

John Lewis and his SNCC also assisted Martin Luther King's bedraggled band of marchers from Selma to Montgomery. Also joining his friends and compatriots in the march was none other than Pete Seeger. One reporter wrote: "Folksinger Pete Seeger, his guitar slung across his back, sat on a car and discussed with some of the marchers the songs they have made up along the road."[62] Their favorite song, however, was old faithful, "We Shall Overcome."

Since truth is oftentimes stranger than fiction, it is not surprising to find, as is pointed out in the last chapter, that Pete Seeger's record album, "We Shall Overcome," has been recorded and distributed by Columbia Records. Why this one time respectable record company would disc this Communist revolutionary song and other songs of Pete Seeger, Malvina

Reynolds, Len Chandler and Bob Dylan is still a mystery.

John Hammond, a top Columbia official, was openly given the credit for drawing Bob Dylan into a Columbia contract.[63] And now Pete Seeger's albums carry the name of John Hammond as producer including Seeger's album, "Dangerous Songs!?" Here Seeger offers such gems as "Draft Dodger Rag" (written by Phil Ochs), "The Pill" and "Mao Tse-tung."

In defending Columbia's practice of discing and distributing pro-Communist materials by Marxist minstrels, Columbia's attorney, Lawrence Harris, maintains that the record company's primary concern "is not their political affiliation, but their artistic ability."[64]

Such a position overlooks the simple truth that an identified member of the Communist Party is not merely a political affiliation. Mr. J. Edgar Hoover, in his *Masters of Deceit*, wrote, "Communists are not American. The Communist Party, U.S.A. endeavors, in every possible way, to convince this country that it is American. This is a typical Aesopian trick. Communism stands for everything America abhors: slave camps, rigged elections, purges, dictatorships ... The Communist movement was born abroad, was imported into the United States, and grew up under the personal direction of Russian leaders in Moscow. How can Communism be American when it employs every form of treason and trickery to bring about ultimate domination of the United States by a foreign power?"[65]

The pro-Communist influence exerted by Pete Seeger through the prestige given him by Columbia Records is inexcusable. The damage already done to this country through his influence is impossible to calculate. It would therefore seem, not from a monetary, but certainly from a patriotic position, that Columbia Records should cease and desist in its production and distribution of singers and songs of subversion.

Columbia Records' attitude toward songs of subversion, however, can be measured by consulting Dr. Hook's "Sloppy Seconds" copyrighted by CBS in 1972. The record, though rock and not folk, contains every form of degradation and corruption for youth. Maybe that is why the lyrics are copyrighted by "Evil Eye, Inc."

But perhaps more startling than any of the above is the fact that the late President Johnson incorporated the Communist revolutionary slogan in his voter-rights address to the American people[66] and again following the revolt in Watts. *Sing Out!* magazine remarked, " 'We Shall Overcome' has been unofficially (but effectively) banned from South African music shops after John Harris sang it on the gallows in Johannesburg early in August. The Pete Seeger recording is the most difficult to get. Until the hanging, government authorities did not realize that it was an American freedom song . . . Meanwhile, in America, we find a photograph of President Johnson on the cover of the sheet music of the song because he quoted the words on a TV broadcast to the nation. While he spoke of freedom in America, he was depriving countless thousands of freedom and life in Vietnam. It's not fair."[67]

James Farmer, former national director of CORE, who had recently returned from an African tour during which he conferred with the Congolese Communist rebels, proudly boasted, "The President is proclaiming our slogans."[68] Farmer's claim was heard in his militant keynote address before the National Conference on South Africa Crisis and American Action. Columnists Allen and Scott reported that two members of the Soviet delegation to the United Nations were prominent throughout the three-day deliberations of the National Conference Guerodot Garilovich Tchernouchtchenko, representing Byelorussia, and Sergi Tinofeevich Shevchenko, of the Ukraine, huddled "constantly with the conference leaders and African diplomats, particularly from Algeria and Ghana."[69]

Such then is the influence of the Red folksingers among the Marxist Negro revolutionaries.

Chapter XXVI

FOLK MUSIC AND THE COLLEGE REVOLUTION

Jules Dubois, former Latin American correspondent for the *Chicago Tribune*, reported in the bulletin of the American Security Council that the Kremlin in 1964 established an unlimited "global solidarity" fund to finance Communist-led student agitation throughout the world, with $100,000,000 allocated for 1965 to Latin America alone. He also observed that the outbreak of student agitation and lawlessness at the University of California, with numerous Communists involved, was not isolated from the Kremlin global plan, but followed the usual pattern.[1]

The experiential togetherness of Marxist guitar-playing folksingers and student rioters is as obvious as girls screaming in Beatle concerts. The University of California at Berkeley provides an excellent illustration of this fondness, and undergirds our thesis regarding the Communist use of folk music.

Irwin Silber, in a *Sing Out!* article, "Songs From Berkeley," admits, "songs and singing were an integral part of the now historic battle on the California campus spearheaded by the Free Speech Movement (FSM) . . . it is a reflection of the sure hold folksinging has on the campus — and the great flexibility of the topical folk song tradition that lends itself to spontaneous expression . . . Leading folksingers (Joan Baez, Barbara Dane, the Freedom Singers, Malvina Reynolds) have lent their voices to the battle — and a whole bevy of writers and songleaders have played a leading role in the movement."[2] Silber cites one of the students' newly-created folk songs entitled "Hey, Mr. Newman." The lyrics contend:

> You call me a Commie, say that all my friends are Red,
> But we've been freezing here for freedom
> While you've been sleeping in your nice warm bed.
>
> Yes, my hair is long, and I haven't shaved in days,

But fighting for my freedom
While clean-cut kids just look the other way.

My boots are old, and my collars don't button down
But you don't need no tuxedo
When you're fighting for the rights of man.[3]

On December 3, 1964, police arrested over 800 persons who had sprawled all night in the University of California administration building in a demonstration described by the state's governor as "anarchy." More than 500 police, sheriff's deputies, and highway patrolmen cleared the four-story Sproul Hall at 3:15 p.m. when they carried or dragged the last of the limp resisters to the patrol wagons.

Rebellious students retaliated by trying to organize a campus-wide general strike. The rebels demanded that trucks entering the campus with foodstuffs and other supplies observe their picket lines. Indeed, if one were not aware of the locale, one could easily mistake the antics in Berkeley for the Communist antics in Africa or Latin America. Nearly every paragraph of the news dispatches emanating from the campus mentioned the "rebellious students" or the "rebels."

According to the press, "The first person to be arrested was a non-student, Robert Treuhaft, Oakland attorney and husband of Jessica Mitford, author of the book about funeral practices, *The American Way of Death.*"[4]

In "The Role of the Communist Lawyer," a government document, "Robert Treuhaft was identified as a member of the Communist Party in sworn testimony before the Committee on Un-American Activities on December 2, 1953, by Dickson P. Hill and on December 3, 1953, by Charles D. Blodgett. He was again identified in June 1957 by Dr. Jack Patten."[5]

An Associated Press dispatch said one of those arrested was Mario Savio, 21, a rebel leader. His key aide in directing the demonstrations was Bettina Aptheker, who was identified by university officials as the daughter of Herbert Aptheker, listed by the House Committee on Un-American Activities as a Communist theoretician.[6]

Not only has Bettina Aptheker, since the riots, admitted

publicly that she is a Communist,[7] but surprisingly enough won a position on the campus Rules Committee. In an editorial, "A Victory by UC Minority," the *San Francisco Examiner* stated, "The Rules Committee election on UC's Berkeley campus fulfilled an old law — that people get the kind of government they deserve. Most of the 27,000 students sat out the election. But the campus far-outers, VDCers and filthy worders didn't. So the election went the way they wanted it. They cared. Few others did. Bettina Aptheker, a Communist and proud of it, was the leader of seven undergraduates for committee membership. The radical political organization, Slate, elected all 26 of its candidates to a constitutional convention. The Graduate Coordinating Committee, a moving force in last year's Free Speech Movement, won all of the 23 graduate seats in the convention. These are the fruits of minority rule."[8]

Bettina Aptheker has been active in the Berkeley chapter of the W.E.B. DuBois Clubs, which were described by the late F.B.I. Director J. Edgar Hoover as "dominated and controlled by the Communists."[9] W.E.B. DuBois, for whom the clubs were named, was a Communist Party member and is buried in Ghana.

Mario Savio, himself a member of a Trotskyite Communist organization,[10] speaking to the Young Socialist Alliance, a Trotskyite organization, said that student revolts against established authority can be understood by those who study Karl Marx.[11]

For a full account of the Communist, pro-Communist and extremist organizations and individuals participating in this Communist-led and directed riot, we strongly recommend a series of articles in the *San Francisco Examiner* entitled "Behind the UC Rebellion."[12]

However, a particularly significant news item reported, "Joan Baez, guitar playing folk-singer, sang the civil rights anthem, 'We Shall Overcome,' as the students swarmed into the building yesterday, but the recording artist left the campus last night before the arrests began."[13] The California Senate Factfinding Subcommittee on Un-American Activities reported, "At 12:30 Baez and Savio began singing 'We Shall Overcome,' and led the march into Sproul Hall. Like the children of Hamelin following the Pied Piper, about five hundred of the assembled multitude followed their leaders into the building . . ."[14] Immediately before the arrests began, however, the report states, "Joan Baez and other FSM (Free Speech Movement) leaders who were considered too important to be immobilized by arrests, escaped from the building and disappeared into the crowd."[15]

Miss Baez was only one of many guitar-playing folksingers present, but she was by far the most popular. In TV films of the riot, one could observe many unshaven, unwashed, guitar-playing folksingers, with their sandals, sweatshirts and tight pants. The situation was a natural for these dustball creatures and what better means of excitation than guitar-strumming and *Sing Out!* folksongs!

In fact, *Sing Out!* has published an ode to non-conformity entitled "See the Beatnik."

> See, the beatniks in the Village
> See, the beatniks on Macdougal Street
> See, the beatniks in the Village
> And they all look just the same.
>
> . . . the boys all wear dungarees,
> and the girls all wear sandals,
> And they're all non-conformists
> and they all dress just the same.
> And they all go to the university
> And they all major in philosophy,
> And they're all deep thinkers,
> And they all think the same.
>
> And they all like folk music,
> And they dig Woody Guthrie,
> And just like Bob Dylan, they
> All sound the same.[16]

The Communist *Worker* reported that Miss Joan Baez was among those wiring greetings to the newly launched and Communist-spawned DuBois Clubs of America.[17] This Red organization played a vital role in the Berkeley revolution.

In a recent Harlem Rally where Jesse Gray, identified member of the Communist Party and mayoralty candidate for New York City, received a standing ovation when he declared "We don't need our troops in South Vietnam, the Marines should be sent to Selma," Joan Baez, according to *The Worker*, entertained the rally.[18] She sang, "We Shall Overcome."

It was this same Joan Baez, along with Judy Collins, who entertained the "more than 20,000 student radicals who swarmed into Washington Saturday, picketing the White House, and staging a protest march against President Johnson's policies in Viet Nam."[19] The key song again was "We Shall Overcome." The crowd was admittedly beatnik and folknik, but then, according to *Sing Out!* beatle-niks, beatniks and folkniks are entirely compatible.[20]

Allen and Scott in their daily news column reported, "The Communist Party definitely had an important hand in this so-called student march on Washington last Saturday to demonstrate against U.S. policy in Viet Nam. As far back as March 5, the Communist Party National Organization Department sent a letter to all district officials, directing vigorous support of this then secret project. Also that month, the national headquarters of the W.E.B. DuBois Clubs, the party's youth organization, dispatched a directive to its branches throughout the country, calling for their full backing."[21]

Of course, Miss Baez's sympathies have not been hidden. While in Paris sometime back where she gave a concert at the Palais de Chaillot she said she would agree to perform in Hanoi if asked, "but I would not perform for United States forces in Saigon."[22] Not unexpectedly her next stop was Moscow, Leningrad and Kiev. A year and a half later while collecting draft cards to send to President Nixon at her Inglewood, California, concert, she admitted, "I am a revolutionary. I wanted to show that you don't just speak out if you are a revolutionary, you act it out."[23] She further acted out her revolutionary role by appearing before the French Communist Party's Festival of Humanity where she was "paid her usual fee and won applause for talking about her 'pacifist-anarchist' views."[24]

Miss Baez, a Pete Seeger disciple,[25] not only proudly displays her talents to revolutionary dregs of pseudo-intellectualism, but also enjoys portraying her anti-Americanism. For example, she said, "I used to sing 'The Star Spangled Banner' when I was tiny — it was just part of the day — but I never liked it. By high school, I wouldn't sing it anymore because I knew even then it was just so much trash. [Our emphasis.] At President Kennedy's Inauguration I remember thinking what a drag it was when they had to sing that same old 'bombs-bursting-in-air' song. It's so phony. As far as 'God Bless America' is concerned, when they used to sing about going through the night with a light from above, I always pictured this old bum standing under a street lamp. That's all the song ever meant to me."[26] (*Fact* magazine, which printed her testimonial, is presently lobbying for a new national anthem. "We Shall Overcome" by Pete Seeger and "This Land Is Your Land" by Woody Guthrie are both being pushed to replace "The Star Spangled Banner.")

At a recent Business Executives Move for Vietnam peace rally she repeatedly dropped the American flag to the floor as a symbolic gesture of what she really thinks.[27]

Dr. Jere Real, in his analysis of Joan Baez, states, "It is not surprising that her repertoire includes a rock 'n' roll parody of the House Committee on Un-American Activities and such musical propaganda devices as 'Strangest Dream' (a 'peace' ballad). She describes herself as 'earnestly political' and takes part in 'peace' marches, Ban-the-Bomb campaigns, and 'Civil Rights' agitation. 'I feel strongly,' she said in a *Look* interview,[28] 'about things like murdering babies with fall-out [one wonders if she's against abortion, too] and murdering spirits with segregation.' Miss Baez, who has said that 'money is just an excuse for a guilt complex,' has withheld large portions of her federal income tax — 'the 60 per cent. . . that goes to armaments.'[29] Although Joan Baez refuses to pay her taxes to the United States government, since it is fighting a war against Communists in South Vietnam, Miss Baez evidently had no scruples in helping the United Nations war effort in putting down anti-Communist Katanga. According to Florence Fowler Lyons, the two heaviest private donors to the United Nations in fiscal 1962 were Nelson Rockefeller and Joan Baez, who gave $1,361.60. Miss Lyons also points out that Joan Baez's father, Albert, 'holds down one of the highest paid jobs in the UNESCO

Secretariat in Paris.' "[30]

Joan Baez's Institute for the Study of Nonviolence in Carmel Valley, California, won its case before the Monterey County Board of Supervisors and can be operated from 8 a.m. to 6 p.m., Monday through Friday. The Institute was established, against the better judgment of 450 interested petitioners, for the purposes of meditation, nonviolent exercise and rigorous study of Thoreau and C. Wright Mills[31] (authority on Castro-type revolutions). In analyzing the various schools recently established and based on the new leftist idea of "counter-institution" (setting up a protest organization parallel to an established one in order to expose and eventually change it), *Newsweek* admits the "movement really began in late 1964 at the Berkeley campus of the University of California during the Free Speech Movement revolt."

It also admits that "Marxism is standard fare."[32] Although Miss Baez characterizes her school as one designed to "purge violence from their [students'] personalities," one can be sure that sooner or later her much exercised, muscle-bound toughs will be attempting to stop troop trains or throwing another flying wedge in Sproul Hall.

Broadside made a great deal over Joan Baez's participation in an organization called Artists' Civil Rights Association, Inc., located at 156 Fifth Ave., New York. Artists included in this group were to contribute one day's earnings to the Fund, preferably February 12, 1965 (*Lincoln's Birthday*). Assisting Baez in this "worthy" cause were Peter, Paul and Mary, Harry Belafonte, Godfrey Cambridge and fifty other entertainers, including Steve Allen.[33]

It is no secret that Miss Baez refused to appear on the popular ABC Hootenanny program while it barred Pete Seeger and The Weavers. In commenting on the situation, *The Worker* reminded ABC that "doing a 'Hoot' without Pete is like playing baseball without a baseball ... The term 'Hootenanny' was virtually invented by Seeger."[34] Theodore Bikel, in the *International Musician*, agrees with *The Worker* regarding the origin of the "Hootenanny." Bikel states, "The word 'Hootenanny' belongs to the people. Pete Seeger, Woody Guthrie and Lee Hays of the Old Weavers have given it its present manner, namely that of a folk song get-together."[35] *The ABC-TV Hootenanny Song Book* frankly admits, "It was under the auspices of People's Songs that the first 'Hootenannies' were presented on a large scale, and the initial ventures into magazine and songbook publishing took place."[36] The irony of this particular situation is that while the American Broadcasting Company barred Seeger from its television program, it permitted Seeger and his two associates, Silber and Silverman, to dominate and even edit the *ABC-TV Hootenanny Song Book.*

The last chapter on the Communist use of folk music has yet to be written. Only in April, 1973, "bi-sexual" Baez (she now admits enjoying women as well as men) entertained the French Communist Party while walking along Ho Chi Minh and Karl Marx avenues. (*Time*, Sept. 27, 1971, p.48) She also endorsed the 1968 Communist student upheavals in France. There is little doubt that Marxist folksingers are hand in glove with student demonstrations and riots. The long arm of Seeger's People's Songs, Inc. is very much in evidence, not only through his protege Joan Baez and her bearded friends, but also through *Sing Out!* magazine. Future campus riots can be confidently predicted as a very essential part of the Communist program of incitation and agitation.

There is little doubt that the Communist youth movement in the United States would have been crippled if state and university officials had acted quickly and vigorously in Berkeley. Every student arrested and convicted of disobeying a university rule should have been expelled. Every person who participated in any kind of demonstration that disturbed peace and order at the university should have been arrested and prosecuted.[37] Instead, one of the agitators, Robert Treuhaft, identified under oath as a member of the Communist Party, was invited to speak on "extremism" at the Pacific School of Religion.[38]

As Dan Smoot put it, "Negotiating and compromising with student rioters means surrender of our universities, and ultimately our nation, to agitators and subversives."[39] Unless we alert loyal and patriotic college and university students to the growing menace we face, we could well pay the ultimate price for an apparently innocuous music corporation, established in 1946 and known as People's Songs, Inc.

PART FIVE
COMMUNIST USE OF ROCK 'N' FOLK

"How do you think the enemy will feel with a tune like that No. 1 in America?"

— Bob Eubanks, Los Angeles,
Disc Jockey,
Time, September 17, 1965,
p. 102.

Chapter XXVII
DEFINITION OF ROCK 'N' FOLK

The combination of the dangerous beat of rock 'n' roll with the potentially dangerous lyrics of folk music has been christened rock 'n' folk.

This synthesis alone could spell the doom of the United States of America, for no nation can long endure with its younger generation singing itself into defeatism, pessimism, a peace-at-any-price mentality, disarmament, appeasement, surrender, fear of death, hatred toward the South, atheism, immorality, drugs, revolution and negation of patriotism. *Newsweek* magazine in an article on rock 'n' folk observed, "The folky rollers protest against being put down, being hung up, being drafted, Vietnam, Selma, the F.B.I., the Bomb."[1]

The marriage of rock 'n' folk music presents a "natural" for Communist exploitation and manipulation, since the folk field has been, in the main, under their domination for twenty years. The rock 'n' roll companies interested in discing the folk-rock sound have to come their way for copyright reasons.

In an article entitled "Don't Throw Rocks at Rock 'n' Roll," *The Worker* insisted that rock 'n' roll become more serious and adopt lyrics downgrading life in the United States. The writer, Gene Williams, realizing the tremendous potential in such a marriage, stated, "Beneath all the jukebox jive there exists an idiom capable of narrating the millions of young lives confined to the ghettos of our cities."[2]

Moving into the rock 'n' folk arena, Gene Williams confesses, "I've sung tunes like 'Woke Up This Morning With My Mind on Freedom' and 'Ain't Gonna Let Nobody Turn Me Round' countless times, but at each singing the baritone bops a little harder, the handclapping becomes more syncopated; and I begin to identify the throb of the music with the pulse of the struggle."[3]

"The music that throbs with the pulse of the struggle" is an interesting definition of the new "soul of the sidewalk" music presently known as rock 'n' folk. Rome burned while a fiddle played, but the United States may well burn with a drum and guitar.

Chapter XXVIII

POWER OF THE BALLAD

Andrew Fletcher, Scot writer, orator, patriot and one time member of the Scottish Parliament, stated on the floor of Parliament in 1704, "I knew a very wise man who believed that if a man were permitted to make all the ballads, he need not care who should make the laws of a nation. And we find that most of the ancient legislators thought they could not well reform the manners of any city without the help of a lyric and sometimes of a dramatic poet."[1] When one realizes the background of many of the new-type songs presently being disced and played around the clock over huge radio transmitters located strategically throughout the United States, Fletcher of Salton's warning merits attention.

The power of the ballad put to music has been known by some from the beginning of human history.[2] Peter, Paul and Mary frankly admitted, "We could mobilize the youth of America today in a way that nobody else could. We could conceivably travel with a presidential candidate, and maybe even sway an election . . . Not that we're going to use this power. It's enough to know that we have it."[3] The Marxists have no such inhibitions!

Chapter XXIX

FOLKWAYS AND METRO-GOLDWYN-MAYER

Billboard, the international music-record newsweekly, headlined a story by Aaron Sternfield, "Rock + Folk + Protest = An Erupting New Sound."

According to the front page article, dated August 21, 1965, and five full months after *The Worker* demanded such a music, we are informed that "a hybrid, combining the best and instrumentation of rock music with the folk lyric — usually a fresh urban lyric, and often a lyric of protest — is selling across the board."

Although he doesn't mention the fact that "lyrics of protest" are generally anti-American and pro-Communist, Sternfield does mention that one company now discing the new sound is Folkways Records.[1]

As pointed out in our chapter on the Communist use of folk music, the founder and director of Folkways Records is Moses Asch. Asch has also been co-owner and co-publisher of *Sing Out!* magazine,[2] and for some time has had his Folkways' offices at 165 West 46th Street, New York City, along with *Sing Out!* and Oak Publications. Asch was a sponsoring member of the old People's Songs, Inc.,[3] which was cited subversive by the California Senate Fact-Finding Subcommittee on Un-American Activities.[4] He has been a lifelong intimate of Pete Seeger, Woody Guthrie and Irwin Silber.

Sternfield points out in *Billboard*, "Verve-Folkways, the label that came into being as a result of a distribution deal between Moe Asch's Folkways Records and the MGM organization, will branch out from its folk music base and become a specialty label for MGM."[5]

The artists to perform for the new label, according to Sternfield, include Pete Seeger, Woody Guthrie, Leadbelly, Cisco Houston, Mike Seeger's group, Peter LaFarge and Dave Van Ronk. *Sing Out!* in its November 1965 issue advertised these very Verve-Folkways records as distributed by MGM.[6] American young people can now be assured of the best anti-American ballads from one of America's most pro-Communist music houses, Folkways Records. In the future, no doubt, one can anticipate such Marxist jewels as "Songs of the USSR," "Songs of Hanns Eisler," "Songs of W.E.B. DuBois" and "Songs against the Senate and House Internal Securities Subcommittees" — all geared to destroy the United States or praise international Communism.

Chapter XXX

PRINCE OF ROCK 'N' FOLK

The crown prince of rock 'n' folk is Bob Dylan. *Newsweek* magazine announced it in very patriotic terminology: "The Patrick Henry of this revolution is twenty-four year old Bob Dylan, a bony, prophet-haired poet of protest."[1] Even *Time* magazine admitted, "Folk 'n' rock owes its origins to Bob Dylan, 24, folk music's most celebrated contemporary composer."[2] Dylan, a faithful disciple of identified Communist Woody Guthrie,[3] has reached heights never before available to one steeped in the traditions of Communists like Brecht, Lorca and Yevtushenko.[4] Even Allen Ginsberg, the San Francisco poet who openly advocates promiscuous relations among sexes,[5] says that Dylan is "the most influential poet of his generation."[6] Dylan in turn thinks Ginsberg should have been invited to the Kennedy inauguration instead of Robert Frost.[7]

International Publishers, official Communist publishing firm in the United States,[8] goes into some historical detail concerning Dylan in its work on Marxist folk music, *Freedom in the Air.* The author, Josh Dunson, is not only an associate editor of the pro-Communist folk journal, *Broadside,*[9] but a recent addition to the *Sing Out!* staff.[10]

According to *Freedom in the Air,* Bob Dylan left the University of Minnesota during his freshman year and bummed around the country. As irony would have it, he was rejected by Folkways Records but accepted by Columbia Records. It seems that, at first, Dylan found himself in the position of having recorded his songs for Columbia and not having them released. However, with time and assistance from leftist John Hammond,[11] Columbia released his topical (pro-Communist) songs in the record album *Freewheelin'.* According to *The Bob Dylan Story,* "Hammond had received advance notice of the Dylan talent from his own son, a singer, who had heard Bob previously and raved about him."[12] Of course, the book fails to point out that Hammond is connected with the pro-Communist operations emanating out of the

Highlander Center, Knoxville, Tennessee.

Even International's folk critique had to admit that "Bob Dylan's best record is *Freewheelin'*."[13] Columbia spent a great deal of money building and advertising the album which included "Blowin' in the Wind," "Hard Rain," "It's All Right" and "Masters of War." In the latter, Dylan expresses bitter hatred toward the generals and war manufacturers who, he says, rule the world and are about to destroy it. Irwin Silber, writing in *Sing Out!*, praised Dylan's album by stating, "He is a rare bird, this Bob Dylan, a phenomenon in his own time, a guitar-picking poet who has somehow reached out and touched the nerve center of his generation. In less than two years, this fiercely talented 22-year-old has rocked the folk music world and the popular music industry with an outpouring of the most startling new songs heard in these parts since Woody Guthrie."[14]

The *Freewheelin'* album made Dylan a national figure and before long *Life* magazine published a feature article describing him as "sloppy, disheveled, unshaven ... talks angrily and irreverently,"[15] and Steve Allen presented him to his audience on The Steve Allen Show.

International Publishers says of the album *Freewheelin'*, "This record spread more radical[16] ideas to more people in a few short months than all the northern protest meetings and marches since 1960."[17]

But the first and most basic influence on Dylan, according to *Freedom in the Air*, "was that of Woody Guthrie."[18] In fact, in *Young Folk Song Book*, Dylan has a "Song to Woody" in which he tells Guthrie about a world that seems sick, tired, torn, and dying although it's hardly been born — no doubt referring to the United States, but assures Guthrie of "a coming new world."[19] One can only surmise whether or not he is referring to William Z. Foster's or Langston Hughes' Soviet America, but then Guthrie would not be interested in any other America. Not only has Guthrie been identified under oath as having been a member of the Communist Party,[20] but Dunson points out that Guthrie wrote a column for the *Daily Worker* entitled, "Woody Sez."[21]

Dylan, as pointed out in our previous chapter on folk music, has been a contributing editor of the pro-Communist *Broadside* journal and a fellow-traveler of the *Broadside* movement from its inception. In fact, he openly admits that *Broadside* gave him his start.[22] And *The Bob Dylan Story* further admits, "Lots of his songs were being published — in *Broadside, Sing Out!*, and even by an 'uptown' publisher. His picture appeared on the cover of *Sing Out!*. John Hammond brought him to the attention of Mitch Miller, who was interested in his music. He appeared in hootenannies at Carnegie Hall and Town Hall. He played Boston. He taped a topical song program for FM radio with Pete Seeger, Sis Cunningham and Gil Turner. He went to England to do a few concerts and tape a program for BBC television. He took part in the great Freedom March on Washington."[23]

And even though some maintain Mr. Dylan has lost contact with movements, it should be noted that he "contributes lavishly to SNCC."[24] He also acknowledges that pro-Communist Bertold Brecht is his favorite poet and his attitude toward the United States in contrast to his pro-Russian feelings betrays his conscious motivations. It should be remembered, too, that Dylan's promoter for some time, Harold Leventhal, is the same Leventhal who manages Pete Seeger and The Weavers.[25]

The International Publishers' book, *Freedom in the Air*, admits that Dylan's best poem is "Hard Rain." Interestingly enough, it also acknowledges that this poem "appears in a poetry anthology edited by a leading American man of letters, Walter Lowenfels."[26] What the book fails to print is the fact that Lowenfels himself has been identified under oath as having been a member of the Communist Party,[27] and that his book *Poets of Today* was published by Communist publishing company, International Publishers. It also failed to point out that *Poets of Today* was highly praised by Gus Hall, leading American Communist Party member, in *Political Affairs*, the recognized theoretical journal of the Communist Party, U.S.A.[28] Dylan's poem is found on page forty-one in the book, and according to copyright acknowledgements, Dylan permitted Lowenfels the usage of his poem. The poem was written at the height of the Cuban missile crisis[29] and was geared to instill fear into the hearts of Americans over the possibility of a nuclear war.

For Dylan's usefulness to the Communist Party and his open

and defiant attitude toward anti-Communists, the Communist front, Emergency Civil Liberties Committee,[30] presented Dylan its Tom Paine Award. According to Dunson, Dylan was quite taken back with ECLC's display of finery, but took the award nevertheless.[31] *The Bob Dylan Story* seeks to soften the blow by pinning the award to that catch-all, "civil rights." Says the Ribakoves, "In December he was given the coveted Tom Paine Award of the Emergency Civil Liberties Committee in recognition of his work for civil rights."[32] However, Mr. and Mrs. Ribakove failed to inform their many readers that the "Emergency Civil Liberties Committee, established in 1951, although representing itself as a non-Communist group, actually operates as a front for the Communist Party. It has repeatedly assisted, by means of funds and legal aid, Communists involved in Smith Act violations and similar legal proceedings. One of its chief activities has been and still is the dissemination of voluminous Communist propaganda material."[33]

Josh Dunson then seemingly gives away the mystique of Dylan's recent switch from a sloppy, disheveled Castro-looking cultist to the more respectable rock 'n' folk composer and singer. Dunson says, "He wants to reach more Americans by using many of the melodic phrases of the Beatles, a popular rock 'n' roll group imported from England."[34] He also admits, "In the light of the general level of popular tunes, I think most people would be very pleased if Dylan's latest songs made the hit parade."[35] The trouble is — his songs have not only made the hit parade — but landed right on top! And even now we are informed by Katy Woolston of the *Albuquerque Tribune* that "Hovering on the horizon may be the hairy style of Bob Dylan, folk rock 'n' roller from Gallup, classed by music trade journals as the No. 1 influence on teenagers."[36] *The Bob Dylan Story* observes, "Much as he may wish to escape, he will not be allowed to abdicate his position as spokesman for rebellious youth. Ten years ago, young people might have ignored him; the pendulum had not yet begun to swing away from middle-class virtues and ideals. But today's youngsters do not want conformity — they want individuality, the wilder the better . . . Still, most of them know they will not get what they want, the majority will turn away reluctantly from radical ideas (emphasis ours) and head back to the middle of the road."[37]

Sy and Barbara continue to write, "The highschoolers are not well equipped to follow his difficult symbolic poetry," referring to Dylan, "and when they are moving to the beat, they can hardly come away with more than a general impression of rebellion. Actually, they are more at home with 'Eve of Destruction' . . . and the anti-war songs of England's Donovan Leitch."[38]

For parents whose daughters believe Dylan to be a fine, uplifting musician, one need only notice his answer to a question asked recently by a national magazine concerning his kind of girl. Said Dylan, "I want my woman dirty looking as though I'd just found her in some alley. Dirt is very attractive. It triggers the animal emotion. I want dirty long hair hanging all over the place.

"I hate shaved legs or arms. I hate cleaning or astringent lotion because those antiseptic smells revolt me. I hate girls who like Rock Hudson."[39] The columnist for the *Des Moines Register*, Donald Kaul, asks, "Now, would you want a man like that to marry your cocker spaniel" and concludes, "I Want a Girl Just Like the Girl That Bobby Dylan Hates."[40]

Irwin Silber, editor of *Sing Out!* and identified under oath as having been a member of the Communist Party,[41] has both praised and condemned Dylan.[42] Phil Ochs, author of "Draft Dodger Rag," "Ringing of the Revolution" and other pro-Communist pieces, eulogizes Dylan with, "As for Bob's writing, I believe it is as brilliant as ever and is clearly improving all the time. On his last record, 'Ballad in Plain D' and 'It Ain't Me Babe' are masterpieces of personal statements that have as great a significance as any of his protest material. How can anyone be so pretentious as to set guidelines for an artist to follow?"[43] In *The Bob Dylan Story*, the writers point up the fact that Ochs sincerely believes Dylan will have to leave the country.[44] For some strange reason the authors fail to relate the two countries suggested by Ochs — Cuba or France.[45]

Dylan himself, however, acknowledges, "I know in my own mind what I'm doing. If anyone has imagination, he'll know what I'm doing. If they can't understand my songs they're missing something. If they can't understand green clocks, wet chairs, purple lamps or hostile statues, they're missing something, too."[46]

Moses Asch, on the other hand, and Silber's co-publisher at *Sing Out!* as well as director of Folkways Records, has only praise for Dylan.[47] And since *Sing Out!* has accepted the advertisements of Verve-Folkways, the publisher of the new rock 'n' folk music, and since Asch is in at the bottom of the new sound and co-owner of *Sing Out!*, one can predict with some certainty that Bob Dylan's newest albums will be pushed through its pages.

Chapter XXXI

THE ROCK 'N' FOLK MAGAZINE

Moving into the publishers' vacuum created by the new music is the *Rock Folk Song Folio.* It is the first popular rock 'n' folk magazine. Presently being published quarterly by the Onyx Publishing Co., it mails from the Charlton Building, Derby, Connecticut.

In its first issue, the magazine eulogizes P.F. Sloan, author of "Eve of Destruction"; Bob Dylan; Joan Baez; Phil Ochs and Pete Seeger.

It refers to Sloan as "a wide-eyed young man of 19 with startled eyes and a cap which seems to grow on his head."[1] One of his more recent pieces, "Sins of a Family," probes into the adolescent mind of the female. The song was copyrighted by Trousdale Music Publishers, Inc., and reads in part:

> She had a bad childhood while she was very young
> So don't judge her too badly
> She had a schizophrenic mother who worked in the gutter,
> Would have sold herself to the devil gladly
> What a sad envir'nment, a bug ridden tenement;
> And when they couldn't pay the rent
>
> It's cause her father was out gettin' likkered
> Oh, the stone's been cast and blood's thicker than water;
> And the sins of a family fall on the daughter
> And the sins of a family fall on the daughter.[2]

His "Eve of Destruction" is analyzed in the next chapter.

Bob Dylan is introduced with the admission that he has "systematically shaken, upset, overturned and finally re-routed the entire course of contemporary folk music. There isn't a singer in the folk field today who hasn't in some way been influenced by him, in his writing, his performing, even in his appearance."

From the article one notices that Dylan has invaded England, too. On a recent tour there he "managed to surpass The Beatles, The Rolling Stones, The Animals and all the rest of them on the record charts; suddenly everyone stopped dancing and started listening."

He even has the Beatles intrigued, according to the Song Folio. "He's the most popular American export over there since Elvis Presley, and has received the approval of virtually everyone in the business, including the Beatles, who are acknowledging him as a great influence on their own music and on the whole Mersey sound."[3]

Joan Baez also has her place in the new trade magazine. Naturally the youth are not told how she feels toward our National Anthem ("The Star Spangled Banner is just so much trash"[4]). It might prejudice the young minds! Instead we are informed that "Joan likes to sing topical protest songs, but she feels there are very few around that mean anything."

She also admits that "Phil Ochs is one of [my] favorite writers." His song, "There But For Fortune," was a big hit for her recently in England. She also "likes Bob Dylan's songs for their beauty both as poetry and music." Referring to Dylan, she states that he would "grow more and more important."

"Regarding the future of folk music," the article points out, "she simply wants to keep singing and try to do something to keep the bomb from falling."[5]

Instead of alerting the rock 'n' folk fans to the works of Phil Ochs and his position with the pro-Communist *Broadside* journal, the magazine prints one of Ochs' more notorious pieces, "I Ain't Marching Anymore."[6] The song has been taken off some radio stations for its pro-Red bias. Perhaps in the next issue of *Song Folio* the editors will print his "Talking Vietnam" or "Draft Dodger Rag"; it did print Seeger's "Flowers" song!

Indeed, never have so few anti-American folksters influenced so many young people with so much un-American propaganda. And many respectable newspapers and journalists have fallen prey to the plot.

The Chicago Tribune, known for its anti-Communist position, in an article entitled, "Why Do They Dress Like That," totally capitulates to the enemies of American culture.

Mary Merryfield, writing for the *Tribune*, states, "O.K., what about the boys' beards and long hair, the girls' bell-bottom sailor trousers, the craze for back-zippered engineer boots, swamp jackets, turtlenecks, tunics, and ponchos? Do they spell revolution?"[7]

Since the article reads like Dylan fan mail, it seems quite evident that Miss Merryfield hasn't listened to Dylan's "The Times They Are A-Changin' " or talked to some of these beards who are openly atheistic and strongly antichrist. And, as portrayed at Berkeley, it is also evident that they are violently anti-American, pro-Viet Cong and pro-Communist.

The amazing element in the *Tribune* article is the by-line which reads, "copyrighted by M. Witmark and Sons, quoted by permission." If the *Tribune* writer obtained her information from Witmark, one can be assured of a pro-Dylan response, since Witmark holds the copyright to most of his songs and Witmark isn't about to reveal Dylan's pro-Red affinities.

The *Tribune* isn't the only newspaper to push the praises of Dylan. Grace Nies Fletcher, writing a series of articles for a number of newspapers entitled, "What's Right With Our Young People," states some disturbing reactions to folk singers. She mentions our youth are "translating their singing philosophy into action in many cities and towns, in youth juries and youth councils, and in trying to clean up the debris of illiteracy.

"Certainly the teen-agers," continues Miss Fletcher, "who would fight the next war have a right to sing out what is in their minds. There is no more blood-chilling indictment of nuclear horror than Bob Dylan's 'Masters of War.' "[8]

She certainly isn't aware of the fact that this song, "Masters of War," according to the Communists themselves, "spread more radical ideas to more people in a few short months than all the northern protest meetings and marches since 1960."[9]

Miss Fletcher reveals her complete naivete concerning the Communist use of folk music when she writes, "Today's folk singing reflects the teenager's bitter disillusionment with things as they are. Such a song is 'Little Boxes,' written by Malvina Reynolds of Berkeley, California, who is extremely popular with the guitar-twanging crowd for her tongue-in-cheek comments of 1966 suburbia.

"The people who live in these ticky-tacky houses all wear gray flannel suits, go to the same universities, marry the same dull girls, drink the same martinis, and, when their own children are born, they repeat the identical process.

"Could there be a more devastating indictment of modern carbon copy living? The fact that our cool-fingered young guitarists realize this and yet can sing about it is comforting, for it means they are achieving a sense of proportion, a determination to be themselves, whether it means marching from Selma to Montgomery with a group of Negroes or making themselves heard on campuses from Cambridge, Mass., to Los Angeles."[10]

Miss Fletcher doesn't seem to mind the fact that Malvina Reynolds lent her voice to the Free (filthy) Speech Movement on the Berkeley campus![11] But if this is what's right with our youth movement, then the United States has already signed its death warrant. If Malvina Reynolds is in fact a "cool-fingered young guitarist" achieving a "sense of proportion," then America is doomed to die.

Never in the history of American music have so few made fools of so many. Never have so many sheep been led into singing the enemies' songs. Never in the history of the world has a nation survived with such mental and spiritual brainwashing. "Such apparently slight causes destroyed Greece and Rome, and will destroy England and America."[12]

Chapter XXXII

"EVE OF DESTRUCTION" AND "LIKE A ROLLING STONE"

One dated but telling example of rock 'n' folk music is P.F. Sloan's subversive "Eve of Destruction," sung by Barry McGuire. Sternfield, writing in *Billboard*, remarks, "The beat is solid but the lyrics, aimed at teenagers, deals with the dropping of a nuclear bomb."[1] The song was at the top of the hit parade for a number of weeks. Lou Adler, president of Dunhill Records, noticed, according to *Time*, "a beautiful change" in his prize songwriter P.F. Sloan. "Phil's complexion was very bad," he says. "He had acne all over his face. Now it's cleared up — perhaps because his mind has cleared up."[2] A syllogism of the above would reveal more than just an excluded middle!

Jack Williams, recently named program director at WIND (Chicago), termed the "Eve of Destruction" lyrics "sick." He said, "It's not the sort of record we want to play for our audience."[3]

The lyric in part reads:

> The Eastern World it is exploding
> Violence flaming, bullets loadin'.
> You're old enough to kill, but not for votin'
> You don't believe in war,
> But what's that gun you're totin'
> And even the Jordan River has bodies floatin'.

The words, copyrighted by Trousdale Music Publishers, Inc., 1965, are obviously aimed at instilling fear in our teenagers as well as a sense of hopelessness. "Thermonuclear holocaust," "the button," "the end of the world" and similar expressions are constantly being used to induce the American public to surrender.

Naturally, no one in the United States believes in aggression, but this is beside the point when war is thrust upon a nation. Marx and his followers discovered (created would be more accurate) a state of war and have sworn to fight until the world rests securely in the arms of totalitarian dictatorship. "Eve of Destruction" will hasten that day.

And for the writer to equate Red China with Selma, Alabama, and overlook Soviet Russia is not accidental. It betrays the mind of the writer. Red China has murdered and butchered thirty to sixty-four million human beings in cold blood over the past twenty years. Yet we are to suppose the conditions existing in Red China and the town of Selma to be equal. Communist Russia's campaign of hatred toward the United States has never been equaled, and yet the writer very conveniently overlooks it and the millions that have perished at the hands of the Communist commissars. A few more years of this type of music and Langston Hughes' infamous poem, "Put One More S in the USA" (to make it Soviet) will cease being a fiction.

Encouragingly enough, WLS (Chicago) removed the song, "Eve of Destruction," from its airwaves for being "Gloomy and maybe un-American."[4] Los Angeles disc jockey, Bob Eubanks, asked, "How do you think the enemy will feel with a tune like that No. 1 in America?"[5] And perhaps more consequential than anything verbally stated or written is the fact, as printed in *Newsweek*, that "During the recent riots the record 'Eve of Destruction' was pulled off the air in Los Angeles, and some radio stations no longer play it because of protests from listeners who brand it 'leftist' propaganda."[6] The degree of influence this type of music had on the revolutionists is hypothetical, but one can be sure it had its effect.

Commenting on Dylan's new rock 'n' folk number, "Like a Rolling Stone," Phil Ochs writes, "Rolling Stone is, I think a much more revolutionary song than EVE OF DESTRUCTION because it's much better — much better written and much more thought out. And it's a long song — six minutes. It's the first time this has ever happened that a song of that revolutionary quality in writing got on the charts and hit so hard. I think LIKE A ROLLING STONE and a new single called YESTERDAY sung by one of the Beatles, where they have cellos and an almost classical arrangement, a beautiful quiet ballad — I think that these two songs are more revolutionary than EVE OF DESTRUCTION."

Ochs' other reactions to Dylan are interesting: "I can even foresee his having to leave the country — go to France, go to Cuba, and sit there and write." He also plainly states, "Dylan is doing much more psychological things than that (i.e., than having a good time singing rock 'n' roll). He's doing it in much more psychological terms and going much deeper in his words." He says that Dylan has "gotten inside so many people's heads — Dylan has become part of so many people's psyche, and they're so many screwed up people in America, and death is such a part of the American scene now." In analyzing Dylan's effective performances, Ochs writes, "It's a form of hypnosis. It's not that everybody sits there listening to him with a single-track mind; Dylan has managed to convene a very dangerous neurotic audience together in one place, who are all hipped on him on different levels."[7]

Little wonder Ralph J. Gleason, columnist for the *San Francisco Chronicle*, commented, "Dylan alone is one of the great warning voices of our time. In his small boy's anti-formal manner he is advocating a moral and social revolution that is long past due."[8]

In ending this brief analysis of the Communist use of rock 'n' folk, one definite conclusion seems inevitable unless a drastic change occurs in the recording, transmitting and listening fields. With Verve-Folkways discing an announced 275 albums; with Bob Dylan recognized as a significant influence on today's teenagers and with *Newsweek's* recognition of Irwin Silber and Moses Asch as the new, respectable authorities on rock 'n' folk music,[9] one is almost forced to agree with Thoreau that music will destroy America.

PART SIX

CONCLUSION

"Let the word of Christ dwell in you richly in all wisdom; teaching and admonishing one another in psalms and hymns and spiritual songs, singing with grace in your hearts to the Lord. And whatsoever ye do in word or deed, do all in the name of the Lord Jesus, giving thanks to God and the Father by him."
—Paul, *Colossians* 3:16 and 17

Chapter XXXIII

MUSIC HATH CHARM

"Music hath charm to still the savage beast," wrote the noted English author, William Congreve. This book has not sought to deny this fact, but Anatole France's words should also be remembered, "Songs have overthrown kings and empires."

We have attempted to point out that the power of music is a two-edged sword; it can instigate and produce savagery as easily as it can calm the same force. It is a matter of selectivity, and the central purpose of this book has been to demonstrate to young people, parents and community leaders, as well as religious and educational leaders, that there is another side to music — a harmful, unhealthy, destructive, and yes, even a sinister dimension.

Secondly, and perhaps implicitly, we have tried to insist that the reader make an educated, knowledgeable choice between exalted, happy, healthy, inspirational music and the "sick" variety so prevalent today.

Music is a mood-setter, and no doubt the most effective such influence in existence. Few men and women have failed to thrill to the strains of the "Washington Post March," "Stars and Stripes Forever," "The Marine Hymn" or "Anchors Aweigh" as they observed a Fourth of July parade. Few churchgoers — and fewer Christians — can resist the inspirational impact of "Blest Be the Tie That Binds," "He Lives," "Holy, Holy, Holy" or "The Hallelujah Chorus" as they join a congregation in worship.

Mothers find peace, confidence and solace in the soft lullaby. People of all ages, races and social backgrounds thrill to the notes of Beethoven, Mozart and Liszt, and the same people find happiness and joy in the rollicking refrains of good, solid musical comedies, or the catchy rhythms of the spirituals and camp meeting songs of just a few years past.

Music has been a rich part of the American tradition, and its role has been portrayed vividly for us by Dr. Samuel Eliot Morison in his *Oxford History of the American People*. In ending each chapter of American history with a fitting song of that period, Dr. Morison includes such proven favorites as "Am I a Soldier of the Cross," "Hail Columbia," "Dixie's Land," "Battle Hymn of the Republic," "Tenting Tonight," "Oh, How I Hate to Get Up in the Morning," "Of Thee I Sing" and "Camelot." Each is a far cry from the jungle noise that is flooding the air waves, waiting for some quasi-historian to label it music.

And today there are still literally thousands of outstanding musical selections (religious, classical, semi-classical and popular) from which to choose a healthy, happy and enjoyable musical diet.

In this book, however, we have sought to publish the dangers of an unwise and pernicious musical diet which could lead not only to indigestion, but outright lead poisoning. Nations throughout the world are being toppled by youth, incited to revolution by the use of songs and chants.

The Rolling Stones' "Street Fighting Man" contains the admonition "Now is the time for violent revolution" and we have already seen where the Beatles admit their music is capable of causing emotional instability, disorganized behavior, riot and revolution!

Since our homes, schools and churches are under the most subtle attack imaginable and since we as a nation are in a fight for national survival, action taken now by concerned Christians and patriotic Americans is of the utmost importance.

In concluding our study of the power of music for both good and evil, we rest our case with: (a) an observation on some important spiritual implications, (b) a guide to action for schools plagued with Young People's Records, (c) a program for alerting and reaching our youth, (d) a call for action by our official committees on un-American activities, (e) a suggested program of action for the Internal Revenue Service and (f) a plan for making these facts known to the greatest nation on earth, the United States of America.

Chapter XXXIV

SPIRITUAL IMPLICATIONS

Since atheistic Communists are vulnerable in the sphere of the spiritual, it should be apparent that our responsibility must be to build solidly upon a spiritual foundation; including a positive reaffirmation of our faith in the Lord Jesus Christ.

Professor Jeffrey Hart (Dartmouth) wrote an article, "The Rebirth of Christ," relative to our present discussion. Since the spirit of the age is naturalistic, Professor Hart quotes C.S. Lewis to the effect that "the uncritical acceptance of the intellectual climate common to our own age and the assumption that whatever has gone out of date is on that account discredited" is a false premise. According to Lewis, one "must find why it went out of date. Was it ever refuted (and if so by whom, where, and how conclusively) or did it merely die away as fashions do? If the latter, this tells us nothing about its truth or falsehood."

Professor Lewis concludes, "From seeing this, one passes to the realization that our own age is also a 'period,' and certainly has, like all periods, its own characteristic illusions. They are likely to lurk in those widespread assumptions that are so ingrained in the age that no one dares to attack or feels it necessary to defend them."[1]

The present hostility to religious beliefs is demonstrated by Professor Hart's reference to Edmund Wilson's charge that "religious belief is an impossibility for any intelligent modern person, and further, that no intelligent person can now suppose Jesus to have been divine."

Professor Hart answers, "Wilson himself is intelligent and well-read; his ratiocinative powers are far from contemptible; he would have known at once that both of his statements are completely untrue — if he had paused to examine them. Whether or not religious propositions are true or not, it is simply a matter of fact that men who are both intelligent and modern affirm that they are true; Eliot, Lewis, Martain, Tate, Auden, Gilson, Waugh, Claudel — all believe precisely those propositions which Wilson asserts, no intelligent modern person can believe. They are intelligent. They are modern. And Wilson himself knows no pertinent fact they are not aware of. When he made those statements Wilson was acting as a spokesman for the spirit of the age. He supposed that the assault upon Christianity has been intellectually conclusive merely because it has been, in many places, historically successful."

Referring to the Resurrection of Christ, Professor Hart says, "the best recent study is by Hans Freiherr von Campenhausen of the University of Heidelberg. In his *Tradition und Leben: Krafte der Kirchengeschichte* (1960) he includes a lengthy study of the Resurrection narratives. He attaches great weight to the historical evidence of I Corinthians 15, pointing out that the epistle was probably written in 56 A.D., less than thirty years after the Crucifixion, and that Paul, in touch with the leaders of the Church in Jerusalem, would hardly have confined his conversations with them to the issue of whether Gentiles should be taken into the Church. Von Campenhausen concludes that probably no more than ten years had passed between the Resurrection itself and the day on which Paul received firsthand information concerning the events of Christ's life from those who had direct knowledge of them. It is this knowledge that he claims to have transmitted to the Corinthians when he led them to Christ. 'It is only rarely,' observes Stephen Neill, 'that we have such good historical evidence for anything in the ancient world.' "[2]

Frank Kluckhohn, former State Department employee and author of *The Naked Rise of Communism*, pointed out that during his employment with the State Department, it was his assignment to escort Khrushchev's son-in-law, Alexi Adzhubei, and seven other leading Communist diplomats around our country. At one point of the tour the delegation stopped to see the film, "A Man Called Peter," the life story of Peter Marshall. One of the Russians translated the words for the group. After the lights were turned on, all of the Communists, including Adzhubei, were weeping profusely and apparently without shame. This experience convinced Mr. Kluckhohn that God was indeed the Achilles heel of the Reds. Naturally, Christians have known this for many years, but now that it has been portrayed so vividly for us by Mr.

Kluckhohn, it is time to take the offensive with this truth and point out that atheism, among other things, is an outdated eighteenth century philosophy.

Frank Garlock, professor of music theory at Bob Jones University and graduate of the Eastman School of Music, in his book *The Big Beat* quotes Johann Sebastian Bach to the effect that "the aim and final reason of all music should be nothing else but the glory of God and the refreshment of the spirit."[3]

He also uncovered a quote from Giovanni Pierluigi la Palestrina over 400 years old in which Giovanni laments, "there exists a vast mass of love songs of the poets, written in a fashion entirely foreign to the profession and name of Christians. They are the songs of men ruled by passions, and a great number of musicians, corrupters of youth, make them the concern of their art and their industry; in proportion as they flourish through praise of their skill, so do they offend good and serious-minded men by the depraved taste of their work. I blush and grieve to think that once I was of their number. But while I cannot change the past, nor undo what is done, I have mended my ways. Therefore, I have labored on songs which have been written in praise of our Lord Jesus Christ."[4]

Any serious Christian young person can see that rock music in particular lures us from true Christian living, washes our minds in cheap filth, evokes riotous and degrading feelings and incites to rebellion, drugs and promiscuity. It should also be obvious to Christian young people that "The Hallelujah Chorus" might indeed welcome us into God's presence, but rock bands playing "Hellfire," "His Satanic Majesty," etc., will be the welcoming committee at hell's gates. It's for this and similar reasons that Paul tells us not to be conformed to this dark age (Romans 12:1,2; Galatians 1:4), but rather to be transformed and sing spiritual songs which manifest God's grace in our hearts (Colossians 3:16,17).

Chapter XXXV

GUIDE TO ACTION

In the unpopular task of removing from our schools the mentally contaminating products of Young People's Records, Pram and Children's Record Guild, we found that many concerned parents were unable to cope with the situation. Therefore, we are presenting a do-it-yourself article written specifically for this purpose by one of our good friends who worked so hard to dispose of these records in Torrance, California. Mr. Bruce S. Glenn, the author of this article, is a high school teacher. He participated in the founding of the Young Americans for Freedom at Sharon, Connecticut, and was the individual responsible for naming Dr. Hargis' book, *Distortion By Design.* His policy of action for removing these hypnotic records from our school systems is workable and should be practical in removing these same records from our churches and homes.

"The information and evidence contained in this book convincingly presents a solid indictment against several record companies, i.e., Young People's Records, Children's Record Guild, Pram and Folkways. Recordings made by these firms are to be found in many of our nation's schools, both elementary and secondary. If this information and evidence is to be put into effective use, it must be directed at eliminating such records from our schools. For, if armed with this knowledge, we continue to allow our nation's students to be subjected to them, do we not fail to meet our responsibility to God and country?

"Assuming your answer to be affirmative to the question above, let's examine what must be considered in seeking removal of these records from our schools. Our efforts will most certainly come to nothing, and could well harm the entire Conservative cause, if we open fire before making sure that our powder is dry.

"Research should be the touchstone of all who would work effectively to rid our land of the many manifestations of the cancer of Communism. It means a willingness to be more than a 'paper patriot' (a check-writer) or a 'vocal volunteer' in the cause of Christ and Country. It means that literally hours of research must come before even our neighbors learn of our opinions. Half-baked ideas usually come from half-bright people. And we need all the light we can get on this subject! So study — not just reading — of this book is necessary. Then follow up any new clues or ideas you may come upon. Make sure the records are actually in daily use in your school. Try to get photocopies of the documents in question. Failing this, be sure to supply those whom you are petitioning with all specific information (page, volume, etc.) and necessary addresses so they may check its accuracy and authenticity.

"A full and complete report should be prepared based on your research. It would be well to concentrate on the subversive backgrounds of the several companies involved, possibly omitting any reference to the records' content. This will lessen the chances of your effort becoming a debate between music critics or psychologists, resulting in an affirmative action. The evidence is abundant, . . . and it is conclusive. The tactics and techniques employed by several of the companies, i.e., Young People's Records and Children's Record Guild, to cover the tracks follow almost classic Communist-front methods as outlined in United States Senate document No. 117 entitled, 'The Communist Party of the United States of America, 1956.' This information should be in your report. And photocopies of all documentary evidence you are able to obtain should also be attached. Your report should conclude with a formal request for the removal of the subversive records.

"This completed report should be delivered by hand or mail to the chairman of the school's board. Another copy should be delivered to the editor of your local newspaper. It should include a cover letter from parents in the school concerned. No attempt should ever be made to raid another district. If your assistance is asked for, you can and should give it. For this is a matter of grave concern to all informed and alert Americans. But it would seem advisable to avoid setting up even an ad hoc committee. Parent action will prove more effective. No outside group, be it Conservative or otherwise, should be allowed to 'capture' your effort.

"At the board meeting at which this question is to be discussed, as large a delegation of parents and concerned citizens as possible should be encouraged to attend. Spokesmen should be informally selected beforehand. Every effort should be made to prevent anyone from sidetracking the board's attention from the companies' subversive backgrounds. Failure on this point may cost you victory. Above all, the keynote of your board appearance should be respect. Do not let any would-be opponents cause you to make intemperate remarks. Be alert to the techniques of 'shifting ground' and 'reversal.' Be a broken record; reiterate, re-emphasize and repeat the findings of your report. Then sit down.

"The chances are good that your school board, if you have conscientiously attempted to follow this guide and they are reasonable, responsible men, will remove these records. Should the board carry the question over several weeks — or even months — and thus by attrition attempt to defeat your effort, remain in the battle. Hold the fort! Should the board arbitrarily turn down your request for removal, a taxpayer's suit may be necessary. Or a request for a county grand jury investigation may be advisable. Make your decision according to your particular situation.

"The bare-bones of this guide to action rest upon four important R's: research, report, respect and removal. They should be ever-present in your planning to rid your school of all subversive records. For if we are to defeat the Communist conspiracy we must somewhere, at some time, defeat them on some issue. Let's see what we can do on our own doorsteps on this issue!"

Chapter XXXVI

OPERATION ALERT

For the well being of our youth as well as our country, it is important to alert our high school, college and university students to the truth concerning Pete Seeger, Bob Dylan, Phil Ochs, Guy Carawan, "Freedom" Singers, Joan Baez, Malvina Reynolds and the whole *Sing Out!*-Folkways network. Students interested in seeking to check a Soviet-inspired revolution must be alerted to the true nature and intent of those Marxist minstrels who are presently using folk music as a tool of subversion. Also, students should associate themselves with organizations that are sounding the alarm concerning the subversion of our youth today. Young Americans for Freedom has filled a huge gap in our college life and Young Life, Intervarsity and many local Conservative clubs have provided needed forums for the claims of Christ and conservatism. Schools like The Summit, Box 207, Manitou Springs, Colorado, should also be attended for further concentrated study in Christianity, Americanism and anti-Communism, and now, of course, the American Christian College, Box 42, Tulsa, Oklahoma 74102 is strongly recommended.

Chapter XXXVII

H.C.I.S., S.I.S.S. AND CALIFORNIA'S FACT-FINDING COMMITTEE

The government's anti-subversive investigating agencies, as well as various state investigating agencies and even county grand juries, if necessary, should be called into action to exhaustively investigate: (1) Young People's Records, (2) Children's Record Guild, (3) Pram, (4) Living Languages Courses, (5) Traffic Publishing Company, (6) Franson Corporation, (7) Greystone Corporation, (8) *Sing Out!*, (9) *Broadside*, (10) Oak Publications, (11) Folkways Records and its many tributaries and particularly its new association with Scholastic Magazines, Inc. and Metro-Goldwyn-Mayer and (12) Columbia Records for its part in releasing *Broadside* and *Sing Out!* materials, including a record of the official Communist folk song, "We Shall Overcome," by Pete Seeger. As previously mentioned, the California Senate Resolution 270 has asked the California Senate Fact-Finding Subcommittee on Un-American Activities to investigate Young People's Records. The resolution offered by former State Senator Schmitz stated, "Relative to an interim study of the use of subversive recordings in the public schools.

"Resolved, by the Senate of the State of California, That the Senate Committee on Rules is requested to assign to an appropriate interim committee for study, the subject of the problems created by the presence and use in the public schools of recordings marketed by record companies which have been cited as subversive by the California Senate Fact-Finding Subcommittee on Un-American Activities." We would suggest the California Committee investigate all the above record companies.

Chapter XXXVIII

INTERNAL REVENUE SERVICE

Since the Internal Revenue Service should not knowingly give aid and comfort to the enemy, it should look into rulings of the tax exemption of the Highlander Center, Student Nonviolent (National) Coordinating Committee and the Metropolitan Music School, Inc. The latter organization was formerly cited subversive with the following comment: "Committee hearings showed clearly that the Metropolitan Music School is controlled by Communists. Twenty-four identified Communists have been on the faculty of the school."[1] If the IRS needs its memory refreshed concerning these Communist and pro-Communist fronts, interested individuals should write The Internal Revenue Service, Washington, D.C., and point out these facts. An investigation should be called for with the aim of removing such organizations found subversive from tax-exempt status.

Chapter XXXIX

OPERATION DISTRIBUTION

Copies of this book should be placed in the hands of radio and television disc jockeys and officials; music store owners and managers. Many are totally unaware of the subversion within this great nation, although most realize the tremendous influence music possesses over youth. Also, ministers, Sunday School teachers and superintendents, teachers, principals, school board members, parents, in short, everyone connected with the youth of this nation should be made aware of the Communist use of music operating within the United States of America.

Music, as pointed out by Dr. Hanson, is a powerful instrument for good or evil, and in the hands of subversives could well lead to the annihilation of our country. Thoreau's prophecy, that music will one day destroy America, may be fulfilled before our very eyes, for in August, 1965, trained revolutionists, with their disgruntled lackeys and always present dupes, destroyed acres of Watts territory with gasoline bombs and a bloodcurdling riot cry borrowed from a Los Angeles disc jockey, "Burn, baby, burn!"[1] Rennie Davis boasted that youth were lured to Chicago for the 1968 Democratic National Convention with "music and sex"[2] and now Jerry Rubin admits, "We've combined youth, music, sex, drugs and rebellion with treason — and that's a combination hard to beat."[3]

In concluding this work it might help some of our readers to know that even the Los Angeles *Free Press* (the nation's leading underground leftist newspaper) finds the overall thesis of this work convincing. Reviewing the author's earlier work *Rhythm, Riots and Revolution* (of which this present volume is an outgrowth), the *Free Press* states, "You can certainly make a good case for the project [that rock-folk music is a major medium for revolution]. Today's teen-agers are sloppily dressed, dope-smoking bohemians, active in left-wing organizations of every stripe, non-aggressive, (basically), non-violent, non-patriotic and substantially more revolutionary than their counterparts of ten years ago. The rise in teen-age rebellion has exactly paralleled the rise in popularity of rock 'n' roll music."[4]

The *Free Press* also admitted that "direct connections through card-carrying Party members [Communist Party] are . . . established up through the folk movement."[5] And concludes, "I wouldn't be at all surprised if it were true. Maybe Ralph Gleason was right all along when he said 'Rock is the Revolution.' "[6]

PART SEVEN

APPENDIXES

"The wise man's words are like goads that spur to action. They nail down important truths. Students are wise who master what their teachers tell them."

—Solomon, Ecclesiastes 12:11

Appendix I

Testimony of Dr. William J. Bryan

Transcript of Dr. William J. Bryan's remarks concerning Young People's Record Guild on October 24, 1961, after listening to "The Little Puppet" (Side one, Children's Record Guild).

"Pretty bad. I didn't realize it was this bad. That's terrible. Well, do you want to just discuss this one first and then go on?

"Well, in the first place, the thing that strikes me immediately is that the tempo is the same as the pulse rate, approximately eighty-two beats per minute, and Hans Sutermeister (I believe I'm correct, this is the *British Medical Journal of Hypnotism* written by Hans Sutermeister) commented on a research program of this very thing, i.e., when sound stimuli are presented at the same rate as the average pulse, they tend to make the suggestion given at the same time — they seem to greatly increase the force with which the suggestions are given at that particular time.

"Now we notice, for instance, in the picture 'Psycho.' You remember, I think I can demonstrate this for you, when Janet Leigh was murdered in the bathtub, if you saw this thing, and the guy came up and pulled the knife, and he stood up like this (jab, jab, jab) (at this point, Dr. Bryan demonstrated the stabbing, using . . . as the victim) and you see there's not much emotion to that, but they had a high pitch noise at the same rate as the pulse to introduce that and suddenly you get (noise, screaming sound). You feel the difference? You see how it gets to you? Well, now this is what they did there.

"And this was also a factor in this . . . the psycho killer who was going out and strangling those three women. He is now under sentence of death at San Quentin, and there's an appeal in to the California Supreme Court based on the fact that we were not allowed to present that information in court and the fact that he was unduly influenced at that time. Now, that part has never been published before, but should be brought to the fore since it is the exact same thing you have here . . . There would be no reason in the world why we should leave that out . . . No reason in my mind why we can't bring it out.

"Now this is certainly — I'm sure I could use this very definitely as an induction record for children . . . I would be happy to take ten children and, with a few words, play that record for them, and show you that you could induce every one of them into a state of hypnosis with that record . . . I'm sure that is probably exactly what's been done and what's been going on in the nurseries around here. These children are being hypnotized without their knowledge and that's the real insidious part about this . . . this is really an induction.

"Lift your arms, drop them, lift them, drop them. Repetition. These are all the things you use in an induction of hypnosis. Repetition, moving one way or the other, lift, drop, lift, drop, continued commands, over and over again. Always giving the command — it's the same thing they utilize in the training of the Army. They give a preparatory command and then a command of execution over and over until the person obeys without thinking. The idea in the Army is that you do this for a person's own good. If you say 'lie flat,' or something, 'the bombs are dropping,' the guy doesn't think — he just drops and consequently it saves his life. But this is not being used for that. This is being used for evil, apparently, and you can prove that too, because after he gets them inducted, then what is the suggestion? He gives them an induction all the way through, continued and repetitious, over, over, over and over, and then after the induction he implants the suggestion. And he does it with a single command, 'boo, did you FALL, little puppet?' "

After listening to side two, Dr. Bryan comments:

"He gives, first, the child the thought that he has fallen, that he has injured himself in some way. Now this is a very traumatic thing, tremendously traumatic. Much more than the average person would ever understand. A tremendous thing. I don't think I've ever heard anything as insidious as this. Now, I know that I can take ten children and put them in hypnosis produced with this record and show you how this would be done. You can do it in front of a group if you want to, take pictures of it, and everything else. If you think about it, this is a very insidious thing. This is induced hypnosis. Then, given the suggestion that you have implanted a sense of failure into the particular child, there is a feeling in this thing of impending disaster throughout that whole thing. There's nothing happy about that at all.

"I noticed there are some other things, i.e., 'lower and still lower.' This is just like 'down deeper and deeper'; it's obvious induction, a deepening technique, every one of these things, and the exact fact that the person, as soon as he says 'drop them' and 'boom' and you then get the reaction of the drum following as though the thing is well on its way to completion. This is strictly an induction record, it's the only thing you can say about it, an absolute hypnotic induction, and then with the suggestion given at the end, that you 'fall,' in other words, that you're a failure, and then, of course, the obvious answer is that, being a puppet, he's pulling the strings and you're doing the job exactly as he says.

"I didn't think they could produce anything as insidious as that — oh boy!

It gets worse and worse, doesn't it — gee whiz! I don't think you even need an explanation on that, it's so perfectly obvious to me, whew! When you loosen up the strings and fall down — it's obviously placing the idea in the subconscious of the child that unless the string puller is there he can't do anything by himself without the specific direction of the Communist boss, or whoever it happens to be. Wow! It really takes the entire control away from the child, and then after he gets through three or four of these deepening things, he says, 'I can make you jump much higher than that,' and then he goes on to prove it. Whew!

"And here it is (reading from the record label) 'recommended by *Parents' Magazine*, and guaranteed by *Good Housekeeping*'; how in the devil can they do this? 'Approved by the Board of Education and daily used in thousands of schools in forty-eight states and in Canada for creative children and parents who want them to understand and grow with good music.' (Recent record labels say 'fifty states.') *Parents' Magazine*, boy, they certainly are all duped, aren't they?"

After listening to "The Sleepy Family" (Young People's Records), Dr. Bryan comments:

"Well, certainly the inference to this is what it already states on the back of the record folder: 'Daddy's song was such a sleepy tune that it put Mother to sleep, then put baby to sleep, then if you listen to it quietly, it might put you to sleep, too,' which is obviously the inference of the thing, and, of course, the idea that these records are going to be used in nurseries, and then when you put them into the state of hypnotic sleep, which is the kind of sleep they're talking about there, then what suggestions are going to be instilled at that time? In other words, in both cases, you have hypnotic induction, that's all. And then, of course, what comes after that is whatever suggestion is placed in the child's head.

"You see, one of the tremendous increases in mental illnesses in this country today, according to Dr. Van Soulsted, who spoke at the 4th International Psychiatric Congress in Barcelona, is the tremendous increase in the 'accidental' hypnosis that is going on. Now you can call it hypnosis, concentration of the mind, or whatever it is, that's all hypnosis is anyway, is the concentration of the mind in which the individual has a tremendously increased susceptibility to suggestion.

"Now when a suggestion is placed in your mind under such circumstances, you accept it with such force that this can become a compulsion with you, and that's one of the reasons why we see so many compulsions, so much compulsive behavior, and this is the cause of a lot of juvenile delinquency, it's the cause of a person's insomnia; the symptoms can be as varied as life itself. But the underlying cause is the same, mainly the accidental hypnosis that results in the acceptance of the subconscious suggestion which the patient is acting out.

"Now, I'll give you some copies of the *Journal of the American Institute of Hypnosis* in which some of the features have been shown with actual case histories. One of the recent articles that I just finished in the June issue was, 'The Walking Zombie Syndrome,' and that is that there are many, many people today walking the streets that have actually accepted the suggestion that they are dead. Now this is a really terrifying thing, there is no idea how bad it can be and how many people are involved. There are really hundreds of thousands of people involved with this thing. And the only answer — hypnotic analysis. Only with deep probing into the subconscious do we find this out. And these people come with every type of symptom. They say, 'Well, I'm an alcoholic, I'm this, or that, or the other thing.' They're not any of these things, they are actually a walking zombie. I think if you read this article through, you'll see how it's possible, it's happening; not only possible, it's being done all the time.

"This started clear back in 1938. Alexander E. Kabaleski, an Austrian physicist, escaped from the Kharkov Institute of Physics, Kharkov, Russia, and told them that they had research projects going on with hypnotic techniques and brainwashing and so forth that were based on these very things. Then we know about it, and still — there's not one single research project in the United States today by any of the Armed Forces or the Central Intelligence or the National Security Administration, not one of these have one single research project dealing with this."

After listening to "Tom's Hiccups" (Young People's Records), Dr. Bryan comments:

"Well, you've got a number of things here. In the first place, every bit of this has appeared both in the American and Russian psychiatric literature. First, you have symptom substitution. I think every psychiatrist is familiar with this. In other words, we can remove any symptom and another takes its place and you are placing in the child the idea that this is exactly what's going to happen to him. As he has symptoms of things happening to him in the future, for instance, if he gets asthma or something, you remove asthma and he'll get migraine. If you remove the migraine, he'll get something else. In other words, it's placing difficulty in the way of treatment in any type of illness in the future. So whenever the child becomes ill, he will immediately have a sense of substitution occur so that he does become ill again. Oh, it's very insidous.

"Now, that's one thing. The second thing you have here is the fact that you have the thing right at the end where he hiccups to show that he never really gets over any of it; that he's always going to go around, around, around and around.

"Now, the third thing he has told you, that the only real way to get rid of this is to forget it. In other words to repress whatever started this to begin with which, of course, is another way of saying that you should forget it; then you're not able to remember the causes of your illness, and if you're unable to remember the cause of illness — it goes on and on by itself as if you were unable to bring out this cause from the subconscious mind.

The fourth bad thing about this is that it ties in all these things that actually produce the disease in people with songs which we all know. Every time the child hears these familiar tunes, he will be tempted to fall into one of these categories of illness; each one of these representing to the child the child's illness, but as he grows up and becomes an adult he will take on adult illnesses in the same fashion."

(The familiar tunes which Dr. Bryan referred to include such well-known songs as "Oh, Suzanna," "How Dry I Am," "The Merry Widow Waltz," and "The Stein Song.")

"What is now a harmless snore or yawn will turn into insomnia. What is only sneezing as a child will turn into hay fever or asthma as an adult, and what is merely a shaky voice as a child will turn into a chronic stutterer later on who is unable to get along, and so forth and so on. And the hiccups may lead to alcoholism and so forth. So that what he's doing is breeding a tremendous race of people who are going to be mentally ill. It's terrible, really horrible; the scope of this thing is FANTASTIC — this is for the age group two to five.

"This is terrible, I've never seen anything so bad as this; scares you to death. You can see why when Khrushchev says, 'We're going to bury you, we won't need to go to war, we're going to have you in seven or eight years,' well, obviously, when these school pupils grow up we won't be able to defend America. When you control the minds of the people that push the button of the A-Bomb, what good is the bomb? Nothing. Well, it's very well known that illness has always been a greater incapacitator, accounting for a greater percentage of any Army in any war, than all the bombs and everything in the history of wars. And it's obvious that they're approaching it from this standpoint. And, if that's true, then why not make everybody sick and unable to defend themselves? And the easiest way to cause it insidiously is through mental illness programs."

Appendix II

The "Sing Out! — Broadside" Axis

The officially recognized and cited Communist publishing firm in the United States is the International Publishers (*Guide to Subversive Organizations and Publications*, December 1, 1961, p. 90). This firm printed a paperback edition on folk music entitled *Freedom in the Air.* In its suggested reading materials, *Freedom in the Air* stated, "Two magazines are essential for an understanding of the topical and freedom song movements, *Sing Out!* (semi-monthly, 589 Broadway, New York) and *Broadside* (monthly, 215 West 98th Street, Apt. 4D, New York)," p. 117.

The following list of artists and songs is merely a general outline of the *Sing Out! — Broadside* axis. Omission does not imply that other artists and songs are not Marxist-oriented, e.g., Joan Baez sings the works of some of the following song writers in "Farewell, Angelina."

Some of these individuals have their own Song Books, but their more revolutionary-slanted songs and Marxist-slanted propaganda pieces are to be found in *Sing Out!* Oak Publications and *Broadside.* If the song merits a recording, the disc is generally pressed by Folkways Records.

I. Almanac Singers
   1. Ballad of Harry Bridges
   2. Reuben James
   3. Strange Death of John Doe
   4. Wildwood Flower

II. David Arkin
   1. A-Travelin' Through
   2. The Dove (Hille)
   3. Last Stop on the Jim Crow Train (Hille)

III. Guy Carawan
   1. Ballad of the Student Sit-Ins
   2. Been in the Pen So Long
   3. Sinner Man
   4. Three Little Piggies

IV. Len Chandler
   1. Beans In My Ears
   2. Father's Grave
   3. Need A Job
   4. Quitting Time
   5. Rally Song
   6. Secret Song
   7. Turn Around Miss Liberty

V. Sis Cunningham
   1. Anthem For the Space Age

VI. Barbara Dane
   1. You Just Can't Make It By Yourself

VII. Josh Dunson
   1. Harp in the Air

VIII. Bob Dylan
   1. Ain't Gonna Grieve No More
   2. All I Really Want To Do
   3. Ballad of Emmett Till
   4. The Ballad of Hollis Brown
   5. Blowin' in the Wind
   6. Boots of Spanish Leather
   7. Don't Think Twice
   8. Fare Thee Well
   9. Hard Rain's A-Gonna Fall
   10. Hattle Carroll
   11. I Will Not Go Down

12. John Brown
13. Lay Down Your Weary Tune
14. Masters of War
15. Only A Hobo
16. Only A Pawn in the Game
17. Oxford Town
18. Paths of Victory
19. Playboys and Playgirls
20. Restless Farewell
21. Song to Woody Guthrie
22. Talking John Birch
23. The Times They Are A-Changin'
24. Train A-Travelin'
25. Who Killed Davey Moore

IX. Hanns Eisler

1. East Germany's National Anthem
2. Comintern Song
3. Lenin Cantata
4. Peace Song
5. Raise High Soviet Banner
6. United Front

X. Woody Guthrie

1. Been in Jail
2. Biggest Thing Man Has Ever Done
3. Billy the Kid
4. Dust Pneumonia Blues
5. Hard Traveling
6. I've Got to Know
7. Ludlow Massacre
8. Moneyless Children
9. New York Town
10. The 1913 Massacre
11. Pittsburgh (Almanac Singers)
12. Poor Lazarus
13. Pretty Boy Floyd
14. Slip Knot
15. Song of the Deportees
16. Talking Subway Blues
17. This Land Is Your Land
18. Tom Joad
19. Vigilante Man
20. You Souls of Boston (praise of Sacco and Vanzetti)

XI. Lee Hays
1. Ballad for Un-American Blues (Lowenfels)
2. Hold the Line (Weavers)
3. The Lighthouse (Seeger)
4. Lonesome Traveler
5. Peace On Earth (Hanns Eisler)
6. The Rankin Tree (Lowenfels)
7. The State of Arkansas
8. Times Gettin' Hard
9. Tomorrow Is A Highway (Seeger)
10. Wasn't That A Time (Lowenfels, Seeger, Haufrecht)

XII. Fred Hellerman
1. House of the Rising Sun (Gilbert)
2. I Never Will Marry

XIII. Joe Hill
1. Casey Jones — The Union Scab
2. Mister Block
3. The Preacher and the Slave
4. The Rebel Girl
5. Should I Ever Be A Soldier
6. Stung Right
7. There Is Power
8. Workers of the World, Awaken!

XIV. Cisco Houston
1. The Gambler
2. Make Me A Bed On Your Floor
3. Railroad Bill

XV. Peter La Farge
1. Black Stallion
2. Coyote, My Little Brother
3. Custer
4. Drums
5. Faubus Foibles
6. Ira Hayes
7. Strangers In Your Town

XVI. Huddle Ledbetter (Leadbelly)
1. Bourgeois Blues
2. It's Almost Done

XVII. Julius Lester
1. Talking Vietnam Blues

XVIII. Walter Lowenfels
1. Brain-Washed

XIX. Ewan MacColl
1. The Blantyre Explosion
2. The Bonnie Shoals of Herring
3. Canily, Canily
4. Come Me Little Song
5. The First Time Ever I Saw Your Face
6. Five Fingers
7. Go Down You Murderers
8. The Spring Hill Disaster

XX. Ernie Marrs
1. Ballad of Hervert Lee (Carawan)
2. The Birmingham Bull
3. Boxholder Local
4. Bull Connor's Jail
5. Dan Smith, M.P.
6. Inflation Marches On
7. The People Are Scratching (Harold Martin)
8. Plain Bill Brown
9. Plastic Jesus
10. Talking Studebaker Blues

XXI. New Lost City Ramblers
1. Brown's Ferry Blues
2. Chewing Gum
3. Franklin D. Roosevelt's Back Again
4. Tom Dooley

XXII. Phil Ochs
1. The A.M.A. Song
2. Ballad of William Worthy
3. Celia
4. Draft Dodger Rag
5. I Ain't Marching Anymore
6. Links On the Chain
7. Ringing of Revolution
8. Talking Cuban Crisis
9. Talking Vietnam
10. This Old World Is Changin' Hands
11. What Are You Fightin' For

XXIII. Tom Paxton

1. Bottle of Wine
2. Brand New Baby
3. Death of Medgar Evers
4. I Can't Help But Wonder
5. Marvelous Toy
6. Ramblin' Boy
7. The Rats
8. Six Men Riding
9. The Train For Auschwitz
10. What a Friend We Have In Hoover
11. What Did You Learn In School Today
12. The Willing Conscript

XXIV. Malvina Reynolds

1. Billy Boy (parody on HCUA)
2. The Birch Society
3. Bury Me In My Overalls
4. Dialectic
5. Do Something Wrong
6. Faucets Are Dripping
7. H.C.U.A.
8. It Isn't Nice (Dane)
9. Little Boxes
10. The Little Generals
11. Oh, Doctor
12. Peace Isn't Treason
13. Playing War
14. Rand Hymn
15. Sing Along (Silverman)
16. Turn Around
17. We Hate To See Them Go
18. What Have They Done to the Rain

XXV. Earl Robinson

1. Abe Lincoln
2. Ballad of the Boll Weevil
3. The Ballad of Doctor Dearjohn
4. Black and White
5. Joe Hill
6. Spring Song

XXVI. Buffy Sainte-Marie

Subject Catalog of *Sing Out!*, Oak Publications and *Broadside* Songs.

A. Praise for Communists and Communism
   1. Ballad of Harry Bridges, *People's Song Book*, p. 118.
   2. Ballad of William Worthy, *Broadside* No. 22, March 1963.
   3. Bay of Pigs, *Broadside* No. 4, Mid-April 1962.
   4. Celia, *Sing Out!* p. 12, November 1964.
   5. Do Russian People Stand For War?, *Broadside* No. 13, September, 1962
   6. Hans Beimler, *Sing Out! Reprint*, p. 20.
   7. Hymn of the 14th of June Revolutionary Movement, 1959, *Sing Out!* p. 32, September 1965.
   8. Jarama Valley, *Sing Out! Reprint* Volume 3, p. 15.
   9. Joe Hill, *Lift Every Voice*, p. 37.
   10. Moscow Nights, *ABC-TV Hootenanny* p. 132 and *Sing-Out!* Volume 7, p. 36.
   11. The Rebel Girl, *Songs of Joe Hill*, p. 39.
   12. Ringing of Revolution, *Broadside* No. 60, July 15, 1965.
   13. Should I Ever Be A Soldier, *Songs of Joe Hill*, p. 18.
   14. Song to Woody, *Young Folk Song Book*, p. 38.
   15. Songs of Hanns Eisler, *Sing Out!*, May 1965, p. 84.
   16. Songs of Joe Hill, People's Artists Publication now printed by Oak Publications.
   17. Songs of the FLN, *Sing Out!*, May 1965, p. 84.
   18. Songs of the Lincoln Brigade, *Sing Out!*, May 1965, p. 84.
   19. This Old World Is Changin' Hands, *Broadside* No. 52, November 20, 1964.
   20. Times They Are A-Changin', *Broadside* No. 39, January 7, 1964.
   21. United Front, *The People's Song Book*, p. 62.
   22. You Souls of Boston, *Sing Out! Reprint*, Volume 6, p. 44.

B. Fear Technique
   1. The Ballad of Major Eatherly, *Broadside* No. 45, May 15, 1964.
   2. Brain-Washed, *Broadside* No. 26, May 1963.
   3. The Devil Is Talking, *Broadside* No. 15, November 1962.
   4. Duffy Square, *Broadside* No. 2, March 1962.
   5. The H-Bomb's Thunder, *Broadside* No. 19, January 1963.
   6. Hard Rain's A-Gonna Fall, *Broadside* No. 31, September 1963.
   7. Mack the Bomb, *Broadside* No. 13, September 1962.
   8. Modern Mother Goose, *Broadside* No. 4, Mid-April 1962.

9. Peace March Song, *Broadside* No. 5, May 1962.
10. Picket Line, *Broadside* No. 31, September 1963.
11. Strontium 90, *Sing Out!* Reprint, Volume 7, p. 9.
12. Take It Away, *Broadside* No. 19, January 1963.
13. Talking Atomic Blues, *People's Song Book*, p. 114.
14. What Have They Done to the Rain, *Young Folk Song Book*, p. 20, *Broadside* No. 38, January 20, 1964.

C. Songs of Immorality
1. Blow the Candles Out, *Hootenanny Tonight*, p. 44.
2. Careless Love, *ABC-TV Hootenanny Song Book*, p. 24.
3. Four Nights Drunk, *ABC-TV Hootenanny Song Book*, p. 24.
4. House of the Rising Sun, *ABC-TV Hootenanny Song Book*, p. 98, *Sing Out! Reprint*, Volume 2, p. 37.
5. The Husband With No Courage In Him, *Sing Out! Reprint*, Volume 15, p. 32.
6. Knaves Will Be Knaves, *Hootenanny Tonight*, p. 80.
7. Maids When You're Young Never Wed An Old Man, *ABC-TV Hootenanny Song Book* p. 114.
8. Matty Groyes, *Young Folk Song Book*, p. 103.

D. Suicide and Murder
1. The Ballad of Hollis Brown, *Young Folk Song Book*, p. 42, *Broadside* No. 21, Late February 1963.
2. Ballad of Sam Hall, *Sing Out! Reprint*, Volume 1, p. 64.
3. Fair Ellender, *Sing Out! Reprint*, Volume 4, p. 60.
4. Go Down You Murderers, *Sing Out! Reprint*, Volume 2, p. 50.
5. Here's To A World That's All Right, *Broadside* No. 28, Late June 1963.
6. The Suicide Song, *Hootenanny Tonight*, p. 122.
7. Tom Dooley, *People's Songs Bulletin*, p. 13.

E. Defamation of Anti-Communists
1. The Ballad for Un-American Blues, *People's Songs Bulletin*, p. 81.
2. Billy Boy, *Little Boxes and Other Handmade Songs*, p. 20.
3. The Freedom Fighters, *Broadside* No. 11 and 12, August 1962.
4. The H.U.A.C., *Broadside* No. 18, Late December 1962.
5. Hold The Line, *Sing Out! Reprint*, Volume 4, p. 34.
6. The Investigator's Song, *The People's Song Book*, p. 102.
7. The Jack Ash Society, *Sing Out! Reprint*, Volume 3, p. 48.

8. The Rankin Tree, *People's Songs Bulletin*, p. 94.
9. Talking Riot Blues, *Broadside* No. 20, February 1963.
10. Talking Un-American Blues, *Sing Out! Reprint*, Volume 3, p. 48.
11. Twelve Legions, *Broadside* No. 9 and 10, July 1962.
12. What A Friend We Have In Hoover, *Broadside* No. 54, January 20, 1965.
13. What Shall It Profit A Man, *American Folksong*, p. 34.

F. Deceitful Anti-War Propaganda for United States Consumption
1. The Conscientious Objector, *Broadside* No. 16, Mid-November 1962.
2. Ding Dong Dollar, *Broadside* No. 3, April 1962.
3. Draft Dodger Rag, *Sing Out!*, March 1965, p. 26.
4. Hitler Ain't Dead, *Broadside* No. 61, August 15, 1965.
5. Hole In The Ground, *Broadside* No. 58, May 15, 1965.
6. I Ain't Marching Anymore, *Broadside* No. 54, January 20, 1965.
7. I've Got to Know, *Broadside* No. 57, April 1965.
8. Masters of War, *Young Folk Song Book*, p. 47, *Sing Out! Reprint*, Volume 7, p. 40.
9. Napalm, *Broadside* No. 60, July 15, 1965, *Sing Out!*, January 1966, p. 21.
10. Only A War, *Broadside* No. 62, September 15, 1965.
11. Playing War, *Broadside* No. 50, September 22, 1964.
12. Portland Town, *Sing Out! Reprint*, Volume 1, p. 39.
13. Strange Death of John Doe, *Sing Out! Reprint*, Volume 5, p. 44.
14. Talking Vietnam, *Broadside* No. 32, September 20, 1963.
15. Talking Vietnam Blues, *Broadside*, No. 56, March 10, 1963.
16. Two Brothers, *Broadside* No. 36, December 10, 1963.
17. Vietnam, *Broadside* No. 14, October 1962.
18. What Are You Fighting For, *Broadside* No. 40, February 1964

G. Praise For Criminals
1. Captain Kidd, *Sing Out! Reprint*, Volume 4, p. 26.
2. Jesse James, *ABC-TV Hootenanny*, p. 40

H. Sacrilegious
1. Cannons of Christianity, *Broadside* No. 59, June 15, 1965.

2. The Cherry Tree Carol, *ABC-TV Hootenanny*, p. 47.
3. Plastic Jesus, *Sing Out!*, November 1964, p. 51, *Broadside* No. 39, February 7, 1964.
4. The Preacher and The Slave, *People's Songs Bulletin*, p. 58.
5. There Is Power, *Sing Out! Reprint*, Volume 2, p. 43.

I. Phony "Peace," "Freedom" and "Justice" Songs

1. And Freedom too, *Broadside* No. 58, May 15, 1965.
2. Blowin' In The Wind, *Sing Out! Reprint*, Volume 6, p. 38.
3. The Flowers of Peace, *Sing Out! Reprint*, Volume 6, p. 15.
4. The Hammer Song, *Lift Every Voice*, p. 84.
5. One Man's Hands, *Sing Out! Reprint*, Volume 5, p. 17.
6. Peace Isn't Treason, *Broadside* No. 58, May 15, 1965, *Sing Out!*, September 1965.
7. Peace On Earth, *People's Songs Bulletin*, p. 76.
8. Put My Name Down, *Lift Every Voice*, p. 20.
9. Talkin' Peace, *Broadside* No. 35, November 20, 1963.
10. We Shall Overcome, *Sing Out! Reprint*, Volume 6, p. 63.
11. Where Have All The Flowers Gone, *ABC-TV Hootenanny*, p. 95.
12. Will You Work For Peace, Or Wait For War?, *Broadside* No. 1, February 1962.
13. World Youth Song, *Lift Every Voice*, p. 80.

The pro-Communist folk songs in *Fireside Book of Folk Songs*, Simon and Schuster, 11th printing and found in People's Songs, Inc. Song Book.

1. Come Fellow Workers, p. 228.
2. Freiheit, p. 210.
3. Joe Hill, p. 48.
4. Los Cuarto Generales, p. 218.
5. Meadowlands, p. 200.
6. Moscow, p. 206.
7. Tachanka, p. 214.

Appendix III

Jesus Christ Superstar

"Jesus Christ Superstar," is blasphemous, sacrilegious, irreverent, profane, desecrating, apostate and anti-Christian.The 89-minute rock opera, put together by two unbelievers (Rice and Webber), was produced as a recording looking at our Lord from a "purely human standpoint." As one reviewer put it, "The work is spiked with enough doubts about traditional Christian beliefs and middle-class values to satisfy cynics. Christ is presented as a dolt; the apostles as idiots and Judas a tool of God the Father.

Rice and Webber have Christ complaining, "Can you show me now that I would not be killed in vain? Show me just a little of your omnipresent brain. Show me there's a reason for your wanting me to die. You were far too keen on where and how and not so hot on why . . . Why then am I scared to finish what I started? What you started — I didn't start. God! Thy will is hard. But you hold every card. I will drink your cup of poison, nail me to the cross and break me, bleed me, beat me, kill me, take me now — before I change my mind."

Christ, before Pilate, is made to say, "There may be a kingdom for me somewhere — if I only knew."

When Christ appears before Herod, the latter comes forth with such jewels as, "Prove to me that you are divine. Change my water into wine." and "Prove to me that you are no fool — walk across my swimmming pool" and "Feed my household with this bread — you can do it on your head."

The apostles are made to look even worse with such comments as, "Always hoped I'd be an apostle. Knew that I would make it if I tried. Then when we retire we can write the gospels, so they'll still talk about us when we've died."

Mary Magdalene laments, "I turn my head, I back away; I wouldn't want to know; he scares me so; I want him so; I love him so."

"Superstar's" treatment of Judas (a traitor in Christian teaching) is sympathetic. He comes off partly as the self-appointed house Liberal, constantly badgering Jesus to plan and organize before all control of the movement and life itself are lost.

Some observers have wondered if Judas is not the opera's real protagonist rather than Christ. Barry Kittleson, a New York press agent for Rice and Webber, said that both writers were fascinated with him as a character and were convinced that he had been given unfair treatment.

In the opera, Judas actually blames God the Father for the death of His

Son. Judas says, "My God, I am sick. I have been used. You knew all the time. God! I'll never ever know why you chose me for your crime. You have murdered me. You have murdered me." (Read John 13: 27 and I Cor. 2: 8 for the real reason.)

The attempt to blame the Father for the death of His Son, of course, is not new. A few years ago, the World Council of Churches printed a new hymn for our modern time with the lines, "It was on a Friday morning that they took me from the cell; And I saw they had a carpenter to crucify as well. You can blame it onto Pilate, you can blame it on the Jews. You can blame it on the devil, it is God I accuse. It is God they ought to crucify instead of you and me."

A *St. Louis Post Dispatch* reviewer said, "Philosophically, too, 'Superstar' has something for just about everyone. Although it maximizes the human weaknesses of Christ and His followers, Jesus' relationship to God and the other men remains mysterious. The question of his divinity and the resurrection somehow remains open."

This is not exactly true. If anything, the deity of Christ is subtly denied and the resurrection is certainly junked when Christ is forced to say, "To conquer death, you only have to die. You only have to die." The Scriptures contend that to conquer death, one has to be raised again. To only die, is to be conquered by death!

Of course, from a Christian standpoint, when Christ is made to shout to the Father, "You are far too keen on where and how and not so hot on why," this is proof enough that the rock opera originated in the pit of hell. Wormwood's advice to Screwtape really struck pay dirt! Our Lord knew why He suffered and died. (Luke 19:10; John 20:30, 31) The Scriptures read very clearly that Jesus Christ "died for our sins." (I Corinthians 15:3,4)

This truth, however, is not exactly popular with apostates.

With such obvious blasphemy throughout the opera, Vatican radio nevertheless announced that, "Nothing like this has been played on Vatican radio before, but we think this is a work of considerable importance."

It also said it is going to "play the record because in the modern piece the suffering of Christ is seen with more insight and the Redeemer is brought closer to mankind than through Holy Scripture."

The liberal *Christian Century* maintains that "Superstar," "is not only a landmark in the field of contemporary music but worthy of thoughtful response. The lyrics are theologically provocative and laden with double meaning."

The Episcopalian notes the album does an effective job of "stressing the need of faith by leaving the question of Christ's divinity unanswered."

Approval has also come from such sources as the Anglican Dean of St.

Paul's in London. Such commendations remind one of the accolades paid to John Lennon when he came forth with, "Christianity will go, we're more popular than Jesus now." Those who thought John Lennon was right were wrong; and those who think Rice and Webber are an improvement over Lennon are also wrong. The Great White Throne will someday reveal just how wrong they were.

Appendix IV

"Hair"

What Jerry Rubin's book *Do It!* is to literature, *Hair* is to music! When Rubin says, "We've combined youth, music, sex, drugs and rebellion with treason — and that's a combination hard to beat," he perfectly describes *Hair* with its hippie youth, rock music (which Rubin admits, "marked the beginning of the revolution"), sex of all varieties and plenty of drugs and rebellion.

Time magazine (May 10, 1968, p. 72) described the tribal love rock musical (which is being staged by numerous *Hair* casts around the world) with these words, "The religion that *Hair* preaches, and often screeches, is flower power, pot and protest. Its music is pop rock, and its dialogue is mostly graffiti. *Hair* is lavish in dispraise of all things American, except presumably liberty. The play itself borders on license by presenting a scene in which half a dozen members of the cast, male and female, face the audience in the nude."

In its December 12, 1969 issue (p. 76), *Time* commented, "*Hair* is America's first tribal love-rock musical . . . and all with four-letter words and the nude scene solidly intact."

The *Saturday Evening Post* (August 10, 1968, p. 66) related, "*Hair* is a shaggy happening set to rock music that grooves along with pot, peaceniks and a startling tableau of nudes." One page later the *Post* commented, "The four-letter words, the frankness regarding bodily functions, the nudity, the acceptance of adolescent drug-taking, the anti-Establishment attitudes, the mockery of patriotism . . .."

Clive Barnes, liberal/liberal writer for the *New York Times* (April 30, 1968, p. 40) remarked that he could not spell out the four-letter words for the *Times* "remains a family newspaper." He also said you "don't have to be a supporter of Eugene McCarthy to love it, but I wouldn't give it much chance among the adherents of Governor Reagan." Barnes didn't say what he thought God would say although Genesis, chapter 19, might provide a clue!

But he did admit "from the first slow burn opening with half naked hippies statuesquely slow-parading down the center aisle — to the all-hands-together, anti-patriotic finale" that *Hair* did have some questionable touches. "Frequent references — frequent approving references — are made to the expanding benefits of drugs. Homosexuality is not frowned upon. The American flag is not desecrated, but it is used in a manner that not everyone would call respectful. Christian ritual also comes in for a bad time, the authors approve enthusiastically of miscegenation, and one enterprising lyric catalogues somewhat arcane sexual practices more familiar to the pages of the 'Kama Sutra' than *The New York Times.*"

Others have described the production as "a landmark in vulgarity" and a "theatrical breakthrough for all types of obscenity, profanity and perversion."

Since *Hair* productions vary from city to city (depending on what each cast feels it can get away with) not everything mentioned in this article will be true of every performance. For example, the Los Angeles cast (involving Tommy Smothers) is not allowed to perform the show on Broadway because it has added new filth which the producers fear will push Broadway audiences too far. In fact, when James Rado and Gerome Ragni (who wrote *Hair's* lyrics) returned to New York fresh from Los Angeles performances they were barred from performing by Butler himself because "their behavior on stage had become increasingly offensive" (*The New York Times*, April 13, 1969, p. 60).

Robb Baker, drama critic for the *Chicago Tribune* saw *Hair* at Chicago's Shubert Theatre and later in Toronto. On January 29, 1970, he wrote, "Chicagoans will probably find it hard to believe that the show could be more outrageous anywhere than at the Shubert, but it is — Toronto."

The cast is usually made up of 32 players (equally divided between male and female; black and white). One dressing room behind stage usually suffices since all help each other undress for the performance. On stage one segment consists of a couple undressing each other and simulating copulation while using juicy four-letter words. In another performance, 20 members are cast in their birthday suits with no curtain drop and anything but dimmed lights. After the nude scene (which is usually part of *Hair's* publicity) the actors and actresses leave the stage grabbing, poking, pinching one another, etc., and one commentator remarked, "and that was the least offensive thing in the play."

Scenes of mock masturbation (sometimes involving the American flag); couples engaged in acts of perversion and other actions repulsive to all Christians are usually stock-in-trade. *The New York Times* (June 6, 1970, p. 22) reported that Capt. James A. Lovell, Jr., and John L. Swigert, Jr., walked out of the rock musical *Hair* over what they considered to be slurs directed toward the American flag. In that particular performance one of the actors wrapped himself up in the flag and later used the flag to cradle one of the performers.

One wonders if the *Hair* cast would treat the North Vietnamese flag in such a manner while singing in benefits for the Vietnam Moratorium Committee (*The New York Times*, January 29, 1970, p. 33); or the United Nations flag which it seemingly endorses since eight *Hair* companies are engaged in raising $225,000 for the UN World Youth Assembly (*The New York Times*, May 19, 1970, p. 1). Being anti-Establishment doesn't apply to the established United Nations — only the United States.

Commenting on its pot content, Gene Lees, writing in *High Fidelity* (July, 1969, p. 108) stated, "As for its eager advocacy of pot-smoking, I smoked it for years." According to *Harper's* magazine (September, 1968, p. 107), "a pregnant young girl comes out briefly to eulogize pot and try to find a husband; and there is a brief transvestite moment later."

In one scene, one of the actors remarks that he would like to hang on a cross and eat cornflakes. At another time he says, "This is the body and blood of Jesus Christ and I'm going to eat you." After making the sign of the cross he bursts into some litany song of sexual perversion.

At another time an actor wearing nothing but a dirty jock strap reaches inside, pulls out a rosary and strangles a kneeling Buddhist monk. In other performances the strangling is committed by a mini-skirted, mini-moraled nun.

One critic felt that the forces of evil devised in *Hair* a diabolically efficient system of propaganda, unparalleled in history, to inject into the minds of mankind doses of poison which eventually will destroy us. Maybe George S. Schuyler (author of *Black and Conservative*) was right when he said our theatres "are heavily infiltrated by crypto-Communists, homosexuals, and fellow-travelers whose favorite outdoor sport is lending support to subversive movements." I know for sure he was right when he said that if Lot's wife were alive today she would be turned into a pillar of salt no matter which direction she looked!

Since *Hair* has all the ingredients of a revolutionary composition (drugs, perversion, rock and rebellion against Family, Church and State), it should come as no surprise to our readers to discover that the one who produced it for consumption back in 1967 (*Life*, April 17, 1970, p. 83) was another atypical Fifth Amendment patriot named Joseph Papp. His testimony before the House Committee on Un-American Activities, June 19, 1958, can be read in a House report entitled *Communism in the New York Area*, pp. 2549-2558.

In his testimony, Papp stated, "I am not now a member of the Communist Party." The Staff Director for the committee asked him "Were you a member of the Communist Party at any time since you received your subpoena to appear before this committee?" Papp replied, "I must decline to answer that question on the grounds of self-incrimination."

Papp taught at the Communist controlled California Labor School and when asked if he were a member of the Communist Party while teaching there he said, "I must decline to answer on the same grounds." The California

Labor School was placed on the Attorney General's list of subversive organizations on April 29, 1953 (see *Guide to Subversive Organizations and Publications*, 1961, p. 239).

Papp was further connected with the People's Drama School of Theatre and the Actor's Laboratory Theatre. The latter organization has also been cited subversive. The government's *Guide to Subversive Organizations* (1961, p. 207) said of it, "A 'red front . . . also referred to as the Hollywood Actor's Laboratory School.' "

And according to the *Fourth Report on Un-American Activities in California*, 1948, p. 104, Mr. Papp (Papirofsky) was on the executive board of Actor's Laboratory Theatre. "The primary function," according to the *Report*, "to draw ambitious young actors and actresses into the orbit of Communist front organizations."

The *Fourth Report* further stated that "Communist Party literature is always available at the Actor's Lab, and the organization has frequently donated funds and talent to help put across pro-Communist demonstrations. Its activities are well publicized in the *People's World.*"

Papp also found time to link himself with the Progressive Citizens of America which has been declared subversive by our government. (See *Guide to Subversive Organizations*, 1961, p. 216.) His role in that organization can be found in California's *Fourth Report*, 1948, p. 356.

Papp staged the first production of *Hair* in his off-Broadway Public Theatre. It was there that Chicago millionaire Michael Butler became interested in its existence and bought into its production. *Life* (June 27, 1969, p. 50B) says that "Papp licensed it to him."

Life not only described Butler as one "born with a silver polo mallet in his mouth." but as "playboy Michael Butler" who made a career out of turning his daddy's assets into deficits. He was a failure at everything. Then he picked up a hippie musical."

It seems that Butler heard the flower gospel from a summertime gardener and part-time hippie. *Look* (August 12, 1969, p. 50) says, "The ethic matched his casual clothes and carefree morality."

According to *Look* Butler believes in astrology (Maria Crummere is his company's astrologer), anarchism, aristocracy and love. His last three wives might doubt the last belief, but then love, playboy style, is a matter of definition. Butler enjoys free-wheeling love. In fact, he says he's dreaming of a "two week communal powwow where tribal love will triumph" (*Look*, Aug. 12, 1969, p. 51).

An anarchist he is, says *Look.* He believes that everyone would be decent and loving if the rules were abolished. He has faith in what he terms "natural laws, laws you know instinctively." He has, says *Look*, "no patience with conventional morality." *Hair* would underscore that point! So would Rousseau's *Emile!*

Look also stated that Butler smokes an occasional pipeful of pot and looks forward to the time he can bring his hairy hippies to Oak Brook, Illinois so they can smoke pot and spread love, freedom, fear and trembling. The citizens of Oak Brook can hardly wait.

Butler's philosophy regarding *Hair:* "I want to get into their [the public's] heads, let them realize a pinch of grass is better for you than a shot of whiskey." He also thinks "modest nudity makes you feel good."

Hair, therefore, was born, bred and transmitted in subversion. It is a perfect reflection of the world, the flesh and the devil. Sodom and Gomorrah are nearly respectable in comparison. It is doubtless part of the revolution.

"Aristocrats and hippies are natural anarchists," says Butler. "The rest of the world has to be educated, only *subtly.*" *Hair* is not subtle!

Appendix 5

Coming Great Day

"The best thing that I did in 1936 was to sign up with the Communist Party," said Woody Guthrie. "I bought and gave away about a dozen of these little blue U.S.S.R. Constitution books since 1936."

This quote and many more like it are to be found in a new book published by the University of Illinois Press ($7.50) entitled *Great Day Coming—Folk Music and the American Left.* Author R. Serge Denisoff is professor of sociology at Bowling Green State University and sometime writer for the pro-Stalinist publication *Broadside* and the underground publication, *Rolling Stone.*

Denisoff's purpose in writing the book: "To examine the use of folk music by the American left, especially the Communist Party, during the '30s and '40s. More specifically, it is an analysis of the use of folk music as a weapon to achieve particular sociopolitical ends ... The book is an endeavor to answer labor historian Archie Green's request for an objective treatment of the role of Communism in the so-called urban folk music 'movement.' "

Although Denisoff has a distaste for government reports, he does admit, "Views expressed in Communist publications can be assumed to reflect political policy and implicit support." Therefore, he documents his case via the *Daily Worker*, *New Masses* and *People's Songs Bulletin.*

When Christian Crusade published *Rhythm, Riots and Revolution* in 1966, exposing the Communist use of folk music, many refused to believe its contents. Denisoff, however, admits the work "made a relatively convincing case." In fact, he says the chapter on Pete Seeger would receive "considerable use in years to come."

Rhythm, Riots and Revolution exposed the Communist use of folk music involving the tactics and strategy of Woody Guthrie, Pete Seeger, Irwin Silber, The Almanac Singers, People's Songs, Inc. ... *Sing Out!* and *Broadside*, etc. Denisoff more than verifies its contents.

He has a chapter on the Almanac Singers. He has a chapter on People's Songs; whole sections on Guthrie and Seeger. At one point he says the Communists were looking for their *Communist Joe Hill* and found him "in an 'Okie balladeer,' Woody Guthrie, and in the Almanac Singers."

Seeger is exposed as one who at one time used the name "Pete Bowers." Also states Denisoff, "Pete was a great favorite of the Stalinist [Denisoff's word for 'Communist'] orbit of New York."

Seeger's group, the Almanac Singers, is referred to as "the engine for a

Communist revolution." And Seeger, along with Guthrie, is said to have "hammered folk songs into weapons of subversion." Denisoff also notes that the Almanacs frequently reflected the Moscow line. "The Almanacs supported nonintervention and the Stalin-Hitler pact," he says, "until the invasion of the Soviet Union. After June 22, 1941, the singing unit became pro-intervention."

"Peace-loving" Seeger, whose fatherland was now under attack, wrote the pro-war song "Dear Mister President." In it he says, "Now I hate Hitler and I can tell you why, He caused lots of good folks to suffer and die. He's got a way of shoving folks around, I figure it's time we slapped him down, Give him a dose of his own medicine . . . Lead poisoning."

Denisoff admits that Lenin and Stalin both realized the importance of music. "Art and music were to play an important part in the plan for revolutionary change," says Denisoff. He also states, "In Communist Party circles, folk music became 'a cry for justice.' " And concludes, "V.I. Lenin and the Bolsheviks appeared to have pointed the American Communists in the direction of folk material."

Denisoff lists two major criticisms of Christian Crusade's *Rhythm, Riots and Revolution*: (1) The author's failure to use original materials and (2) the author's use of the testimony of Harvey Matusow in his citation of Pete Seeger as a member of the Communist Party.

Denisoff admits that had Christian Crusade consulted the *Daily Worker* and *New Masses* it would have found "a great deal of objective evidence of the Communist's relationship to folk music."

The truth of the matter is that the *Daily Worker; Sing Out!; Broadside*, and numerous other original source materials were consulted. However, the task was Herculean and Denisoff's findings only verify the original charge. It is reassuring to know the more he uncovered, the more he found to substantiate our case.

The Matusow affair, however, is a Liberal/Conservative watershed. Therefore, the following points should be noted:

First, Denisoff himself states in his own foreword: "Views expressed in Communist publications can be assumed to reflect political policy and implicit support." Since Seeger has been found in Communist publications for the past 30 years, by Denisoff's own criterion, this should tell us a great deal about Seeger; viz., Seeger reflects Communist political policy and implicitly supports it.

Indeed, at one point, Denisoff admits, "Pete Seeger was surely not the political innocent portrayed in his interview with the Los Angeles Press."

Secondly, Denisoff's whole book, directly and/or indirectly, shows Seeger's role as part of Denisoff's "analysis of the use of folk music as a weapon to achieve particular sociopolitical ends." If Seeger had no significant part in the Communists' use of folk music, then why is he mentioned in nearly half of Denisoff's book?

Lastly, the testimony of Harvey Matusow and his subsequent publication *False Witness* is a classic in Communist tactics and strategy.

For Denisoff's sake (and also for our readers who might be interested) the Senate Committee on the judiciary, April 6, 1955, published a document entitled *The Significance of the Matusow Case.* The document reveals the facts surrounding Harvey Matusow and his testimony.

Denisoff seeks to use Matusow's book *False Witness* as a screen for denying Matusow's original charges of Seeger's affiliations with the Communist Party. The Committee of the Judiciary found Matusow's original testimony sound and his book *False Witness* "a confection of falsehoods." According to the Committee of the Judiciary, the project for the writing and publication of the book was conceived by Nathan Witt and John T. McTernan and initiated by Witt, long before Matusow was first contacted by the Cameron and Khan Publishing Firm. The document also states that both Witt and Kahn invoked the Fifth Amendment in refusing to testify respecting their Communist Party membership.

But most important, and, undoubtedly, the deathblow to those who use the above line of reasoning, is the following statement found in the *Findings and Conclusion* of the report: "Matusow's story was checked by the Department of Justice through other sources. The Department found that 90 per cent of the persons he had identified, while a witness for the government, as Communists, were also identified as Communists by other evidence. The Department found no information to disprove the identification of the remaining 10 per cent."

The 1956 *Internal Security Annual Report* likewise stated, "The Matusow hearings made it undeniably clear that *False Witness* was a total fraud, concocted by the Communist Party in an attempt to discredit Government agencies which uncover the facts about Communism. For example, the subcommittee put into the public record a list of 244 persons whom Matusow, in his past testimony, had linked with Communism. We invited any and all of these persons to come forward and swear that the past statements about them were false. Not one accepted this invitation."

Therefore, if Denisoff does not wish to accept Matusow's original testimony he should at least point out those whom Matusow falsely accused. Since the Government was unable to locate any it should prove enlightening to see what Denisoff produces. Then, too, if Denisoff doesn't like Matusow's testimony he can always consult the testimony of e.g., John Lautner, a former top ranking member of the Communist Party, who exposed the highly secret Cultural Division of the Communist Party whose purpose was "to carry out the general policies of the party in the field of culture" and to "raise finances for the party."

All in all, however, Denisoff's book is generally accurate. Had it been written by our staff it would have been tagged a radical-right work. However, since it was written by left-leaning Dr. Denisoff, it will be appraised, as he says in his Foreword, "an objective treatment of the role of Communists in the so-called urban folk music 'movement.' "

Appendix 6

Rock, Drugs and Communism

On September 12, 1972, Mme. Suzanne Labin, a noted French writer, journalist and lecturer, testified before the Committee on the Judiciary, United States Senate. Her testimony, entitled, "The Hashish Trail," included a section on the role of political subversive forces. The following material is from her remarks relating the interlocking pieces of rock music, drugs and the extreme left.

I shall give a look at the ties between the hippie drug movement and the various species of radical leftism and organized subversion.

Not all the hippies are radicals. As a matter of fact, most of the run-of-the-mill hippies shy away from political, as well as from all organized, commitments. But all those who do indulge in some politicking do it on the side of the extreme left. I was very struck by the fact during my world inquiries, that most of the missionaries of the hippie crusade did not use drugs. They obviously wanted to keep cool heads in order to recruit the greatest number of prospective converts.

The self-appointed Messiah I interviewed in a hippie community of San Francisco, who told me that "The saints of Christ are the new forces for the riots," was of that type. So, also, was a British musician who led hippie bands in the streets of St. Germain des Pres in Paris, who exquisitely explained to me that "Rock-and-roll, drugs, and communism are all of the same essence."

So was the Canadian chieftain of the Hotel Bamyan, in Kabul, whom I mentioned earlier. So was an articulate, never-stoned Chinese chap whom I watched serving as director of conscience in the drug lodges of Nepal. All were fluent and clever to praise — to the others — the drugs they never took, filling their environment with all the subversive slogans about current issues.

The higher leaders of the "drug culture" are even more tainted with the same political color. During the student strikes in Berkeley, Mario Savio welded together a coalition of hippies and left revolutionaries. Allen Ginsberg appears at public meetings at the side of Communist speakers and leaders of the "Fair Play for Cuba Committee."

The Canadian hippie leader, Daniel DePoe, adorns his headquarters with photos of Mao Tse-tung. The French hippie leader, Jean Claude Lamoureux, before dying from a heroin injection, printed a journal called, "The Red Mole." For all the underground hippie press, the only material you find, apart from hippie and drug items, is not discernible from the propaganda stuff of all subversive movements.

And notice that the greatest guru, Timothy Leary, once escaped from jail, went straight to Algeria to offer his services to the Marxist revolution. An incident worth remarking here is that, in the end, Tim Leary was expelled from Algeria, which is in tune with the following, very revealing lines written by the Castroite publicist Susan Sontag, in the April, 1969, issue of *Ramparts*, to defend Castro's stern interdiction of hippieism:

"The American new left is correct to be anarchic, because it is out of power. The freaky clothes, rock, drug, sex, are prerevolutionary forms of cultural subversion and so you can have your grass and your orgy, and still be moral and revolutionary. But in Cuba, the revolution has come to power, and so it follows that such disintegrative 'freedom' is inappropriate."

Through this undisguised confession of Communist double play, Susan Sontag brought unwillingly to light a very important point; namely, that the pro-Communist leanings of those hippies who engage in politics are by no means normal. What naturally belongs to the hippie drug drives is a radical condemnation of the social order existing in the West. But there is no reason why this should entail applauding the Communist order of the East, in which all the vices denounced by the hippies are considerably more severe: Hard discipline, innumerable constraints, intensive labor, oppressive police, black censorship, rigid orthodoxy and strict outlawing of drug addiction, with drug traffickers sentenced to death.

There is, thus a paradox in the fact that the hippies curse a democratic society which treats them nicely and lets their horizons free, while blessing a totalitarian society which oppresses and enslaves men. This paradox can only be understood under one assumption: that the hippies have been manipulated by the subversive propaganda machines.

They are, indeed, easy to manipulate, because of their naivete and ignorance. As they are constantly at odds with the law, which prohibits drugs, they are bound to welcome the "kill pigs" campaigns of black extremist groups against the police. As they love peace and dislike violence, they are biased so as to swallow phony pacifist slogans used by the Communists to undermine the American resistance to Communist aggressions. In support of what I have just said, let me make some quotations.

The hippie press is full of ads publicizing antidraft unions. Their journalists advise the young to convince their draft board that they are either addicts, homosexuals, or incurable psychotics, or to throw a hysterical fit. Many ads offer obscene tatoos on the body, to avoid the draft. The "Sun," which boasts of specializing in "rock, drugs, and fornicating," write that guerrilla warfare ought to include the dynamiting of police vans and recruiting offices.

Jerry Rubin, who burned his draft card, wrote the following in his book, *Do It:*

"We have mixed young people, music, sex, drugs, revolt and treason all together. What other combination would be as effective? . . . What we need is a generation of bizarre, unbalanced, irrational people, obsessed with sex, angry, irreligious, infantile and crazy. People who burn their draft cards, who take marijuana and LSD, who proudly wave the Vietcong flag, who are not afraid to say obscenities on television."

To sum up, we see that all varieties of the leftist subversions had tried to capture the hippie drug movement and to manipulate it.

PREFACE — NOTES

1. Moshe Decter, *The Profile of Communism* (New York: Crowell-Collier Publishing Co., 1961), p. 100.
2. Appropriation testimony of the late John Edgar Hoover; then director, Federal Bureau of Investigation, before the House Subcommittee on Appropriations on March 6, 1961, p. 49.
3. J.Edgar Hoover, "Faith or Fear" *Congressional Record*, June 28, 1960, p. 13653.
4. V.I. Lenin, *Selected Works* (New York: International Publishers Co., 1937), Vol. IX p. 471. The speech, entitled "The Tasks of the Youth Leagues" was delivered at the Third All-Russian Congress of the Russian Young Communist League, October 2, 1920. For further information that involves both Lenin and Stalin's position regarding music and the revolution see R. Serge Denisoff, *Great Day Coming — Folk Music and the American Left* (Urbana: University of Illinois Press, 1971), pp. 3—17.
5. Nicolas Slonimsky, *Music Since 1900* (New York: W.W. Norton & Company, Inc., 1937), p. 549.
6. *ibid.*, p. 554.
7. *ibid.*, p. 555.
8. House Committee on Un-American Activities, *Guide to Subversive Organizations and Publications*, Dec. 1, 1961, p. 89, 90.
9. *Guide to Subversive Organizations and Publications*, Dec. 1, 1961, p. 117. National Council of American-Soviet Friendship, Inc. is cited subversive.
10. House Committee on Un-American Activities hearing, *Testimony of Walter S. Steele Regarding Communist Activity in the United States*, July 21, 1947, p. 99.
11. *ibid.*, p. 101.
12. *ibid.*, p. 100.
13. House Committee on Un-American Activities hearing, *Communism in the Metropolitan Music School*, April 9, 1957, p. 674. *The Worker*, Oct. 5, 1965. p. 5 reports that Finkelstein along with Herbert Aptheker, Hyman Lumer, Henry Winston and Gil Green are on the faculty of the New York School for Marxist Studies.
14. Sidney Finkelstein, *How Music Expresses Ideas* (New York: International Publishers Co., 1952), p. 84.
15. *ibid.*, p. 118.
16. *ibid.*, p. 117, 118. For further information see Eric Burdon, "An 'Animal' Views America"; *Ebony*, December, 1966, p. 161 f.; Arnold Shaw, *The World of Soul* (New York: Cowles Book Co., Inc., 1970),

p. 294; Richard Goldstein, "Wiggy Words That Feed Your Mind"; *Life*, June 28, 1968, p. 67; Burton H. Wolfe, "The New Music and the New Scene"; *The Age of Rock*, ed. Jonathon Eisen (New York: Random House, 1969), p. 33; *Time*, October 19, 1962, p. 58.

17. *Time*, May 21, 1965, p. 84f.
18. Finkelstein, *op. cit.*, p. 118.
19. Jerry Rubin, *Do It!* (New York: Simon and Schuster, 1970), p. 19.
20. *ibid*, p. 85.
21. *ibid.*, p. 249.
22. Jonathan Eisen, *The Age of Rock: Sounds of the American Cultural Revolution* (New York: Random House, 1969), p. 190.
23. *ibid.*, p. 195.

CHAPTER I — NOTES

1. Edward Hunter, *Brainwashing* (New York: Pyramid Books, 1961), p. 230.
2. *ibid.*, p. 18.
3. *ibid.*, p. 229.
4. *ibid.*, p. 229.
5. William C. Bullitt, a Wilsonian liberal, was our first U.S. Ambassador to the Soviet Union. The quotation used was taken from *A Manual For Survival*, p. 40, Church League of America publication, Wheaton, Illinois. For Bullitt's chilling account of the Communist massacre of 11,000 Czarist officers with their wives and children, see House Report No. 2189, Committee on Un-American Activities, pp. 18—19.
6. A few years back this was a nearly self-evident fact. Today the pseudo-liberal is not so sure. For beginner's proof, *Masters of Deceit* by J. Edgar Hoover and *Communism: Its Faith and Fallacies* by Dr. James D. Bales are recommended.
7. Hunter, *op. cit.*, p. 6. "Dr. Joost A. M. Meerloo, a psychiatrist of Dutch origin . . . coined the fine laboratory word menticide — murder of the mind — for this atrocious quack science devised by the Reds to bring about the voluntary submission of people to an unthinking discipline and a robot like enslavement."
8. *American Opinion*, September 1964, p. 52. Dr. R.P. Oliver reviews *In The Presence of My Enemies* by John W. Clifford.
9. A. R. Luria, *The Nature of Human Conflicts* (New York: Grove Press, Inc., 1960). Pertinent quotations from his work will be used in context.

CHAPTER II — NOTES

1. *Republic*, 424c.
2. *Politics*, 1339a; 1340 a,b.
3. *The American Journal of Psychiatry*, Volume 99, p. 317. The quotation is in an address by Dr. Hanson entitled "A Musician's Point of View Toward Emotional Expression," read at the ninety-eighth annual meeting of the American Psychiatric Association, Boston, Massachusetts, May 18-21, 1942.
4. *Seattle Post-Intelligence*, February 2, 1966, p. 13.

CHAPTER III — NOTES

1. I.P. Pavlov, *Conditioned Reflexes and Psychiatry* (New York: International Publishers Co., 1963), p. 164. Also, I.P. Pavlov, *Psychopathology and Psychiatry* (Moscow, U.S.S.R.: Foreign Languages Publishing House), p. 167f.
2. Hunter, *Brainwashing*, p. 213.
3. *ibid.*, p. 13.
4. *ibid.*, p. 14.
5. Ivan Petrovich Pavlov: late Director of Physiological Laboratories, Institute of Experimental Medicine and Academy of Sciences, Leningrad; Late Professor of Physiology, Military Medical Academy, Leningrad; Member of Academy of Sciences of the USSR; Foreign member of several academies and scientific bodies.
6. A.R. Luria: Professor of Psychology at the Academy of Communistic Education; Research Associate, State Institute of Experimental Psychology, Moscow.
7. K.I. Platonov: from 1925 to 1932 conducted experimental work in the laboratory of Physiology of Labor of the Ukrainian Psychoneurological Institute (headed by M. Denisenko); worked in the Physiological Laboratory of the Ukranian Institute of Labor (headed by G. Volborth); worked in the Laboratory of Physiology of Higher Nervous Activity of the Department of Physiology of the Kharkov Pedagogical Institute (headed by Y. Katkov); later labored in a number of laboratories of the Central Clinical Psychoneurological Hospital of the Ministry of Railways.

CHAPTER IV — NOTES

1. I.P. Pavlov, *Conditioned Reflexes* (New York: Dover Publications, Inc., 1960), p. 25.
2. Edward Hunter, *Brainwashing* (New York: Pyramid Books, 1961), p. 22.
3. *ibid.*, p. 240. Also, K. I. Platonov, *The Word As A Physiological and Therapeutic Factor* (Moscow, U.S.S.R.: Foreign Languages Publishing House, 1959), p. 71, 101.
4. A.R. Luria, *Nature of Human Conflicts*, p. 335, 6. "Our experiments with the simple rhythmical reactions were conducted in children beginning at two and a half years of age and concluding with those of school age. The experiments made possible the establishment of certain peculiarities of the neurodynamical processes in the child, which serve as a foundation for further investigations.

   "The technique of the experiment was very simple: the child was seated in front of a pneumatic apparatus, and he was told to make rhythmical pressures at any speed he desired.

   "In older children this constituted the whole procedure; but in the very young ones (those too small to attend school), we reinforced the method by certain measures to ensure their observance of the instructions and their participation in the experiment. One of these was 'the paired experiment,' in which the child at first watched another child several years older running through the experiment; after this the younger one began to imitate him. This method gave excellent results. In certain cases we introduced the element of play, being careful, however, that this did not disturb the basic fundamental setting of the experiment itself.

   "The instructions to make rhythmical movements, generally following one another rather rapidly, presupposes a fairly high development of the cortical processes; only with a fairly well-organized action of the motor cortex, with development of the higher cortical automatisms, could we reckon on obtaining an accurate picture of similar rhythmical pressures.

   ". . . The first thing that strikes us in this material is that each beginning cortical process readily passes over in the young child to the subcortical mechanisms, rapidly depriving this process of its pure cortical character and involving intricate diffused processes. To trace these was not very difficult. The younger the child, the more clearly do we observe these processes."

   p. 344: "In a number of experiments we have seen beyond doubt that the young child, three or four years old, is not capable of delaying its movements, and the reactions which the child gives in this experiment differ only slightly from those which we obtained from him during the usual instructions. Evidently the impulsiveness of the child's reactive system is so powerful that to inhibit them is almost impossible for him . . .

"Every time we tried to produce in a young child a delayed pressure we saw a process having a definite conflicting character."

5. *ibid.*, pp. 210–211. "We attempted to use automatic motor acts to produce this conflict by giving to the subject a definite speed of rhythmical motor reactions and then suddenly trying to change this rate when we gave a signal. . . The instruction to change to a slow tempo produced a collision of the prepared response with a conditioned signal of inhibition . . ."
   Also, K.I. Platonov, *The Word As A Physiological and Therapeutic Factor*, p. 47.
6. A.R. Luria, *op. cit.*, p. xi in author's preface. ". . . it was necessary to create artificially effects and models of experimental neuroses which made possible an analysis of the laws lying at the basis of the *disintegration of behavior.*"
7. *American Institute of Hypnosis Journal*, Oct. 1963, p. 12.
8. A.R. Luria, *op. cit.*, p. 220.
9. *ibid.*, p. 425f. Andrew Salter, What Is Hypnosis? (New York: The Citadel Press, 1963), p.2, ". . . it will be shown that hypnosis is an aspect of the conditioned reflex, probably the most undeniable fact of modern psychology."
10. K.I. Platonov, *The Word As A Physiological and Therapeutic Factor*, p. 11.
11. *ibid.*, p. 244.
12. Leonard Gilman M.D., and Frances Paperte, *Music and Your Emotions*, (New York: Liveright Publishing Corporation, 1952), p. 36, "I am quite convinced that our music activity reaches the subcortical centers of the brain, where other activities do not . . ."
13. *American Journal of Diseases of Children*, 1933; 45:355-370, "In normally intelligent children the reflexes are easily conditioned."

CHAPTER V – NOTES

1. H.C.U.A. hearing, *Investigation of So-Called "Blacklisting" In Entertainment Industry*, Part 2, p. 5299. "There has been testimony, most of it correct but some of it lacking in depth, as to the inability of the Communists to put propaganda on the air, and I say that is not entirely correct because it is a too-simplified formulation of propaganda. Certainly the Communists do not try to extol Marxism-Leninism over the air, but we did have instances, for example in 1947, when Norman Corwin made his 'One World Flight,' of pro-Soviet propaganda." Corwin's Communist-front activity is staggering. For a partial insight into his activities consult the H.C.U.A.'s *Review of the Scientific and Cultural Conference For World Peace*, April 19, 1949, p. 2, 5, 8, 9, 19, 22, 29, 32-35, 38, 39-45, 48-50, 53 and 58. This hearing could well be the single most important government document on the Communist use of culture in the United States. On the opening page we are informed that the purpose of the Scientific and Cultural Conference was to "discredit American culture and to extol the virtues of Soviet culture."
2. Psychopolitics is defined as the art and science of asserting and maintaining dominion over the thoughts and loyalties of individuals, officers, bureaus, and masses, and the effecting of the conquest of enemy nations through "mental healing."
3. For some time Norman Corwin was serving on the Board of Advisors to the University of Southern California Idyllwild School of Music and the Arts, *Summer Session 1965 Bulletin*, p. 2.
4. California, *Fourth Report of the Senate Fact-Finding Subcommittee on Un-American Activities*, 1948, p. 392.
5. Quotation found on the record jacket. We are also instructed that "Pram Records are Baby's Best Toy."

CHAPTER VI — NOTES

1. H.C.U.A. hearing, *Communism in the New York Area* (Entertainment), June 19, 1958, p. 2576.
2. *Guide to Subversive Organizations and Publications*, Dec. 1, 1961, p. 94. Also, see Organizations Designated Under Executive Order No. 10450, the Attorney General's list of subversive organizations.
3. H.C.U.A. hearing, *Communism In the New York Area* (Entertainment), June 19, 1958, p. 2575f.
4. *100 Things You Should Know About Communism and Education*, p. 17. This report was prepared and released by the Committee on Un-American Activities, U.S. House of Representatives and is available from the Superintendent of Documents, U.S. Government Printing Office, Washington 25, D.C.
5. *Guide to Subversive Organizations and Publications*, May 14, 1951, p. 126.
6. Senate Internal Security Subcommittee, *Scope of Soviet Activities in the United States*, Part 27, June 14, 1958, pp. 1477-1478.
7. *Torrance Press-Herald*, June 9, 1965, p. 1. (Torrance, California) In a letter from Herman Singerman (on Franson Corporation stationery) to Dr. J.H. Hull, administrator of the Torrance Unified School District, Mr. Singerman, with tongue in cheek, states "discovery of discoveries — yes, there is a Traffic Publishing Company. Seriously there is a Traffic Publishing Company occupying space on the Tenth Floor of 100 Sixth Avenue (Franson Corporation is on the Third Floor)." Since Mr. Singerman was the manager of Traffic Publishing Company, his electrifying discovery of his own organization's existence is reassuring. Yes, Virginia, there is a Herman Singerman — discovery of discoveries! According to the *Torrance Daily Breeze* (January 13, 1966) the Traffic Publishing Company is still distributing Young People's Records. In an article by staff writer John Farley, "The records [YPR] are distributed." he says, "by Traffic Publishing Co., believed to be a subsidiary of Franson Corp."
8. House Committee on Un-American Activites, *Communist Political Subversion*, Part I, p. 7427. Exhibit 185c. Herman Singerman was involved in the Provisional United Labor and People's Committee for May Day, an organization cited subversive by our government. See *Guide to Subversive Organizations and Publications*, December 1, 1961, pp. 162-163.
9. Contained in a letter to Bruce S. Glenn, from Mr. Robert J. Wentworth, Assistant Director of Public Relations Department of the AFL-CIO. Also,

see *Thirteenth Report of the Senate Fact-Finding Subcommittee on Un-American Activites*, 1965, p. 8.
10. Contained in a letter to Mr. Glenn from Karl Prussion, June 15, 1965.
11. Fourth Report of the *California Senate Fact-Finding Subcommittee on Un-American Activities*, 1948, p. 390.
12. Contained in a letter from R.E. Combs, counsel for the committee, April 26, 1965.
13. *Fourth Report of the California Senate Fact-Finding Subcommittee on Un-American Activities*, 1948, p. 392.
14. *Eleventh Report of the California Senate Fact-Finding Subcommittee on Un-American Activities*, 1961, p. 382.
15. Letter from Hugh M. Barns, president pro-tem, California Legislature, to the author, Nov. 30, 1965.
16. *Los Angeles Times*, June 18, 1965, Part II, p. 6.
17. "It is surprising how much of the meaning of a song is absorbed by a child while singing it. The message of some contemporary 'folk' songs carries greater weight in song than in plain language. These songs make a deeper and a more lasting impression than twenty lectures on the same subject." Columnist Jack Lotto, writing on the indoctrination of children through songs, quoted a pro-Communist magazine. Taken from *FACTS*, Volume XI, No. 6, p. 7. Editor and Publisher is Francis P. Bartlett, P.O. Box 2056-D, Pasadena, Calif.

The following, while not directed to children gives abundant evidence of the Communist use of music: " 'Red China is singing herself into the Communist ideology,' Mrs. Inez McLaughlin told the Port Angeles Reading Club Friday . . . Mr. McLaughlin reviewed the book *The Power of Song* by F. Olin Stockwell. The author was a prisoner of the Red Chinese for over two years at a center where the government was training its cadre.

"He said that after a morning of studying Communist doctrines prisoners spent the afternoon in mass singing. The songs were catchy, easy-to-remember tunes combined with words in the Communist theme and propaganda.

"In this way, the author said, the government is able to sing itself into the minds and hearts of the trainees and prisoners. This method is being used in the schools, offices and armies of Red China.

"Mrs. McLaughlin said that song has power whether it is patriotic, religious or folk music. It grips the emotions and these emotions determine people's actions often more than logical thought does.

"According to Stockwell, 'If we would win over the Communists, we must not only out-think them, out-live them, but out-sing them.' " *Port*

Angeles Evening News (Washington), November 14, 1961, p. 4.

18. The Progressive Book Shop at 1806 West Seventh Street in Los Angeles, California, is managed by Frank Spector. House Report No. 259, *Report on the Southern California District of the Communist Party*, April 3, 1959.

    Fourth Report of the California Senate Fact-Finding Subcommittee on Un-American Activities, 1948, p. 222, "Frank Spector was subpoenaed and appeared before the committee in Los Angeles on Wednesday, Feb. 18, 1948. He stated that he was born in Russia and that he is an alien . . . On Sept. 14, 1939, he was appointed organizer for the Communist Party in San Francisco County . . . He was connected with Herbert K. Sorrell (identified by Walt Disney as a Communist) in the recent Hollywood strikes."

19. *Fourth Report of the California Senate Fact-Finding Subcommittee on Un-American Activities*, 1948, p. 390.

20. (1) Dr. W. Horsley Gantt; (2) William H. Harris; (3) Walter B. Cannon and (4) Adolph Meyer.

    (1) Dr. W. Horsley Gantt: Translated A.R. Luria's work *Nature of Human Conflict.* In the translator's preface, Dr. Gantt states: "My sojourn of six years in the Union of Soviet Socialistic Republics as the first American following the Revolution to do extended research in the laboratories and medical institutes of the new Russia just emerging from chaos, my intimate and cordial relations there with the scientists and my admiration of their zealous strivings and achievements, together with my natural interest in the problems Luria illuminates, have made the opportunity to cooperate in the presentation of another scientific book from Russia too great a temptation to let pass."

    Gantt is Professor Emeritus of Psychiatry, Johns Hopkins University School of Medicine. At the school, Dr. Gantt translated and edited Ivan Pavlov's work *Lectures on Conditioned Reflexes*, published by a Communist press here in the States, International Publishers. Title pages of work contain the following: "Translated and edited by W. Horsley Gantt, M.D., D.S.C. Medical Director Leningrad Unit American Relief Administration, 1922, 23; Co-worker in Pavlov's laboratory, Institute Experimental Medicine, 1925-29; Associate in Psychiatry and Director Pavlovian Laboratory, Johns Hopkins University."

    Dr. Gantt's Communist front activity is spelled out in Appendix IX: On pages 336, 368, 475, 1104, 1202, 1249, 1338, 1450 and 1603, one finds Dr. Gantt sponsoring the following Communist fronts: American Council on Soviet Relations, American Propaganda Agencies For the Soviet System, Greetings to the Red Army on its 26th Anniversary,

National Council of American-Soviet Friendship, National Federation for Constitutional Liberties, National Wartime Conference of the Professions, the Sciences, the Arts, the White-collar Fields, Writer for Communist Party and Party line publications such as *Soviet Russia Today* and *New Masses.*

(2) William H. Harris: Mr. Harris in 1940 was the Communist Party Candidate for State Assembly of Pennsylvania, *H.C.U.A., Appendix IX,* p. 1411.

(3) Walter B. Cannon: Took part in writing *Physiological Basis of Psychiatry*, and wrote the introduction to Pavlov's work, *Lectures On Conditioned Reflex*. At the time, he was the George Higginson Professor of Physiology, Harvard University.

Dr. Cannon's Communist front activity can be comprehended by referring to the following pages in Appendix IX: 328, 330, 335f, 349, 353, 358f, 369, 380, 382, 489, 669, 689, 941, 944, 977, 980, 1200, 1203, 1212, 1338, 1611, 1648, and 1702. These pages include some of the following Communist fronts cited by the United States Government: American Committee for Democracy and Intellectual Freedom; American Committee for Protection of Foreign Born; American Committee to Save Refugees; American Council on Soviet Relations; American Friends of Spanish Democracy, etc.

(4) Dr. Adolph Meyer: In the foreword of his *Experimental Basis for Neurotic Behavior*, Gantt states, "The Pavlovian Laboratory was started in 1929 on the initiative of Dr. Adolph Meyer." Dr. Meyer's Communist front activity, according to Appendix IX, includes the following: American Council on Soviet Relations, American Propaganda Agencies for the Soviet System; Greetings to the Red Army on its Twenty-sixth Anniversary.

21. (1) American Council on Soviet Relations, (2) Communist Party Candidate writers, (3) National Wartime Conference — sponsors, (4) Communist Party Publications — writers, (5) "Soviet Russia Today" — writers, (6) National Council on American-Soviet Friendship — open letter, (7) American Committee For Democracy and Intellectual Freedom, (8) Abolish the Dies Committee, (9) American Committee for Protection of Foreign Born, (10) American Committee to Save Refugees, (11) Committee For Defense of Public Education, (12) The Teachers Union Arts Committee, (13) American Peace Mobilization, (14) American Propaganda Agencies for the Soviet System, (15) American Youth Congress, (16) Musicians' Committee to Aid Spanish Democracy, (17) Artists' Front To Win The War, (18) International Workers Order, (19) People's Songs, Inc., (20) Joint Anti-Refugee Committee, (21)

League of American Writers, (22) League of Women Shoppers.

22. (1) Genevieve Taggard, (2) Douglas Moore, (3) Mary F. Langmuir, (4) Howard Hanson, (5) William Schuman, (6) Randolph Smith.

(1) Genevieve Taggard: Her Communist front activities span Appendix IX on the following pages: 354, 375, 480, 487, 520, 535, 589, 641, 657, 730, 758, 939, 968, 974, 977, 1006, 1128, 1150, 1163, 1202, 1340, 1351, 1391, 1456, 1460, 1602f, 1617, 1640, and 1772. *The Eighth Report of the Senate Investigating Committee on Education*, 1951, Senate of the State of California, lists her on pages 52 and 56. *Fourth Report of the California Senate Fact-Finding Subcommittee on Un-American Activities*, 1948, finds her on pages 97, 114, 181, 194, 227, 228, 244, 270, 274, 277, 390, and 391.

(2) Douglas Moore: Appendix IX lists Moore on the following pages: 348, 1252. In the *Fourth Report of the California Senate Fact-Finding Subcommittee on Un-American Activities*, 1948, he is listed on pages 240, 317, 331 and 390.

(4) Howard Hanson: Appendix IX lists Hanson on page 1139 with the Musician's Committee to Aid Spanish Democracy. The *Fourth Report of the California Senate Fact-Finding Subcommittee on Un-American Activities*, 1948, lists him in pages 311, 317, 390 and 391.

(5) William Schuman: Appendix IX on page 1338 with the National Wartime Conference of the Professions, the Sciences, the Arts and the White-Collar Fields. *H.C.U.A. Fourth Report*, 1948. p. 331.

(6) Randolph Smith: *H.C.U.A., Appendix IX* lists Smith on pages 1110, 332, 334, 1126, 1237 and 1366.

23. (1) Edith Sidorsky, (2) Lucy Mitchell, (3) Raymond Abrashkin, (4) Thomas Glazer, (5) Eleanor Reich, (8) Alex North, (9) Sam Wanamaker, (10) Charity Bailey, (11) Jack Elliott, (12) Pete Seeger, (13) Woody Guthrie, (14) Jean Ritchie, (15) Huddie Ledbetter, (16) Cisco Houston, and (17) Alan Lomax.

(1) Edith Sidorsky: Former instructor at the Harriet Johnson Bank Street Schools and Riverside Church Nursery Schools.

(2) Lucy Mitchell: Quoted as an authority on children's records by the Book-of-the-Month Club's *Your Child Is Musical*, p. 1. *Appendix IX* lists Lucy Mitchell on pages 638, 660, 694, 1006, 1008, 1110 and 1202.

CHAPTER VII — NOTES

1. *American Institute of Hypnosis Journal*, 8833 Sunset Boulevard, Los Angeles, California, October 1963, p. 14.
2. K.I. Platonov, *The Word As A Physiological and Therapeutic Factor* (Moscow, U.S.S.R.: Foreign Languages Publishing House, 1959), p. 47. "Thus, some of our subject, repeatedly put into the state of suggested sleep by verbal suggestion accompanied by metronome beats, lapsed into this state while awaiting their turn in the reception room as soon as they heard the metronome beats coming from the laboratory. Thus, the sound of the rhythmic metronome beats, which had theretofore been indifferent to these people, became a conditioned stimulus of the first signal system . . ."
3. *ibid.*, Platonov, p. 26, ". . . we very well know that monotonous, lengthy and rhythmic sounding of a lullaby, the ticking of a clock, the rustle of trees, the rhythmic and protracted stimulation by a weak source of light, or long-continued rocking which stimulates the vestibular apparatus of the internal ear, and stroking some part of the body — all invariably aid in the development of sleep inhibition in the stimulated cortical cells . . ."
4. Letter from Dr. Granville F. Knight to Mrs. Irene Johnson, Nov. 8, 1963.
5. *Los Angeles Evening Herald Express*, October 23, 1961. The writer of the article entitled "New UN Book Key to Children's One World Ideas" makes mention of the fact that two record companies the UN endorses (YPR and CRG) are cited as Communist. In fact, the author states: "developed in Russia and financed in America."
6. Letter from Dr. J.A. Boucher to Mrs. Irene Johnson, Jan. 10, 1963.
7. The Lyrics and Music of "The Little Puppet" were written by Judith Sidorsky, formerly instructor at the Harriet Johnson and Riverside Church Nursery Schools.
8. The same technique is used in folk music. Dr. Wm. J. Bryan, Jr., states: "Sometimes a well-known folksong's tempo will be changed to the same beat as the normal pulse beat which makes it more effective for induction." *American Institute of Hypnosis Journal*, Oct. 1963, p. 3.
9. While pulse rating is always approximate, adults are usually in the 60s, teenagers in the 70s, children in the 80s and infants anywhere from 100 to 120. *Seattle Post-Intelligence*, January 22, 1965, p. 17, "Dr. Johannes Kneutgen of the Max Planck Institute for Behavioral Psychology at Seewiesen says: 'If a person whose heart beats normally 70 times a minute listens to an alarm clock ticking 100 times a minute, his pulse will begin beating 100 times a minute after one half-hour. A slowly ticking

clock will decrease his heartbeat to 55 beats per minute.'"

10. Contained in a six-page transcript taken by a stenographer on Oct. 24, 1961. The transcript embodies Dr. Bryan's remarks concerning Children's Record Guild and Young People's Records. The transcript is in our files. See Appendix I for full context of testimony by Dr. Bryan.
11. K.I. Platonov, *The Word As A Physiological and Therapeutic Factor*, p. 46. "It is known that a successful induction of sleep in one person in the presence of another who is not suggestible aids in putting the latter to sleep according to the mechanism of the initiative reflex."
12. *ibid.*, Platonov, p. 82. "As the date of I. Pavlov's laboratory and numerous clinical observations show, the hypnotic state also plays a rather important part in the process of formation of certain neurotic states, often manifesting itself under certain conditions independently, without the purposeful induction of suggested sleep. The hypnotic state, as we know, may vary in intensity, beginning with a barely perceptible 'hypnoid' state, 'hardly distinguishable from wakefulness' (I. Pavlov). The slightest drop in cortical tone, however, is likely to give rise to the paradoxicality of force relations under which heightened suggestibility is produced." Also Andrew Salter, *Conditioned Reflex Therapy*, (New York: Capricorn Books, 1961), p. 20. "Hypnosis is a term of convenience which has become attached to certain aspects of conditioning. It is all conditioning, and when this is constantly kept in mind hypnosis — or, more broadly, conditioning — becomes an instrument of the most fantastic power, and the person under treatment needs neither faith, nor hope, nor confidence . . ."
13. *ibid.*, Platonov, p. 47.
14. Contained in letter sent to Mr. Dean Riggins on April 15, 1964. We have the letter on file.
15. See Appendix I.
16. K.I. Platonov, *The Word As A Physiological and Therapeutic Factor*, p. 47.
17. A.R. Luria, *Nature of Human Conflicts*, p. 240. "We undertook to produce synthetically a complete model of a stable neurosis . . .

    "All the difficulties which we have referred to might be successfully removed by the help of the hypnotic method. In hypnosis we can count on obtaining a conflict of fair stability and intensity . . .

    "The hypnotic method opens up for us some very interesting possibilities, capable of helping us in the experimental setting to obtain those stable conflicts which are limited in their influence by the artificially provoked model of neurosis . . .

    "We may easily cause a collision between our suggested activity and the natural setting of the personality; we may investigate the stages in which the personality orients himself to the suggested intrusion as to something extraneous, and this conflict conditions the deep-lying neurodynamic changes. We may further oppose the activity produced in the hypnotic state by the subsequent instructions given in the waking state, excluding the free manifestations of the former activity; then we have a collision of activities characterized by compulsion or tension with a subconscious motive. Finally, we can introduce into the psyche of the subject the entire conflicting process by suggesting during hypnosis two equally obligatory and opposed tendencies: for example, having made the subject incapable of expressing something imperative for him.

"In all these cases we were able artificially to produce a model of compulsion and to oppose it by some physiological measure, beginning with a natural reaction of the personality and ending with a motor delay called out in a state of hypnosis. It is obvious that for the artificial creation of acute processes of disorganized human behavior, and for a study of its laws, the situation of the hypnotic experiment offers many favorable opportunities."

18. See Appendix I.
19. The words of the record state: "My name is Tom (hic) — I am so sad. 'Cause these old hiccups (hic) — Make me feel bad. I'd like to cure them (hic) — Wouldn't you, too? 'Cause I (hic) all day, And I (hic) all night, What can I (hic) do? (hic) !" Following the hiccups, Tom gets the whistles, the stutters, the sneezes, the yawns and the snores. The cure at the end of the record goes: "My name is Tom and I feel so grand. My voice now is wonderful, the best in the land! I sing the whole day through — That's what I do — With my snore all gone, and my yawn all gone, and my sneeze all gone, and my shake all gone and my hiccups gone! I feel so grand. (hic) Oh-Oh!"
20. Platonov, *op. cit.*, p. 151, ". . . it is possible to produce by verbal suggestion during suggested sleep not only hysterical syndromes, but also more complex pathological states, such as the epileptic fit in man." Also see p. 265.
21. "Oh, Suzanna, " "How Dry I Am," "The Merry Widow Waltz" and "The Stein Songs."
22. Platonov, *op. cit.*, p. 145, "According to Pavlov's teachings, the cerebral cortex represents a mosaic picture of excited and inhibited sections . . . On the basis of these considerations and of experimental data, we can assert that by suggesting a past age we can really reproduce the former dynamic structure relating to a corresponding earlier period of life."
23. See Appendix I.

24. A.R. Luria, *op. cit.*, pp. 335-336, "Our experiments with the simple rhythmical reactions were conducted in children beginning at two and a half years of age . . ."
25. Edward Hunter, *Brainwashing*, p. 238, "If brainwashing can make a single individual neurotic, what about the inhabitants of a village, or a city, or even a country . . . There is no doubt any longer that this type of mind attack is being waged against entire populations . . ."
26. Platonov, *op. cit.*, p. 244, "A weakening of the volitional traits may occur only if a special verbal suggestion aimed precisely in this direction is made, which, of course, is opposed to the basic moral principles of a physician . . ." This could well be the key passage in seeking to understand Communist mind warfare. Physicians might have basic moral principles, but Communist psycho-politicians have no such scruples.

Chapter VIII — Notes

1. Bertrand Russell, *Bolshevism: Theory and Practice* (New York: Harcourt Publishers, 1920), p. iv. Admits that he is a Communist, although in a later edition of the work (1948), Russell changed the word "Communist" to "Socialist." In Dagobert D. Runes, *Pictorial History of Philosophy* (New York: Philosophical Library, Inc., 1959), p. 269, Dr. Runes refers to Russell as one who "delighted in attacking the United States as a monger of atomic warfare, advocating a general acceptance of Soviet Russian world dominance." Russell is a member of the Fabian Society of Great Britain — an organization of Red-fronters and atheists. See *Fabianism In the Political Life of Britain 1919-1931*, Dr. M. Margaret Patricia McCarran, and *Keynes at Harvard*, Veritas Foundation, 150 East 35th Street, New York 16, N.Y.
2. Bertrand Russell, *The Impact of Science on Society* (New York: Simon and Schuster, 1953), pp. 29-30.
3. *ibid.*, pp. 49-50.
4. *American Institute of Hypnosis Journal*, Oct. 1963, p. 13.

CHAPTER IX — NOTES

1. *Book-of-the-Month Club News* for January, 1952. "A check of the authors promoted through the Book-of-the-Month Club against the indicies of government investigating bodies showed that over 30% of the authors of the selections and dividend books of the Book-of-the-Month Club from 1926 through 1957 had Communist front affiliations." *The Great Deceit*, Veritas Foundation, p. 52. Also, "Such poisonous socialist and Communist propaganda items as Bernard Shaw's *Intelligent Woman's Guide to Socialism* and the official Soviet text of New Russia's Primer were distributed by the hundreds of thousands due to the impetus given to them by the Book-of-the-Month Club."
2. *Fourth Report of the California Senate Fact-Finding Subcommittee on Un-American Activities*, 1948, p. 390.
3. Carried on the jacket of the records.
4. Carried on the jacket of the records. Not all records carry it, of course.
5. *The Great Deceit*, Veritas Foundation, p. 37. "In Tamiment Institute activities we find such persons as Frank Stanton of the Columbia Broadcasting System participating along with Leo Rosten of *Look*, and William Nichols of *This Week*. These are individuals who reach millions of people with their peculiar slant on national and world affairs." " . . . the Tamiment Institute and Library is a new name for the old Rand School of Social Science and it has replaced the latter as an adjunct of L.I.D. [League for Industrial Democracy]. It is the American counterpart of the British Fabian Research Bureau." (p. 26)
6. Carried on the jackets of the records that we have on file.
7. See Appendix I.
8. Letter from *Good Housekeeping's* G. Harry Chamberlaine to Mr. Bruce Glenn, July 19, 1965.
9. Letter from *Parent's Magazine's* Marjorie B. Keiser to Mr. Bruce Glenn, July 26, 1965.
10. *The World Almanac*, 1960, p. 188.
11. The National Council of Churches has been in the forefront of many activities looked upon by Bible-believing Christians as subversive; e.g., according to the Communist *Worker* for March 16, 1965, Jessie Gray received an ovation when he declared: "We don't need our troops in South Vietnam, the Marines should be sent to Selma." Also speaking at the Harlem rally were Bayard Rustin, John Lewis and others of their revolutionary type. On page 7 of this *Worker* we are informed that the National Council of Churches helped sponsor the rally. In the Allen and Scott report, found in the *Tulsa Daily World* for April 16, 1965, mention

is made of a National Conference on South Africa Crisis and American Action. Prominent throughout the conference were two Communists from Byelorussia and Ukraine who "huddled constantly with conference leaders and African diplomats, particularly from Algeria and Ghana." The late Robert Spike, then executive director of the Commission on Religion and Race of the National Council of Churches, was also active in the conference. For additional information on the pro-Communist activities of the National Council of Churches, we would suggest a Christian Crusade publication, "Does the National Council of Churches Speak For You?" It presents the Council's position on the recognition of Red China, on H.C.U.A., free-love, J. Edgar Hoover and other vitally important subjects. Also, Christian Crusade's full length book, *The Facts About Communism and Our Churches*, by Dr. Billy James Hargis and Julian Williams.

12. Letter from the N.C.C.'s Agnes Prestrod, Jan. 8, 1965.
13. *Southern Baptist Book Store Catalog*, 1010 Broadway, Nashville, Tennessee, 1965, pp. 152, 153. Also see subsequent catalogs.
14. *Southern Baptist Training Union Quarterly*, July-August-September 1964, p. 6. Also, see James Baldwin's chilling account on our Lord in *National Review*, 150 East 35th Street, New York, Nov. 30, 1965, p. A-22, "belief in Christ is based on an ignorance of 'several elementary historical details,' says Baldwin, such as 'that the real architect of the Christian Church was not the disreputable, sunbaked Hebrew who gave it his name but the mercilessly fanatical and self-righteous St. Paul.' "
15. Dr. Randolph Smith, Edith Sidorsky, Lucy Sprague Mitchell and Eleanor Reich are or have been members of the teaching staff of the Bank Street Schools.
16. Gilman and Paperte, Music and Your Emotions, p. 28. "Experiments of Fere, Tartchanoff, Diserens, and Cripture included studies of the effects of the sound stimulus upon the skeletal muscles. Using musical selections as the stimulus, Tartchanoff observed that (1) music exercises a powerful influence on muscular activity, which increases or diminishes according to the character of the melodies employed; (2) when music is sad or of a slow rhythm, and in the minor key, the capacity for muscular work decreases to the point of ceasing entirely if the muscle has been fatigued from previous work. The general conclusion is that sounds are dynamogenic or that muscular energy increases with the intensity and pitch of the sound stimuli. Isolated tones, scales, motifs, and simple tonal sequences have all been found to have an energizing effect upon the muscles." Ivan Pavlov found only three areas of the human body to condition: (1) muscles, (2) glands and (3) skin areas. These Communist

records for children condition the muscles!

17. Andrew Salter, *Conditioned Reflex Therapy* (New York: Capricorn Book, 1961), p. 17. "... it is a truism to say that the movements of our muscles are associated with the sensory information we receive from without. Consequently, words with their corresponding muscular associativity easily produce conditioned muscular responses in the much-practiced motor system of the body."
18. *Your Child Is Musical*, Children's Record Guild pamphlet distributed by the Book-of-the-Month Club, Inc., p. 5.
19. Norbert Wiener, *Human Use Of Human Beings*, (New York: Doubleday and Company, Inc., 1950), p. 17. "Man is immersed in a world which he perceives through his sense organs. Information that he receives is co-ordinated through his brain and nervous system until, after the proper process of storage, collation, and selection, it emerges through effector organs, generally his muscles." A.R. Luria, *Nature of Human Conflicts*, p. 342."... such an effect is generally seen in the child. His movements customarily reflect directly the intensiveness of the given stimulus; the strengthening of the stimulus brings about the marked reactive impulse, the stimulus having certain normal intensity, passes over into a state of shock and exhibits a disturbed motor reaction."
20. *Grade Teacher*, February 1962, p. 122.
21. *Your Child Is Musical*, Children's Record Guild pamphlet distributed by the Book-of-the-Month Club.
22. *Educational Record Sales*, 157 Chambers Street, New York 7, N.Y., p. 1. *Lyons Elementary School Catalog*, 223 West Lake Street, Chicago, Illinois, 1962-63, p. 55.
24. *ibid.*, p. 57.
25. *Tools of Teaching*, School Service Company, 4233 Crenshaw Blvd., Los Angeles 8, California, p. 157.

CHAPTER X — NOTES

1. *Daily Breeze*, Redondo Beach, California, n.d., "Recordings Will Stay," by Al Butkus.
2. *ibid.*
3. *ibid.*, May 19, 1965.
4. Butkus, *op. cit.*
5. Letter from *Parent's Magazine*, July 26, 1965.
6. Letter from *Good Housekeeping's* G. Harry Chamberlaine to Mr. Bruce Glenn, August 9, 1965.
7. Letter from Federal Trade Commission to author, Feb. 3, 1966.
8. See Senate Internal Security Subcommittee report, *Pacifica Foundation*, Parts 1, 2 and 3, January 10, 11 and 25, 1963.
9. "The records are distributed by Traffic Publishing Co., believed to be a subsidiary of Franson Corporation."

CHAPTER XI — NOTES

1. *Eternity Magazine*, May 1965, p. 8. Dr. Raymond Robertson, Supt., Institute of Juvenile Research, Chicago, Illinois, in an address before the Family Life Section, Division of Christian Education, National Council of Churches, 1965.
2. *Matthew 18:6.*
3. *I Timothy 5:8.*
4. See Appendix I.
5. Edward Hunter, *Brainwashing*, p. 285.

CHAPTER XII – NOTES

1. *Time*, May 21, 1965, p. 85.
2. Henry David Thoreau, *Walden* (New York: The New American Library, 1854), p. 147.
3. House Committee on Un-American Activites hearing, *Communism in the Metropolitan Music School*, April 9, 1957, p. 674.
4. Sidney Finkelstein, *How Music Expresses Ideas* (New York: International Publishers Co., 1952), p. 118.
5. *Time* May 21, 1965, p. 85.
6. *ibid.*, p. 85.
7. *ibid.*, p. 85.
8. Information contained in letter from Joseph Stone, Assistant District Attorney in charge of Criminal Courts Bureau, Sept. 14, 1965.
9. *Newsweek*, November 30, 1959, p. 95.
10. *Jacksonville Journal*, February 23, 1965, p. 1.
11. *Independent*, Long Beach, California, May 17, 1965, p. B-1.
12. *ibid.*, October 24, 1964, p..
13. *The San Francisco Chronicle*, March 8, 1965, p. 18.
14. *Evening Tribune*, San Diego, California, April 3, 1965, p. 1.
15. *Los Angeles Herald-Examiner*, Dec. 6, 1965, Section B, p. 1.
16. *Chicago Sun-Times*, Sept. 5, 1964, p. 24, and *Saturday Evening Post*, August 8, 1964.
17. *Seattle Post-Intelligence*, Aug. 22, 1964, p. 6.
18. *Daily Oklahoman*, Saturday, Sept. 19, 1964, p. 1,2.
19. Ivan P. Pavlov, *Lectures On Conditioned Reflexes* (New York: International Publishers, 1928), Chapter 36. Also, A.R. Luria, *Nature of Human Conflicts* p. 209-211.

CHAPTER XIII — NOTES

1. Edward Hunter, *Brainwashing* (New York: Pyramid Books, 1961), p. 40.
2. *ibid.*
3. *ibid.*
4. "How the Communists Control Thoughts and Attitudes," Herbert A. Philbrick, Freedom Forum XIX, Searcy, Arkansas, April 7, 1958. Also *op. cit.*, K.I. Platonov, p. 11: "Soviet psychotherapy has developed under conditions entirely different from those in foreign countries and in pre-revolutionary Russia. It is being built on the basis of dialectical materialism . . ."
5. *Seattle Daily Times*, August 22, 1964, p. 1. Also, Martin C. Sampson, M.D., *Solacen Tybamage* (New Jersey: Wallace Laboratories), p. 5, lists the following symptoms of psychoneurosis: "crying, apathy, agitation, anorexia, insomnia, hostility, lack of concentration, tension, headache, irritability, anxiety, tension, assaultive behavior, fearfulness, restlessness, nervousness, depression, phobias, psychosomatic complaints, obsessive-compulsive delusions, withdrawn behavior, lack of cooperation, hallucinations, psychomotor retardation."
6. I.P. Pavlov, *Conditioned Reflexes*, Dover edition, 1960, p. 398.
7. I.P. Pavlov, *Conditioned Reflexes and Psychiatry* (New York: International Publishers, 1963), p. 96.
8. *ibid.*, p. 164.
9. I.P. Pavlov, *Conditioned Reflexes*, Dover edition, 1960, p. 395f.
10. I.P. Pavlov, *Conditioned Reflexes and Psychiatry*, p. 64, 105. Also I.P. Pavlov, *Conditioned Reflexes*, Dover edition, 1960, p. 288.
11. I.P. Pavlov, *Lectures on Conditioned Reflexes* (New York: International Publishers Co., 1963), p. 374.
12. *ibid.*, p. 375. Also, I.P. Pavlov, *Conditioned Reflexes and Psychiatry*, p. 84, 164.
13. I.P. Pavlov, *Conditioned Reflexes and Psychiatry*, p. 52.
14. I.P. Pavlov, *Lectures on Conditioned Reflexes*, Volume 1, p. 375. Also, I.P. Pavlov, *Conditioned Reflexes*, Dover edition, p. 311.
15. Rosen, Bahn, Kramer, *The American Journal of Orthopsychiatry*, "Demographic and Diagnostic Characteristic of Psychiatric Clinic Outpatients in the USA," 1961, Volume XXXIV, No. 3, April 1964, distributed by the Health, Education and Welfare Department, p. 457. Also, *Eternity* Magazine, May 1965, p. 8, Dr. Raymond Robertson, Supt., Institute of Juvenile Research, Chicago, Illinois, in an address before the Family Life Section, Division of Christian Education, National Council of Churches, 1965, "between 2.5 and 4.5 million children in our

country are in need of psychiatric help."

16. *The American Journal of Psychiatry*, Volume 101,, No. 3, Nov. 1944, p. 369. The quotation is found in Dr. Hanson's speech before the American Psychiatric Association, "Some Objective Studies of Rhythm in Music." Since the speech was given in 1944, the "wild" music Dr. Hanson refers to is the predecessor of rock 'n' roll, "violent boogie-woogie." His warning has grown in import instead of diminishing and this in itself makes his observations more valuable — perhaps even prophetic.
17. Dr. Howard Hanson, *The American Journal of Psychiatry*, Volume 99, No. 3, Nov. 1942, p. 325.
18. Edward Hunter, *Brainwashing*, p. 238.
19. I.P. Pavlov, *Conditioned Reflexes and Psychiatry*, p. 164.
20. I.P. Pavlov, *Conditioned Reflexes*, Dover edition, p. 397.
21. I.P. Pavlov, *Conditioned Reflexes and Psychiatry*, p. 164.
22. I.P. Pavlov, *Lectures on Conditioned Reflexes*, p. 374.
23. I.P. Pavlov, *Psychopathology and Psychiatry* (Moscow: Foreign Languages Publishing House), p. 147f. Also I.P. Pavlov, *Conditioned Reflexes*, Dover edition, p. 302f.
24. I.P. Pavlov, *Conditioned Reflexes*, Dover edition, p. 318.
25. I.P. Pavlov, *Conditioned Reflexes and Psychiatry*, p. 84. In this passage, Pavlov analyzes his animals' neurotic condition. Not surprisingly, our young people could very easily relate the same following experience. Pavlov writes, "One can conceive in all likelihood that, if these dogs which have become ill could look back and tell what they had experienced on that occasion, they would not add a single thing to that which one would conjecture about their condition. All would declare that on everyone of the occasions mentioned they were put through a difficult test, a hard situation. Some would report that they felt frequently unable to refrain from doing that which was forbidden and then they felt punished for doing it in one way or another, while others would say that they were totally, or just passively, unable to do what they usually had to do."
26. *ibid.*, p. 115.
27. Perverted musical form generally stands in contradistinction to what is musically understood by the expression "Tinpan Alley." Needless to say, the Communists have no use for Tinpan Alley — *The Worker*, March 9, 1965, p. 5. Also, see *How Music Expresses Ideas*, Sidney Finkelstein, p. 109, 115. Such expressions as "Tinpan Alley straitjacket of form" or "formalist Tinpan Alley pattern" are used to slur standard musical form.
28. *Reader's Digest*, Nov. 1964, p. 183.

29. *ibid.*, p. 184.
30. *Parade Magazine*, January 10, 1965.
31. Some contend that individuals will not act contrary to their morals, but Pavlovian scientists have found this to be a mistaken notion. Experiments were conducted in which subjects actually threw acid into the faces of their friends. Heavy glass protected the friends. *Journal of Abnormal and Social Psychology*, 1939, 34:114-117, article by L.W. Rowland entitled "Will Hypnotized Persons Try To Harm Themselves or Others?" *Journal of Abnormal and Social Psychology*, 1941, 11: 63-102, article by W.R. Wells entitled, "Experiments In the Hypnotic Production of Crime." *Psychiatry*, 1942, 5:49-61, article by M. Brenman entitled "Experiments in the Hypnotic Production of Anti-Social and Self-Injurious Behavior." *Journal of Abnormal Social Psychology*, 1947, p. 256ff., Dr. John G. Watkins reported experiments that show that "under deep trance, hallucinations can be set up which will cause some subjects to commit 'socially criminal acts,' even to the extent of murder." He also found that under hypnosis members of the armed forces (although forewarned, in some cases, of what would be attempted) would betray military secrets and try to murder their commanding officers. Also see Andrew Salter,, *Conditioned Reflex Therapy*, p. 10f. Also, Dr. Louis J. West and Dr. Gordon H. Deckert, writing in the *Journal of the American Medical Association*, asserted that hypnosis can be used to lead some folk astray. In writing up the article, John Troan, Scripps-Howard Science writer said, "Contrary to a widespread notion that a hypnotized person 'draws the line at violating the law or his own ethical code,' the doctors cited evidence indicating hypnosis can be used to seduce some individuals or lead them into crime." *Rocky Mountain News* (Denver, Colorado) April 3, 1965, p. 41.
32. Andrew Salter, *Conditioned Reflex Therapy* (New York: Capricorn Books, 1961), p. 26.
33. *Modern Medicine*, 65th Street at Valley View Road, Southdale Park, Minneapolis, Minnesota, July 5, 1965, Volume 33, No. 14, p. 14.
34. House Committee on Un-American Activities, *Communist and Trotskyist Activity within the Greater Los Angeles Chapter of the Fair Play For Cuba Committee*, November 2, 1962, p. 1571. Billy James Hargis, *Distortion by Design*, Christian Crusade Publications, P.O. Box 977, Tulsa Oklahoma 74102, 1965, p. 170f. Fulton Lewis, Jr., *The Top of the News* Sheraton-Park Hotel, Washington, D.C., January 9-13, 1961, p. 4.
35. Appropriation testimony of John Edgar Hoover, director, Federal Bureau of Investigation, before the House Subcommittee on Appropriations on March 6, 1961. Published 1962, p. 49.

36. Aldous Huxley, *Devils of Loudun,* (New York: Harper and Rowe Publishers Inc., 1952), pp. 367-368.
37. As a fellow of the Royal College of Physicians, Dr. William Sargant first came to the United States in 1938 to work at Harvard and the Massachusetts General Hospital on a Rockefeller Foundation grant. Since then he has been frequently invited as a visitor to the United States. A former president of psychiatry section of the Royal Society of Medicine, he is in charge of the department of psychological medicine at one of London's oldest and most famous general teaching hospitals. *Atlantic Monthly* (July, 1964, pp. 88-95) recently published one of his articles entitled, "Psychiatric Treatment."
38. Wilhelm Wundt, *Outlines of Psychology*, p. 162f: ". . . observed that each beat of a given tempo is followed by a rising nervous and muscular tension, on the part of the hearer, in anticipation of the beat to follow. With the succeeding beat the tension would drop and then immediately begin to rise again in anticipation of the next beat. He also observed that a slowing of the tempo, and abrupt halt, or an abrupt change of tempo caused a considerable increase in nervous tension." A.R. Luria, Nature of Human Conflicts, p.210: "We attempted to use automatic motor acts to produce this conflict by giving to the subject a definite speed of rhythmical motor reactions and then suddenly trying to change this rate when we gave a signal."
39. William Sargant, *Battle For The Mind* (New York: Doubleday & Company, Inc., 1957), p. 59. Also, *op. cit.*, K.I. Platonov, p. 120, 206.
40. I.P. Pavlov, *Lectures On Conditioned Reflexes* (New York: International Publishers, 1928), pp. 333-334: "If I have produced a process of excitation and now limit it with one of inhibition, this is trying on the animal; it begins to whine and bark and attempts to free itself from the stand. The only reason for this is that I have brought about a difficult balancing of the processes of excitation and inhibitions. Let any of us consider his own personal life and experiences and he will find many similar examples. If, for example, I am occupied with something — i.e., I am under the influence of a definite process of excitation — and if someone suddenly proposes to me to do another thing, it is unpleasant for me. For it means that I must inhibit the strong excitatory process in which I was engaged, and only after this can I start a new one . . . And even more. A stress of such nature, this difficult conflict between our dogs, produce painful results, i.e., marked disturbances in the normal nervous activity."
41. Sargant, *op. cit.*, p. 50.
42. *ibid.*, p. 145.

43. *Wichita Eagle* (Kansas), February 17, 1965.
44. *The American Journal of Psychiatry*, Volume 101, p. 364.
45. *Reader's Digest*, Nov. 1964, p. 183. "In contrast, rock 'n' roll dulls the capacity for attention; the steady beat creates instead a kind of hypnotic monotony."
46. *Seattle Daily Times*, August 22, 1964, p. 1.
47. Leonard Gilman M.D., was formerly chief of the Psychiatric Section, Walter Reed General Hospital, and is a Diplomat of the American Board of Neurology and Psychiatry.
48. Gilman and Paperte, *Music and Your Emotions*, pp. 30-31.

CHAPTER XIV — NOTES

1. *Look*, December 15, 1964.
2. Jack Staulcup, *Today's Teenager and Dance Music* (Illinois: Metropolis Printing Service, 1964), p. 6, 7.
3. Henry J. Taylor predicted that the National Arts and Cultural Development Act "will soon be subsidizing in the name of art and culture everything from belly dancing to ballet; from Handel to Hootenanny; from Johannes Brahms to the Beatles; from symphonies to strip tease." *Tulsa Daily World*, November 2, 1965, p. 10.
4. *American Mercury*, Sept. 1961, p. 49.
5. *Teen Magazine*, Sept. 1964, p. 84.
6. *U.S. News and World Report*, February 24, 1964, p. 88. Dr. Reisman, one of the authors of the extremely pro-Communist *Liberal Papers*, states on page 30 of the book, "But as the cold war continues, it becomes increasingly difficult for decent Americans, humane enough to prefer peace to an ego-centric national honor, to be outspokenly and genuinely anti-Communist."
7. *Tulsa Daily World*, April 21, 1965.
8. *Los Angeles Herald-Examiner*, Sunday, August 8, 1965, p. J-9.
9. *The American Journal of Psychiatry*, Volume 101, p. 365.
10. *American Mercury*, Sept. 1961, p. 47.
11. *ibid.*, p. 46.
12. *ibid.*, p. 46.
13. *ibid.*, p. 46.
14. *American Journal of Psychiatry*, Volume 101, November 1944, p. 369.
15. *Atlantic Monthly*, July 1964, p. 82. "The statistical facts about the incidence and the prevalence of mental illness have been so widely publicized in the last decade that they have been synthesized in a series of cliches: 'Half the hospital beds in the country are occupied by mental patients;' 'One person in ten is sufficiently sick mentally or emotionally to require professional help;' 'One family in three will at sometime place one of its members in a mental hospital;' 'Mental illness is the country's number-one health problem.' Unfortunately, these are not exaggerations or slogans but the simple truth. At the present time there are 500,000 patients in mental hospitals throughout the country; possibly one million are under treatment in clinics or other outpatient facilities; and countless thousands who need psychiatric help are receiving no treatment of any kind."
16. See Footnote 15, Part III, Chapter XIII.
17. J. Edgar Hoover continually states in his annual report on crime that

delinquency is at an all-time high. In his book, *The Shook-up Generation*, Harrison E. Salisburg, *New York Times* correspondent, states that the one factor always present in the delinquent is "emotional insecurity."

CHAPTER XV — NOTES

1. *Barron's*, May 20, 1968, p. 1.
2. Now the Student National Coordinating Committee. H. Rap Brown is its new director.
3. Senate Internal Security Subcommittee, *The Anti-Vietnam Agitation and Teach-in Movement*, October 22, 1965, p. 16.
4. *Denver Post*, July 7, 1969, p. 1.
5. *Christian Century*, January 15, 1969, p. 92.
6. Jerry Rubin, *Do It!* (New York: Simon and Schuster, 1970), back cover.
7. *Human Events*, May 16, 1970. "The first part of the Yippie program, you know is kill your parents . . . until you're prepared to kill your parents you're not really prepared to change the country, because our parents are our first oppressors."
8. Rubin, *Do It!!*, p. 19.
9. *ibid.*, p. 18.
10. *ibid.*, p. 249.
11. *ibid.*, p. 85.
12. *Denver Post*, July 13, 1969, p. 14.
13. *Tulsa Tribune*, April 12, 1969, p. 14B.
14. *Time*, May 26, 1967, p. 53.
15. *San Francisco Sunday Examiner and Chronicle*, September 25, 1966, Sec. 1, p. 13.
16. Gene Lees, "Rock, Violence, and Spiro T. Agnew," *High Fidelity*, February, 1970, p. 108.
17. *ibid.*
18. *ibid.*, p. 110.
19. *ibid.*, p. 108, 110.
20. *Time*, August 9, 1968, p. 47.
21. *New York Times*, April 2, 1963, p. 9.
22. *Saturday Evening Post*, March 25, 1967, p. 41.
23. *New York Times* magazine, December 1, 1963, p. 124.
24. *ibid.*, p. 126.
25. *Parade*, Sunday supplement, June 27, 1965.
26. *Cavalier*, February, 1969, p. 37.
27. *ibid.*, p. 88.

CHAPTER XVI – NOTES

1. *Central California Register*, July 6, 1967, p. 7.
2. *American Opinion*, May, 1969, p. 59.
3. *Cavalier*, February, 1969, p. 37.
4. *Life*, June 28, 1968.
5. *Time*, May 26, 1967, p. 53.
6. *The Cleveland Press*, July 25, 1969, p. IN.
7. *New York Times*, August 28, 1967, p. 35.
8. *Time*, July 1, 1966, p. 56.
9. *Columbus Citizen Journal*, May 9, 1967.
10. *San Francisco Sunday Examiner and Chronicle*, September 25, 1966, p. 13.
11. *Confidential*, May, 1969, p. 45.
12. House Select Committee on Crime, *Crime in America — Views on Marijuana*, October 14, 15, 1969, p. 17, 18.
13. *ibid.*, p. 79.
14. Harold Kolansky and William T. Moore, "Effects of Marijuana on Adolescents and Young Adults," *Journal of the American Medical Association*, Vol. 216, No. 3, April 19, 1971, p. 487.
15. *ibid.*
16. *ibid.*, p. 491.
17. *ibid.*, p. 492.
18. *Tulsa Daily World*, May 5, 1967, p. 8.
19. *Tulsa Daily World*, September 25, 1969, p. 16A.
20. *Tulsa Tribune*, February 24, 1967, p. 14.
21. *Daily Cardinal*, December 3, 1968, p. 5.
22. Hunter Davies, *The Beatles* (New York: McGraw Hill Co., 1968), p. 281.
23. *Time*, September 22, 1967, p. 62.
24. Davies, *The Beatles*, p. 228.
25. *ibid.*, p. 275.
26. *Time*, September 22, 1967, p. 105.
27. *Life*, June 16, 1967, p. 105.
28. Davies, *The Beatles*, p. 310.
29. *ibid.*, p. 78.
30. *ibid.*
31. *ibid.*, p. 206.
32. *ibid.*, p. 288.
33. *Tulsa Daily World*, July 25, 1967, p. 13.
34. Davies, *The Beatles*, p. 272.
35. *ibid.*, p. 289.

36. *ibid.*, p. 228.
37. *ibid.*, p. 235.
38. *ibid.*, p. 230.
39. *New York Times*, September 11, 1967, p. 53.
40. *Tulsa Daily World*, April 1, 1969.
41. *Des Moines Tribune*, January 18, 1969, p. 3.
42. *Detroit Free Press*, September 5, 1967.
43. *Commonweal*, May 12, 1967, p. 235.
44. *Time*, September 26, 1969, p. 69.
45. *Cavalier*, February,, 1969, p. 37.
46. House Select Committee on Crime, *Crime in America — Illicit and Dangerous Drugs*, October 23, 24, 25, 27, 1969, p. 152.
47. *ibid.*, p. 148.
48. S. Taqi, "Approbation of Drug Usage in Rock and Roll Music," *Bulletin on Narcotics*, Vol. XXI, No. 4, October-December, 1969, p. 33.
49. *ibid.*, p. 32.
50. *ibid.*, p. 35.
51. D.C. Parks, *Narcotics and Narcotics Addiction* (New York: Carlton Press, Inc., 1969), p. 1.
52. *Time*, September 26, 1969, p. 68.
53. John Kaplan, *Marijuana — The New Prohibition* (New York: Pocket Books, 1971), p. 192, 3.

CHAPTER XVII – NOTES

1. *Seattle Post Intelligence*, January 28, 1965, p. 16.
2. *G.O. Scene*, Winter, 1967-1968, p. 89.
3. Roland H. Bainton, *What Christianity Says About Sex, Love and Marriage* (New York: Association Press, 1957).
4. Romans 1:26, 27.
5. Galatians 5: 17-21.
6. *Time*, April 28, 1967, p. 54.
7. Sara Davidson, "Rock Style: Defying the American Dream," *Harpers*, July, 1969, p. 60.
8. *Time, June 23, 1967, p. 53.*
9. *Life*, May 21, 1968, p. 93.
10. *Ft. Lauderdale News*, March 6, 1969, p. 10C.
11. *New York Times*, December 11, 1967, p. 58.
12. *Newsweek*, November 6, 1967, p. 101.
13. Arnold Shaw, *The World of Soul*, (New York: Cowles Book Company, Inc., 1970), p. 262.
14. Davies, *The Beatles*, p. 281.
15. *Commonweal*, May 12, 1967, p. 235.
16. *Time*, July 1, 1966, p. 57.
17. *ibid.*
18. *ibid.*
19. *ibid.*
20. *Parade*, January 10, 1965.
21. *New York Times* magazine, March 14, 1965, p. 72.
22. *Indianapolis Star*, November 28, 1965, p. 1, Sec. 7.
23. *Seattle Times*, August 22, 1964, p. 1.
24. Davies, *The Beatles*, p. 179.
25. *The American Journal of Psychiatry*, Vol. 99, p. 317.
26. Bob Larson, *Rock and Roll* (McCook, Nebraska: Bob Larson, 1968), pp. 48-58.
27. *Los Angeles Times*, November 27, 1966.
28. *Riverside* (California) *Daily Enterprise and Press*, February 11, 1969.
29. *Saturday Evening Post*, March 21, 1964, p. 36.
30. Davidson, *Harpers*, July 1969, p. 57.
31. Davies, *The Beatles*, p. 31.
32. *ibid.*, p. 77.
33. *ibid.*, p. 79.
34. *Parade*, October 4, 1964, p. 12.
35. Davies, *The Beatles*, p. 324.

36. *Newsweek*, April 17, 1967, p. 66.
37. *Penthouse*, October, 1969, p. 32.
38. *ibid.*, p. 29.
39. *New York Daily News*, March 26, 1969, p. 4.
40. *London Sunday Express*, March 30, 1969.
41. *St. Louis Globe Democrat*, Sept. 28, 1971, p. B1.

CHAPTER XVIII — NOTES

1. *Tulsa Tribune* (Alice Widener Column), April 23, 1969, p. 18E.
2. *Life*, April 25, 1969, front cover and p. 34.
3. *U.S. News & World Report*, May 12, 1969, p. 34.
4. *ibid.*
5. *Christian Century*, January 15, 1969, p. 92.
6. *Saturday Evening Post*, August 8-15, 1964, p. 25.
7. *Chicago Tribune*, September 22, 1968.
8. *ibid.*
9. *Manchester Union Leader*, November 14, 1966, p. 22.
10. *Congressional Record*,, March 11, 1969, E 1898.
11. *ibid.*
12. *Riverside* (California) *Daily Enterprise & Press*, February 11, 1969.
13. *ibid.*
14. *ibid.*
15. House Committee on Un-American Activities, *Communism in the New York Area (Entertainment)*, June 19, 1958, pp. 2581, 2582.
16. *Sing Out!* May, 1965, p. 63.
17. Davies, *The Beatles*, p. 19. The New Orleans *Times-Picayune* (Nov. 22, 1971, p. 12) carried the following, "Damage was estimated at $10,000 when part of a crowd of about 11,000 went on a rampage Saturday night during a rock show at the Pacific Coliseum. A spokesman for the coliseum said about 100 seats were slashed and about eight sheets of protective glass around the ice in the coliseum, home of the National Hockey League's Vancouver Canucks, were shattered."
18. Leopold Schwartzschild, *Karl Marx, The Red Prussian* (New York: Grosset & Dunlap, 1947), p. 64, 65.
19. Robert Payne, *The Life and Death of Lenin* (New York: Avon Books, 1967), p. 550.
20. William Z. Foster, *Toward Soviet America* (Balboa Islands [California]: Elgin Enterprises, Inc., 1961), p. 317.
21. *ibid.*, p. 326.
22. Whittaker Chambers, *Witness* (New York: Random House, 1952), p. 712.
23. Phillip Crane, *The Democrat's Dilemma* (Chicago: Henry Regnery Co., 1964), pp. 37-42.
24. Stormer, *None Dare Call It Treason*, p. 26.
25. George Bernard Shaw, *Intelligent Woman's Guide to Socialism*, (New York: Brentanno's Publishing Co., 1928), p. 470.
26. Davies, *The Beatles*, p. 60.
27. *ibid.*, p. 318.

28. *ibid.*, p. 103.
29. *Saturday Evening Post*, August 8-15, 1964, p. 28.
30. *Playboy*, February, 1965, p. 58.
31. *ibid.*
32. John Lennon, *A Spaniard in the Works* (New York: Simon and Schuster, 1965), p. 14.
33. *Dallas Times Herald*, July 11, 1965.
34. *Realities*, Vol. I, No I, October 8, 1965, p. 4.
35. *Parade*, Sunday Supplement, June 27, 1965.
36. Lennon, *A Spaniard in the Works*, p. 90.
37. *Newsweek*, March 21, 1966, p. 52.
38. *San Francisco Chronicle*, April 13, 1966, p. 26.
39. *ibid.*
40. *New York Times*, August 5, 1966, p. 20.
41. *Denver Post*, August 11, 1966, p. 65.
42. Davies, *The Beatles*, p. 210.
43. *ibid.*
44. *New York Times*, August 12, 1966, p. 38.
45. *ibid.*
46. *Christianity Today*, September 2, 1966, p. 54. Also see *Washington Post*, August 15, 1966.
47. *New York Times*, December 12, 1966, p. 57.
48. *Time*, September 6, 1968, p. 60.
49. *News of the World*, March 23, 1969. Also see *Christian Beacon*, April 10, 1969, p. 3.
50. *Chicago Tribune*, September 3, 1966, p. 3.
51. See Part Four, Chapter XXIII.
52. *Sing Out!*, January, 1964, p. 77.
53. Norrie Drummond,, "A Party with the Beatles," *Hit Parade*, October, 1967, p. 14.
54. *Time*, September 22, 1967, p. 60.
55. See Part Four, Chapter XXVI.
56. U.P.I., March 6, 1964.
57. *Insurgent*, Vol. I, No. I, March-April, 1965, p. 12.
58. *Daily World*, February 22, 1969, p. M6.
59. Davies, *The Beatles*, p. 295.
60. *Tulsa Daily World*, May 11, 1967, p. 6. Chicago Tribune, June 30, 1967, p. 3.
61. *Indiana Evening Gazette*, October 7, 1968, p. 14.
62. *Tulsa Daily World*, January 23, 1967, p. 4. Also see *Esquire*, June, 1969, p. 170.

63. Senate Internal Security Subcommittee, *Institute of Pacific Relations hearing*, Part 13, April, 1952, p. 4509.
64. *Time*, October 11, 1968, p. 88.
65. *Daily World*, February 22, 1969, p. M7.
66. *New York Times*, December 1, 1963, p. 126.
67. *Los Angeles Times*, October 23, 1964.
68. *London Sunday Express*, March 30, 1969.
69. *Washington Star*, March 11, 1967.
70. *Holiday*, February, 1968, p. 142.
71. Davies, *The Beatles*, p. 296.
72. *Saturday Evening Post*, August 27, 1966, p. 26.
73. *ibid.*, p. 27.
74. *Manchester Union Leader*, June 23, 1965.
75. *New York Times*, June 17, 1965, p. 3.
76. *Rolling Stone* Magazine, Box 77245, San Francisco, California 94107.
77. *ibid.*, January 7, 1971, p. 39, 40.
78. *ibid.*, p. 40.
79. *ibid.*, p. 39.
80. *ibid.*
81. *ibid.*
82. *ibid.*
83. *ibid.*, p. 40.
84. *ibid.*, February 4, 1971, p. 39.
85. *ibid.*
86. *ibid.sm*,
87. *ibid.*
88. *ibid.*
89. *ibid.*, January 7, 1971, p. 41.
90. *St. Louis Globe Democrat*, Sept. 30, 1971, p. B1.
91. *National Observer*, January 15, 1968, p. 22.
92. *Penthouse*, October, 1969, p. 34.
93. *Life*, June 16, 1967, p. 105.
94. *Cavalier*, February, 1969, p. 37.

CHAPTER XIX – NOTES

1. *The Cleveland Press*, July 25, 1969, p.,1N.
2. Written by Marxist Phil Ochs.
3. *The Cleveland Press*, July 25, 1969, p. 1N. See *Cavalier*, July, 1969, p. 79f, for the new breed of "Rock Jock" playing "progressive" rock.
4. Jacques Barzun, *Darwin, Marx, Wagner* (New York: Doubleday & Co., 1958), p. 231. See also pp. 315, 316. Vetterli and Fort also state in their *The Socialist Revolution* (New York: Clute International Corp., 1968), p. 108, "Wagner, like so many other socialists of the time, fused his anti-capitalism with anti-Semitism, blaming both capitalism and the Jews for the degeneration of the human race. In his early youth, he took active part in the short-lived Dresden uprising with his friend the Russian anarchist Mikhail Bakunin." The two authors further stated, "Wagner bore a fanatical hatred for the Jews. He was convinced that they were out to dominate the world with their money, thus giving his endorsement to the fraudulent declaration called 'The Protocols of the Elders of Zion,' which Hitler also used with impunity."
5. *The Cleveland Press*, July 25, 1969, p. 1N.
6. Davies, *The Beatles*, p. 19.
7. *Tulsa Tribune*, February 22, 1967.
8. *The New York Times*, August 28, 1967, p. 35.
9. *Voice*, Vol. 40, No. 6 (April, 1967), p. 8.
10. *San Francisco Sunday Examiner and Chronicle*, September 25, 1966, p. 13.
11. David Gornston, *Straight Talk* (New York: Gateway Music Co., 1965), p. 16.
12. T. Olga Curtis, "Music That Kills Plants," *Denver Post*, June 21, 1970, p. 8M.
13. *ibid.*
14. *ibid.*
15. *ibid.*, p. 9.
16. *ibid.*
17. *ibid.* p. 11.
18. I Peter 2:24.
19. Hebrews 2:15.
20. Romans 10:9, I Corinthians 15: 3,4.
21. Romans 8:14.
22. The American Social Health Association reports "venereal disease has reached epidemic proportions in this country with more than one million Americans expected to become infected!" And, according to Dr. Joseph

Levin of the Chicago Medical School, a trend toward suicide is to be expected after the teens have been immersed with sex and drugs. Levin points out that suicide already ranks next to accidental fatalities as a cause of death among college students.

CHAPTER XX — NOTES

1. R. Serge Denisoff, *Great Day Coming — Folk Music and the American Left* (Urbana: University of Illinois Press, 1971), Foreword.
2. *Ibid.*, p. 161.
3. *Ibid.*, Foreword.
4. Nicholas Slonimsky, *Music Since 1900* (New York: W.W. Norton, 1937), pp. 549, 555. The chapter was entitled, "The Ideological Platform of the Russian Association of Proletarian Musicians."
5. House Committee on Un-American Activities, *Investigation of Communist Activities, New York Area — Part VII (Entertainment)*, August 18, 1955, p. 2459. Also see R. Serge Denisoff, *Great Day Coming — Folk Music and the American Left*, pp. 106-129.
6. *Fifth Report of the California Senate Factfinding Subcommittee on Un-American Activities*, 1949, p. 544.
7. Josh Dunson, *Freedom in the Air — Song Movement of the 60s* (New York: International Publishers, 1965), p. 19.
8. House Committee on Un-American Activities, *Investigation of Communist Activities*, New York Area — Part VII (Entertainment), August 18, 1955, p. 2459. Also, *Guide to Subversive Organizations*, Dec. 1, 1961, p. 94.
9. Horace Grenell, e.g., former president of Young People's Records, was a member of the board of directors of People's Songs, Inc.
10. *Op. cit.*, *Fifth Report of the California Subcommittee*, p. 543.
11. Mr. Glazer sings for Young People's Records and the Children's Record Guild. *Appendix IX*, Special Committee on Un-American Activities, House of Representatives, 1944, p. 541, finds Mr. Glazer a sponsor of the American Youth Congress. Attorney General Thomas Clark cited this front subversive December 4, 1947.
12. Mr. Hammond, Jr., is presently a sponsor of the Highlander Center, Knoxville, Tennessee. Highlander Center is the new name for the Highlander Folk School of Monteagle, Tennessee.
13. Bess L. Hawes is presently the teacher of Balladry and Folk Music at the University of California, Los Angeles Extension. See *Lifelong Learning*, Volume XIX, No. 31, University of California Extension, Fall, 1965, p. 141, 3. Her background is given in *Sing Out!*, September 1965, p. 26.
14. "Waldemar Hille, the editor of the original People's Songbook, has won a grant from the National Association for American Composers and Conductors for his oratorio called 'Denmark Vesey.' Hille . . . is musical director of the First Unitarian Church in Los Angeles," (*Sing Out!*,

January 1966, p. 5) The pastor at First Unitarian is Rev. Stephen H. Fritchman, a Fifth-Amendment patriot, who refuses to state whether or not he is a Communist.

15. Mr. Robinson has been connected with the Metropolitan Music School in New York for many years. In testimony before the House Committee on Un-American Activites, April 11, 1957, Mr. Robinson refused to testify concerning his Communist Party activity. His activity is staggering. In H.C.U.A., *Appendix IX* alone he is listed 23 times. In subsequent reports of the House Committee he is found numerous times. He served as musical editor for *Young Folk Song Book*, published by Simon and Schuster, New York, 1963.
16. House Committee on Un-American Activities, *Testimony of Walter S. Steele*, July 21, 1947, p. 105, "Walter Lowenfels of People's Songs is a Communist Party leader in Philadelphia." Lowenfels compiled an anthology of poems for the Communist publishing company, International Publishers, New York, entitled *Poets of Today*. The foreword was written by Langston Hughes, author of "Put One More S in the USA to make it Soviet," "Goodbye Christ" and "Ballad of Lenin." (See *Tax-Exempt Foundations*, House of Representatives, Report No. 2681, December 16, 1954, p. 293, 4.) Lowenfels also teamed up with Lee Hays in writing a vicious parody on the H.C.U.A. entitled "The Ballad For Un-American Blues." See Irwin Silber's *Reprints from the People's Songs Bulletin*, Oak Publications, New York, 1961, p. 81.
17. Commenting on *The People's Song Book*, Leonard Bernstein said, "A long- awaited record of a kind of American folk music which should long ago have entered the consciousness of the American people." His comment is found on the back cover of the song book. The book was copyrighted by Sing Out, Inc. in 1959 and Oak Publications in 1961. "At least 49 have given their open support to Communist candidates in election campaigns: Herbert Aptheker, Howard Bay, Leonard Bernstein, Marc Blitzstein . . ." See House Committee on Un-American Activities, *Review of the Scientific and Cultural Conference for World Peace*, April 19, 1949, p. 20. In more recent times Bernstein has raised funds for the Marxist- Leninist Black Panther Legal Defense League and also $35,000 for the Berrigan Defense Fund. (*Religious News Service*, May 12, 1971, p. 23). He has also manifested his anti-Christ colors in his musical *MASS* (assisted by Stephen Schwartz, creator of the blasphemous *Godspell*). See *Time*, Sept. 20, 1971, p. 41f.
18. The Scientific and Cultural Conference for World Peace was arranged by a subversive organization, the National Council of the Arts, Sciences and Professions. (See *Guide to Subversive Organizations and Publications*,

December 1, 1961, p. 118.) The National Council of the Arts, Sciences and Professions "is a descendant of the Independent Citizens Committee of the Arts, Sciences and Professions which was repudiated in 1946 by Harold L. Ickes, its Chairman, because of its Communist character." (See H.C.U.A.', *Review of the Scientific and Cultural Conference for World Peace*, April 19, 1949, p. 2.) The Independent Citizens Committee was also declared subversive in the *Guide to Subversive Organizations and Publications*, Dec. 1, 1961, p. 84. Mr. Copeland was not only a sponsor of the New York Conference for World Peace, but was also affiliated with the Independent Citizens Committee. (Op. cit., *Review*, p. 2) He was also listed as one of 49 who gave "their open support to Communist candidates in election campaigns." (Op. Cit. *Review*, p. 20) But more importantly we are informed, "Twenty-eight have been affiliated with from 21 to 30 Communist-front organizations, and include . . . Aaron Copeland." (Op. cit., *Review*, p. 18) The purpose of the Conference on World Peace was to "discredit American culture and . . . extol the virtues of Soviet culture." (Op. cit., *Review*, p. 1).

19. Paul Robeson, praising the Communist International Publishers' founder, Alexander Trachtenberg, stated, "Way back in 1924, 'Trachty' (as we call AT with affection) began the formidable task of building a publishing organization around books dealing with the scientific basis of our society . . . particularly against the background of the events of 1917 and the emergence of the Soviet Union, and the subsequent struggles for national liberation all over the world . . ." (See International Book Publishers News Letter No. 3, March 1965, 381 Park Ave. South, New York 16.)
20. Moe Asch (Moses Asch) is the production director of Folkways Records and co-owner and co-publisher of *Sing Out!* magazine. Folkways stands in the same relationship to *Sing Out!* as Keynote Recordings originally stood to People's Songs, Inc. Keynote Recordings disced the songs published by People's Songs, Folkways Records discs the songs published by *Sing Out!* magazine. Keynote Recordings was declared subversive by the *California Senate Factfinding Sub-committee on Un-American Activities*, 1948, p. 392.
21. The listing of these names affiliated with People's Songs, Inc. can be found in the House Committee on Un-American Activities, *Testimony of Walter S. Steele*, July 21, 1947, p. 101, or in the *Fourth Report of the California Senate Factfinding Subcommittee on Un-American Activities*, 1948, p. 392.

Chapter XXI — Notes

1. Irwin Silber, *Reprints From The People's Songs Bulletin* (New York: Oak Publications, 1961), p. 3. Oak Publications, Folkways Records and *Sing Out!* have all occupied the same address. Also see R. Serge Denisoff, *Great Day Coming*, pp. 107, 109, 115, 136, 154, 166.
2. *ibid.*, p. 3.
3. Irwin Silber, *Reprints From The People's Songs Bulletin* (New York: Oak Publications, 1961), p. 3. On page 2 of the Second People's Song Book, *Lift Every Voice*, we are informed, "Copyright 1953 by People's Artists, Inc. Assigned, 1957 to Sing Out, Inc." Then, too, *Sing Out!*, Vol. 6, No. 2 (Spring, 1956) is copyrighted by People's Artists, Inc.
4. *Sing Out!*, February-March 1964, p. 3, "Over the past year and a half, our readership has jumped dramatically. Today, *Sing Out!* has a circulation of 15,000 copies per issue — increasing at the rate of more than 1,000 every two months." *Sing Out!*, March 1965, p. 3, "Today, more people are reading *Sing Out!* (25,000 of you) than ever before." According to the *Reader's Digest* (April 1965), p. 191, ". . .more than six million young Americans are today strumming guitars. The top selling instrument of 1963 was, in fact, not the piano, as it has been for most of the 20th Century, but the guitar." The alarming fact is that most of these 6 million will inevitably end up with *Sing Out!* material or those publications that *Sing Out!* recommends, e.g., *Broadside* (New York), *The Little Sandy Review* and *Broadside* of Boston, to mention only three. (See Sing Out!, March 1965, p. 3 for a list of its recommendations.) The obvious deficiency in the *Digest's* articles written by Arnold Shaw is the lack of warning to those six million Americans interested in folk music. Not a word about *Sing Out!*, Silber or Seeger and even praise for Guthrie, Dylan and Reynolds. To praise the latter three is only to further the Communist use of folk music among the American public.
5. *Life* magazine, Oct. 9, 1964. Above the headline, "A Minstrel with a Mission," one is told, "Pete Seeger starts U.S. folk singers on their way."
6. Pete Seeger, *American Favorite Ballads* (New York: Oak Publications, 1961), p. 38.
7. Irwin Silber, *Reprints From Sing Out!*, (New York: Oak Publications, 1961), Volume 3, p. 15, 20. *Sing Out!*, Jan. 1967, p. 11f, Silber and Barbara Dane combine to praise Castro's Cuba.
8. *ibid.*, p. 48, 49.
9. *ibid.*, p. 41, 45. The *Sing Out!* reprint series contains enough evidence in song to clearly portray its official stand. Volume One contains Joe Hill's,

"The Rebel Girl," dedicated to Elizabeth Gurley Flynn (p. 14, 15). Also notice pp. 38, 45, 52, 54, 62 and 64. In Volume Two check pp. 4, 5, 12, 16, 17, 20, 23, 24, 26, 29 and 43. In Volume Four check pp. 4, 26 and 34. A vicious parody on the John Birch Society entitled, "The Jack Ash Society," relates: "The Jack Ashes says that in World War II we should have joined with the Third Reich; Adolph can pass their loyalty test, but not Allen and Milton and Dwight." In Volume Seven check pp. 17, 21, 49, 54 and 58. In this volume, Irwin Silber writes a song based on Woody Guthrie's original. Silber states, "I've got a brother in Stalingrad, I thought you know'd. I've got a brother in Stalingrad, Way down the road. On lots of things we don't agree, But he wants peace, just like me, So he's gonna put his name down."

10. House Committee on Un-American Activities, *Communist Activities Among Youth*, February 6, 1952, p. 3286. Also, *Annual Report of the Committee on Un-American Activities* for the year 1952, p. 72. Identified as members of the Communist Party and members of the singing group, "The Weavers," were Hope Foy, Lee Hays, Ronnie Gilbert, Freddie Hellerman and Pete Seeger. Same Annual Report, pp. 70-73. *The Weavers' Song Book* published by Harper and Brothers was copyrighted 1960 by Lee Hays, Ronnie Gilbert, Fred Hellerman and Erik Darling. According to the *Denver Post*, July 18, 1965, p. 32, Vanguard Records is producing "The Weavers: Reunion at Carnegie Hall." The article states, "The 'Reunion' albums bring back together all the people who, at one time or another, were members of this great group — Pete Seeger, Lee Hays, Ronnie Gilbert, Fred Hellerman, Erik Darling, Frank Hamilton and Bernard Krause." Since Denisoff calls in question the testimony of Harvey Matusow in his work, *Great Day Coming*, p. 158 (he insists Matusow recanted his previous testimony) attention is directed to the Senate's Committee on the Judiciary report, *The Significance of the Matusow Case*, April 6, 1955.
11. Edgar C. Bundy, *News and Views* (July, 1965) 422 North Prospect Street, Wheaton, Illinois.
12. House Committee on Un-American Activities *Annual Report*, 1960, p. 51.
13. House Committee's *Annual Report*, 1961, p. 43-44.
14. *ibid.*, 1962, p. 27.
15. *ibid.*, 1967, p. 88.
16. *The Worker*, Sunday, January 17, 1965, p. 9.
17. *ibid.*, March 7, 1965, p. 6.
18. *ibid.*, February 21, 1965, p. 10.
19. *American Dialog*, 853 Broadway, New York, May-June, 1965, p. 2. In

the Autumn, 1971 issue Seeger writes on "The World Flood of U.S. Pop Music."

20. House Committee on un-American Activities, *Testimony of Walter S. Steele*, July 21, 1947, p. 105.
21. Will Geer sings for Young People's Records and Children's Record Guild.
22. *Thirteenth Report of the California Senate Factfinding Subcommittee on Un-American Activities*, 1965, p. 12, "John Howard Lawson ... has been a member of the Communist Party for a good many years ... is a writer of motion pictures, scenarios and plays, has written several books and frequently lectures to Communist front organizations and at Communist front groups."
23. Waldo Frank was "one of the organizers of the Fair Play for Cuba Committee." See Senate Internal Security Subcommittee report, April 25, May 16, 1961, Part 2, p. 150. One of its members, Lee Harvey Oswald, shot the President of the United States, November 22, 1963.
24. Mrs DuBois is the wife of the deceased W.E.B. DuBois who died a member of the Communist Party and whose name is presently being used by the Communist Party's newest youth group, The DuBois Clubs of America.
25. *Sing Out!*, May 1965, p. 49, 95.
26. *Tocsin*, June 10, 1965, p. 2.
27. House Committee on Un-American Activities, *Communist Youth Activities*, relating to the Eighth World Youth Festival, 1962, p. 1781.
28. *ibid.*, p. 1823.
29. *National Review*, July 27, 1965, p. 664.
30. *Chicago Tribune*, October 25, 1965, p. 6. Also, *Daily Oklahoman*, Oct. 25, 1965.
31. Pre-Convention *Newsletter*, January 1965, No. 1 International Walther League Youth Building, 875 Dearborn Street, Chicago, Illinois.
32. Missouri District Walther League Publication, *Let Love Be Genuine*, August 20-22, 1965, article, "International," by R.J.K. Gluesenkamp, p. 12. Mr. Gluesenkamp served as third vice-president of the Executive Board of the League.
33. Pete Seeger, *The Bells of Rhymney* (New York: Oak Publications, 1964), p. 82.
34. Pete Seeger, *American Favorite Ballads* (New York: Oak Publications, 1961), p. 38.
35. *Broadside*, 215 W. 98th St., New York, 45, May 15, 1964, p. 15.
36. *New York Times*, April 11, 1964.
37. *The Knoxville Journal*, October 26, 1965, p. 4.
38. Edward Bash, *Songs For Today* (Minnesota: The American Lutheran

Church, 1964), p. 9.
39. *ibid.*, p. 93.
40. *Spirit Talk*, Vol. 1, No. 1, Concordia Publishing, St. Louis, Missouri.
41. *Tulsa Daily World*, January 5, 1967.
42. *Denver Post*, August 13, 1968, p. 6.
43. *Penthouse*, January, 1971, p. 35.
44. Communist *Daily World*, February 4, 1971, p. 2.
45. House Committee on Un-American Activities, *Investigation of Communist Activities, New York Area — Part VII (Entertainment)*, August 17, 1955, p. 2447f.
46. *The Westchester Spotlight*, Box 1111, White Plains, New York, April, 1961. Also, *New York Herald Tribune*, April 2, 1961.
47. House Committee on Un-American Activities, *To Amend Section II of the Subversive Activities Control Act of 1950*, August 16, 1961, p. 100.
48. *Presbyterian Life*, August 15, 1968, p. 11.
49. *Christianity Today*, August 16, 1968, p. 3,4.
50. *Risk*, "New Hymns For A New Day." published by World Council of Churches, Geneva 20, Switzerland, pp. 5-10, 43-45.
51. *Boy's Life*, October, 1968, p. 73.
52. Letter from Mr. Oliver S. Johnson to Pastor Charles King, January 6, 1969.
53. *Guideposts*, August, 1970.
54. *Audubon*, March, 1971, p. 80T.
55. Woody Guthrie, "My Constitution and Me," *Sunday Worker*, June 19, 1949, p. 12. Quotation found in Denisoff's *Great Day Coming*, p. 68.
56. John Greenway, "Woodrow Wilson Guthrie (1912-1967)," *Journal of American Folklore*, 81 (Jan-Mar., 1968), p. 63. Material from Denisoff's *Great Day Coming*, p. 135.
57. R. Serge Denisoff, *Great Day Coming*, p. 136.
58. *Ibid.*, p. 76.
59. *Special Committee on Un-American Activities*, Volume 14, May 22, 1941, p. 8463.
60. Josh Dunson, *Freedom in the Air*, International Publishers, New York, 1965, p. 45.
61. House Committee on Un-American Activities, *Guide To Subversive Organizations and Publications*, December 1, 1961, p. 192. *Sing Out!*, March 1965, p. 26, contains Ochs' "Draft Dodger Rag." *Sing Out!*, Nov. 1964, p. 12 contains his "Celia." Celia refers to the wife of an American Marine named Bill Pomeroy who joined the Communist Huk army in the Philippine Islands.
62. *National Review Bulletin*, March 3, 1964.

63. *Broadside* 40, February 25, 1964, p. 11. *Broadside* publishes monthly at 215 West 98 St., New York.

CHAPTER XXII — NOTES

1. Josh Dunson, *Freedom in the Air* (New York: International Publishers, 1965),
2. House Committee on Un-American Activities, Guide to Subversive Organizations and Publications, May 14, 1951, p. 94. "People's Artists . . . has always been friendly to the political line of the Communist Party," according to the Socialist Song Book, 1182 Broadway, Rm. 402, New York.
3. H.C.U.A., Communist Activities Among Youth Groups, Feb. 6, 1952, p. 3288. Silber is identified as "head of the Communist group within People's Songs." Also, see Annual Report of the Committee for 1952, p. 73 (Appendix 14). Also, H.C.U.A., *The Communist Party's Cold War Against Congressional Investigation of Subversion*, Oct. 10, 1962, p. 1480. See Appendixes 14 and 17.
4. House Committee on Un-American Activities, *Communism in The New York Area* (Entertainment), June 19, 1958, p. 2581, 2.
5. *ibid.*, p. 2585. *Sing Out!*, Nov. 1966, finds Silber in Cuba as guest of the Cuban Ministry of Culture.
6. *Sing Out!*, December-January, 1967/68, pp. 28, 29, 41.
7. International Publishers, "Report on the Double Anniversary Celebration," Book News Letter Supplement, No. 3, March, 1965.
8. House Committee on Un-American Activities, *Communist Outlets for the Distribution of Soviet Propaganda in the United States*, Part 1, p. 1593. Also, see H.C.U.A., Subversive Activities Control Act of 1950, Aug. 16, 1961, p. 114f.
9. *Four Continent Book Corporation Bulletin*, 156 Fifth Avenue, New York, February 1964, p. 4a.
10. Jerry Silverman, *The Panic Is On* (New York: Oak Publications, 1966), front cover.
11. *Sing Out!*., November 1964, p. 74, 45.
12. Advertisement distributed by Record, Book and Film Sales, Inc., 165 W. 46th Street, New York.
13. *Sing Out!*, Sept./Oct., 1969, middle insert.
14. *Washington Post*, November 6, 1965.
15. *Fourth Report of the California Senate Factfinding Subcommittee on Un-American Activities*, 1948, p. 392.
16. *Sing Out!*, January 1965, p. 7. Also, see Dunson's *Freedom in The Air*, p. 52.
17. *ibid.*, p. 2.
18. *ibid.*, May 1965, p. 54.

19. *Political Affairs*, Theoretical Journal of the Communist Party, USA, 23 West 26th Street, New York, February, 1965, p. 14.
20. *Sing Out!*, May 1965, p. 91.
21. *ibid.*, p. 84.
22. Nicolas Slonimsky, *Music Since 1900* p. 608, "Hanns Eisler, composer of atonal symphonies as well as eminently tonal mass songs, since 1942 a writer of background music for Hollywood films, leaves the United States as a 'voluntary deportee,' as a result of the actions of the H.C.U.A. alleging that he has 'perjured' his way in and out of the United States at will, going to Soviet Russia and other countries when he pleased."
23. Bernardo Teixeira, *The Fabric of Terror* (New York: Devin-Adair Co., 1965), p. 100.
24. *ibid.*, p. 82.
25. *The Worker*, December 15, 1964, p. 5. Also, in *The Worker*, September 14, 1965, p. 5, one reads, "Folkways Records has issued a delightful LP disc telling the story of the march from Selma to Montgomery, with the aid of Len Chandler, Pete Seeger and the Freedom Voices." Len Chandler, a contributing editor of *Broadside*, was the writer of "Beans in my Ears." The song was banned by many Public Health Boards (*Sing Out!*, May 1965, p. 45) because children were putting beans in their ears.
26. Folkways Records/Record, Book & Film Sales, *Newsletter*, Winter 1964/65.
27. *Lyons Elementary School Catalog*, 223 West Lake Street, Chicago 6, Illinois, 1963, p. 67. *Tools of Teaching*, 4233 Crenshaw Blvd., Los Angeles 8, California, 1964, p. 161. si,Materials List and Course Outlines for Music Education, prepared by Dr. Walter E. Purdy and published by the University of Houston, recommends Folkways Records, p. 37.
28. *Scholastic Magazine* letter sent to high school English teachers over the signature of Turner Dickson.
29. *Sing Out!*, January 1965, p. 34f.
30. Senate Internal Security Subcommittee, *The Pugwash Conference*, 1961, p. 55, 56. Further information on Eisler is contained in the House Committee on Un-American Activities, *Hearings Regarding Hanns Eisler*, September 24-26, 1947, p. 26. In the *Guide to Subversive Organizations*, Dec. 1, 1961, p. 90, Hanns Eisler, one of the founders of the subversive International Music Bureau, states, "Communist music becomes heavy artillery in the battle for Communism."
31. *Fourth Report of the California Senate Factfinding Subcommittee on Un-American Activities*, 1948, p. 224.
32. *Billboard*, August 21, 1965, p. 3.
33. *ibid.*, p. 3.

34. *ibid.*, p. 3.
35. *The Worker*, March 9, 1965, p. 5, 7.
36. *Newsweek*, September 20, 1965, p. 88, 90. Also, *Time*, September 17, 1965, p. 102, admits, "Folk rock owes its origins to Bob Dylan, 24, folk music's most celebrated contemporary composer."

CHAPTER XXIII – NOTES

1. *Broadside*, 215 West 98th St., New York, 10025.
2. Josh Dunson, *Freedom in the Air* (New York: International Publishers, 1965), p. 56. International Publishers is the official Communist publishing house in the United States. Its advertisement of the book carried comments by Pete Seeger, Irwin Silber, Phil Ochs, Mike Newberry, etc.
3. *Sing Out!*, November 1965, p. 98.
4. *Broadside*, 215 West 98 St., Apt. 4-D, New York, 54, Jan. 20, 1965, p. 3.
5. Josh Dunson, *Freedom in the Air*, International Publishers, 1965, p. 25.
6. *Guide to Subversive Organizations*, Dec. 1, 1961, p. 16.
7. Josh Dunson, *Freedom in the Air*, p. 17. Also, see *Broadside*, No. 7, June 1962, p. 13.
8. *Guide to Subversive Organizations and Publications*, May 14, 1951, p. 94.
9. House Committee on Un-American Activities, *Testimony of Walter S. Steele*, July 21, 1947, p. 106.
10. House Committee on Un-American Activities, *Communism in the Detroit Area*, Part 1, February 25, 26, 27, 28 and 29, 1952, p. 2716.
11. House Committee on Un-American Activities, *Communism in the Detroit Area*, Part 1, p. 2742.
12. *Guide to Subversive Organizations and Publications*, Dec. 1, 1961, p. 121.
13. Karl Prussion, *Heads Up*, Box 6519, San Diego 6, California, April 1964, p. 4.
14. *Broadside*, No. 20, February 1963, p. 17.
15. *Broadside*, No. 57, April 10, 1965, p. 18. In Sy and Barbara Ribakove, *The Bob Dylan Story* (New York: Dell Publishing Co., 1966), p. 67, Dylan admits that *Broadside* gave him his start.
16. *Broadside*, No. 38, January 20, 1964, p. 23.
17. *ibid.*, No. 27, June 1963, p. 21.
18. *Guide to Subversive Organizations and Publications*, Dec. 1, 1961, p. 193, referred to the *National Guardian* as "established by the American Labor Party in 1947, as a 'progressive' weekly . . . Although it denies having any affiliation with the Communist Party, it has manifested itself from the beginning as a virtual official propaganda arm of Soviet Russia."
19. *National Guardian*, August 22, 1962. Reprinted in *Broadside*, 31, September 1963, p. 13.
20. House Committee on Un-American Activities,, *Communism In Motion*

Picture's Industry, October 20-30, 1947, p. 497, 8.

21. *ibid.*, p. 494. *Sing Out!*, January 1966, p. 71, reported Ted Bikel touched the "heart and guts" of the 6,000 New Yorkers with a reading from Brecht, at a recent "Sing-In For Peace" rally. Joan Baez, Phil Ochs and Walter Lowenfels were among the participants of the rally.
22. *National Guardian*, August 22, 1962.
23. *Broadside*, No. 32, September 20, 1963, p. 1. In *Sing Out!*, February-March 1966, p. 85, Ochs is quoted as saying, "The Vietcong are right because they provide an extreme answer to the extreme problems of poverty, famine, disease . . . We should support Ho Chi Minh as the last workable bulwark against Communist China in Asia."
24. *Broadside*, No. 58, May 15, 1956, p. 4. Also, *Sing Out!*, Sept. 1965, p. 8.
25. *ibid.*, No. 56, March 10, 1965, p. 9.
26. *ibid.*, No. 61, August 15, 1965, p. 4.
27. *Chicago Tribune*, November 22, 1965. The Senate report made clear that "murder is an instrument of Soviet policy, and, as proof of that, the assassination department of the state security still exists. The name . . . has been changed to the 13th department of state security . . . testimony showed that Soviet agents themselves call it 'the department of blood-wet affairs.' "
28. Josh Dunson, *Freedom in the Air* (New York: International Publishers, 1965), p. 117.

CHAPTER XXIV — NOTES

1. *Playboy Magazine*, February 1965, p. 54, finds John, one of the Beatles, admitting, "But it wasn't until *Time* and *Life* and *Newsweek* came over and wrote articles and created an interest in us that the disc jockeys started playing our records." *Life*, October 9, 1964, gave Pete Seeger an excellent build up entitled, "The Angry Young Folk Singer." Joan Baez and Woody Guthrie have also been written up big in the nation's mass media.
2. Irwin Silber, *The ABC-TV Hootenanny Song Book* (New York: Consolidated Music Publishers, 1963), p. 6.
3. Waldemar Hille, *The People's Song Book* (New York: Oak Publications, 1961), p. 63.
4. Irwin Silber, *The ABC-TV Hootenanny Song Book*, p. 40.
5. *ibid.*, p. 47.
6. Irwin Silber, *The ABC-TV Hootenanny Song Book*, p. 81.
7. *ibid.*, p. 123.
8. *ibid.*, p. 132.
9. Earl Robinson, *Young Folk Song Book* (New York: Simon and Schuster, 1963), p. 20.
10. *Chicago Tribune*, March 10, 1965.
11. *Life* Magazine, April 10, 1964, p. 109.
12. Earl Robinson, *Young Folk Song Book* (New York: Simon & Schuster, 1963), p. 38.
13. *ibid.*, p. 47. Non-violent Bob Dylan, who despises murderers, related the following in the eighth verse of "Masters of War." "And I hope that you die, And your death will come soon. I'll follow your casket by the pale afternoon. An' I'll watch while you're lowered down to your deathbed, An' I'll stand over your grave till I'm sure that you're dead."
14. *Life*, April 10, 1964, p. 114.
15. *ibid.*
16. *Broadside*, 215 W. 98 St., New York City, No. 11-12, August 1962, p. 19.
17. *ibid.*, 51, October 20, 1964, p. 23.
18. Earl Robinson, *Young Folk Song Book*, p. 9.
19. House Committee on Un-American Activities, *100 Things You Should Know About Communism*, May 14, 1951, p. 4, "No Communist, no matter how many votes he should secure in a national election, could, even if he would, become President of the present government. When a Communist heads the government of the United States — and that day will come just as surely as the sun rises — the government will not be a

capitalist government but a Soviet government, and behind this government will stand the Red Army to enforce the dictatorship of the proletariat."
20. Waldemar Hille, *The People's Song Book*, p. 48.
21. Margaret B. Boni, *Fireside Book of Folk Songs* (New York: Simon and Schuster), p. 200
22. *ibid.*, p. 206.
23. Margaret B. Boni, *Fireside Book of Folk Songs*, p. 214.
24. House Committee on Un-American Activities, *Crimes of Khrushchev*, Seven Parts, September 4, 1959-January 8, 1960.
25. Margaret B. Boni, *op. cit.*, p. 228.
26. *ibid.*, p. 210.
27. *ibid.*, p. 218.
28. *ibid.*, p. 46.
29. *ibid.*, p. 48.
30. *Thirteenth Report of the California Senate Factfinding Subcommittee on Un-American Activities*, 1965, p. 163.
31. Barrie Stavis and Frank Harmon, *Songs of Joe Hill*, Oak Publications, 1960, p. 10. Oak is now offering *The Letters of Joe Hill*, *Sing Out!*, Jan. 1966, p. 62.
32. *ibid.*, pp. 42, 43.
33. *ibid.*, pp. 18, 19.
34. *ibid.*, p. 37.
35. *ibid.*, p. 39.
36. *Amalgamated Song Book*, 15 Union Square, New York City.
37. *Sound Off*, Young Christian Workers, 1655 W. Jackson Blvd., Chicago 12, Illinois.
38. Nat Hentoff is a member of the New York Branch of SANE, has taught "non-violence," signed Communist-sponsored petitions on behalf of Red agents Morton Sobell and Junius Scales, and was sponsor of the Communist front "Monroe Defense Committee." See American Opinion, December 1964, p. 23.
39. House Committee on Un-American Activities. *Communist Methods of Infiltration, Entertainment — Part I*, p. 3859.
40. *Guide to Subversive Organizations and Publications*, Dec. 1, 1961, p. 197.
41. *American Opinion* December 1964, pp. 22, 23.
42. James F. Leisy, *Hootenanny Tonight*, (Connecticut: Fawcett Publications, 1964), Foreword.
43. *Sing Out!*, May 1965, p. 63.
44. *ibid.*, September 1965, p. 42.

45. *Sing Out!*, November 1965, p. 112.
46. *ibid.*, p. 113.
47. *ibid.*, March 1965, p. 65.
48. *Los Angeles Times*, January 29, 1965, p. 1.
49. James F. Leisy, *Hootenanny Tonight*, p. 122.
50. *ibid.*, p. 123.
51. *New York Herald Tribune*, February 28, 1965, p. 1.
52. *ibid.*, p. 30.
53. James F. Leisy, *Hootenanny Tonight*, p. 65.
54. Taken from brochure, "Legendary Folk Songs," published by The Longines' Symphonette Recording Society, Symphonette Square, Larchmont, New York.
55. *Reader's Digest*, April 1965, p. 191f.
56. Mary admits her interest in folk music "was stirred by Pete Seeger." (*Saturday Evening Post*, May 30, 1964, p. 35) Irwin Silber, commenting on the trio said, "Peter, Paul and Mary are probably the most frankly political of the current crop of bit-time groups . . . I do not expect Peter, Paul and Mary or the Chad Mitchell Trio to sound like Frank Proffitt or Doc Watson or Jean Ritchie." (*Sing Out!*, Feb.-March 1964, p. 63) According to *Sing Out!*, Nov. 1964, p. 73, "Peter, Paul and Mary entertained at a dinner party in the White House given by President Johnson for U-Thant. . ."
57. *Sing Out!*, January 1965, p. 5.
58. *ibid.*, March 1965, p. 3.
59. *The Ballad Mongers* gives a fairly accurate description of the exploitation of folk music. *Broadside* No. 26, May 1963, p. 5f, gives the book a three-quarter-hearted review.
60. Reprints From *Sing Out!* Volume five, 1963. Also see Appendix 26 for a listing of songs by singers and categories of the *Sing Out! — Broadside* Network.
61. *Tulsa Tribune*, May 5, 1965 (Tulsa, Oklahoma).
62. *McCall's Magazine*, June 1965, article, "Sight & Sound," by Lenore Hershey, p. 8.
63. *Chicago Tribune*, May 18, 1965, p. 20. *The Thirteenth Report of the California Senate Subcommittee on Un-American Activities* reported the same conclusion, ". . . a hard core of Reds took over the so-called Free Speech Movement 'in the greatest student rebellion in the history of the United States on the main campus of the country's largest educational institution.' " *Chicago Tribune*, June 19, 1965, p. 1.
64. Zygmund Dobbs and Archibald B. Roosevelt, *The Great Deceit* (New York: A Veritas Foundation Staff Study, 1964), p. 52.

65. *American Folk Singers and Balladeers* brochure, distributed by the Classics Record Library, a division of the Book-of-the-Month Club, Inc., 345 Hudson Street, New York, N.Y., n.d.
66. *Guide to Subversive Organizations and Publications*, Dec. 1, 1961, p. 90.
67. Josh Dunson, *Freedom in the Air*, (New York: International Publishers, 1965), pp. 73-75.
68. Earl Robinson, *Young Folk Song Book* (New York: Simon & Schuster, 1963), p. 9.
69. *American Institute of Hypnosis Journal*, Oct. 1963, p. 3.
70. *Sing Out!*, May 1965, p. 31.

CHAPTER XXV – NOTES

1. Artuyo Cuyas, *Revised Cuyas Dictionary*, Appleton Century Crafts, Inc., New York, 1960, p. 546.
2. House Committee on Un-American Activities, *Testimony of Paul Crouch*, May 6, 1949, p. 193. Mr. Crouch testified, "His wife, Zylphia, seemed even more pro-Communist than her husband (Myles Horton) and I heard reports in party circles, which I am unable to verify, that she had subsequently joined the party."
3. Senate Internal Security Subcommittee, *Communist Passport Frauds*, July 11, 1958, p. 42. Carawan, then of Los Angeles, California, but now musical director of Highlander, was named as part of a Committee of Fifteen to receive an all-expense-paid trip to and from Red China. This trip was in connection with the World Youth Festival held in Moscow in 1957.
4. Guy and Candie Carawan, *We Shall Overcome* (New York: Oak Publications, 1963), p. 11.
5. Josh Dunson, *Freedom in the Air* (New York: International Publishers Co., Inc., 1965), pp. 29, 30.
6. House Committee on Un-American Activities, *Testimony of Paul Crouch*, May 6, 1949, p. 191.
7. House of Representatives Special Committee, *Investigation of Un-American Propaganda Activities in the United States*, August 13, 1938, p. 126.
8. Senate Internal Security Subcommittee, *Southern Conference Educational Fund, Inc.*, March 18-20, 1954, p. vii. Also see *National Review*, Sept. 20, 1966, pp. 914, 915, for an insight into Horton's relationship with Stokely Carmichael and his "black power" concepts.
9. House Committee on Un-American Activities, *Communism in the New York City Area*, July 7, 8, 13 and 14, 1953, p. 2266. Ward was referred to as ". . . . the chief architect for Communist infiltration and subversion in the religious field."
10. Senate Internal Security Subcommittee, *Southern Conference Educational Fund, Inc.*, March 18-20, 1954, p. 48. According to *The Worker*, Dec. 8, 1964, p. 2, Dr. James Dombrowski was awarded the Tom Paine award by the Emergency Civil Liberties Committee, a subversive organization according to *Guide to Subversive Organizations and Publications*, Dec. 1, 1961, p. 69.
11. *Guide to Subversive Organizations and Publications*, Dec. 1, 1961, p. 121.
12. *Congressional Record*, Wednesday, February 3, 1963, pp. 1916, 7.

13. *Tulsa Daily World*, Monday, April 19, 1965, p. 9.
14. *Chicago Tribune*, May 25, 1965, p. 1.
15. *Newsweek*, March 2, 1970, p. 54. William Kunstler has been listed as a radical campus speaker by the House Internal Security Committee (*New York Times*, Oct. 15, 1970), and is reported to have told college students to bring guns to school and be prepared to use them (Springfield, Mo., *Leader-Press*, Aug. 24, 1970, p. 4).
16. Senate Internal Security Subcommittee, *Southern Conference Educational Fund, Inc.*, March 18-20, 1954, p. 47.
17. Irwin Silber, *The ABC-TV Hootenanny Song Book* (New York: Consolidated Music Publishers, Inc., 1963.), p. 94.
18. *Tulsa Daily World*, April 13, 1965, p. 1.
19. *U.S. News & World Report*, April 12, 1965, p. 20.
20. Georgia Commission on Education, 220 Agriculture Bldg., 19 Hunter Street, S.W., Atlanta 3, Ga. This commission published a broadside entitled *Highlander Folk School.* King was shown in the pictures not only as a student, but also as an instructor.
21. *Atlanta Constitution*, February 23, 1961.
22. Josh Dunson, *Freedom in the Air*, p. 99.
23. Highlander Center, 1625 Riverside Drive, Knoxville 15, Tennessee, letterhead contains Myles Horton, director, and King as one of the sponsors.
24. *Christianity Today*, April 9, 1965, pp. 45, 6.
25. *U.S. News and World Report*, April 12, 1965, p. 11.
26. *Tulsa Daily World*, March 24, 1965, p. 3.
27. *ibid.*
28. *U.S. News and World Report*, April 12, 1965, p. 11. For an accurate account of the debauchery see Albert C. Persons, *The True Selma Story*, (Alabama: Esco Publishers, Inc., 1965).
29. *Los Angeles Times*, March 19, 1965.
30. House Committee on Un-American Activities, *Communist Infiltration and Activities in the South*, July 29-31, 1958, pp. 2604, 2893. The report stated: "The testimony taken by this committee in the course of just the last few months at Atlanta, Georgia, was to the effect that another man, by the name of Carl Braden who has been repeatedly identified as a hard-core agent in the Communist Party, was in session with Mr. Harvey O'Connor . . ." For a full account of Braden's Southern Conference Educational Fund activities, see the *Joint Legislative Committee on Un-American Activities*, Report No. 4, State of Louisiana.
31. Georgia Commission on Education, 220 Agriculture Building, 19 Hunter Street, S.W., Atlanta 3, Georgia.

32. *St. Louis Globe-Democrat*, December 3, 1964, p. 12A.
33. *Congressional Record*, March 30, 1965, p. 6114. Congressman Dickinson incorporated into the record a sworn affidavit of Karl Prussion, a former counterspy for the FBI from 1947 to 1960. In the affidavit Prussion states: "I further swear and attest that at each and every one of the aforementioned meetings, one Rev. Martin Luther King was always set forth as the individual to whom Communists should look and rally around in the Communist struggle on the many racial issues."
34. *Congressional Record*, March 30, 1965, p. 6114.
35. *Guide to Subversive Organizations and Publications*, Dec. 1, 1961, p. 115.
36. *National Review*, April 20, 1965, p. 327.
37. *Saturday Review*, April 3, 1965, p. 16, 17, 57.
38. *Tulsa Daily World*, April 16, 1965, Henry J. Taylor's column.
39. William Z. Foster, *Toward Soviet America* (California: Elgin Publications, 1961), pp. 233, 249 and 304. Also see James W. Ford and James S. Allen's (both Communists) *The Negro in a Soviet America*. Reprints available from Christian Crusade.
40. *Chicago Tribune*, March 11, 1965.
41. *ibid.*, March 29, 1965.
42. *The Worker*, March 16, 1965.
43. *Political Affairs*, August 1963.
44. *Sunday Oklahoman*, November 29, 1964 (Oklahoma City, Oklahoma).
45. *Political Affairs*, January 1965, p. 1.
46. *Tulsa Daily World*, May 11, 1965, p. 6.
47. Robert F. Williams, *The Crusader* (Canada: Cuba via 21 Ellis Gardens, 1964), Vol. V, No. 4.
48. *Chicago Tribune*, October 25, 1965, p. 9.
49. *Tulsa Daily World*, May 22, 1965, p. 5.
50. *Tulsa Daily World*, June 1,1965, p. 1.
51. John Lewis was in Selma (*Chicago Tribune*, March 22, 1965, p. 2) and in Harlem (*The Worker*, March 16, 1965, p. 1).
52. *The Worker*, March 21, 1965, p. 9.
53. *U.S. News and World Report*, April 12,1965, p. 11. Also see *Tulsa Tribune*, March 20, 1965, p. 6.
54. *ibid.*, U.S. News and World Report.
55. *New Republic*, August 22, 1964, pp. 17-21.
56. The *Tulsa Daily World*, Sept. 11,1966, p. 27, finds Ralph McGill, editor of the *Atlanta Constitution*, exposing SNCC as having received Havana money and using "Castro's slogans."

57. *The Weekly Crusader*, June 25, 1965, Christian Crusade, Box 977, Tulsa, Oklahoma, p. 3–5.
58. Josh Dunson, *Freedom in the Air*, p. 64.
59. *ibid.*, p. 64.
60. *ibid.*, p. 65.
61. *ibid.*, p. 100.
62. *Tulsa Daily World*, March 24, 1965, p. 3.
63. Earl Robinson, *Young Folk Song Book* (New York: Simon and Schuster, 1963), p. 36.
64. Contained in a letter from Mr. Harris, July 28, 1965, to one of Columbia's inquirers. The letter is on file.
65. J. Edgar Hoover, *Masters of Deceit* (New York: Pocket Books Inc.,1965),p. 95.
66. *Congressional Record*, March 15, 1965, p. 4925.
67. *Sing Out!*, 165 West 46th Street, New York, November 1965, p. 87, 89.
68. *Tulsa Daily World*, April 16, 1965, p. 8.
69. *ibid.*, p. 8.

Chapter XXVI — NOTES

1. *Chicago Tribune*, February 17, 1965.
2. *Sing Out!*, May 1965, p. 19.
3. *ibid.*
4. *Chicago Tribune*, December 4, 1964, p. 2. For excellent material on Jessica Mitford and her Communist background, see *American Opinion*, June 1965, p. 91.
5. House Committee on Un-American Activities,*Communist Legal Subversion*, February 16, 1959, p. 68.
6. *Chicago Tribune*, December 4, 1964, p. 1
7. *Tulsa Daily World*, November 10, 1965, p. 1.
8. *San Francisco Examiner*, November 26, 1965, p. 38.
9. Federal Bureau of Investigation *Law Enforcement Bulletin*, October 1964. Also *Tulsa Daily World*, December 22, 1964, p. 18
10. *Thirteenth Report of the California Senate Factfinding Subcommittee on Un-American Activities*, 1965, p. 117.
11. *The Reporter*, January 28, 1965, pp. 36—40
12. *San Francisco Examiner*, November 25-27, 1964. Reprints available from the paper's research department. Since the rioters were fomenting the trouble on campus months before the Sproul Hall incident, Ed Montgomery's articles are must reading for background material.
13. *Chicago Tribune*, December 4, 1964, p. 2. For further material regarding Baez' activities at Berkeley see *Thirteenth Report of the California Senate Subcommittee*, 1965, p. 6, 96, 97, 99, 100, 101, 116, 152, 153.
14. *Thirteenth Report of the California Senate Factfinding Subcommittee on Un—American Activities*, 1965, p. 99.15.
15. *ibid.*, p. 101.
16. *Sing Out!* February — March 1964, p. 17.
17. *The Worker*, June 30,1964,p. 7.
18. *ibid*, March 16, 1965, p. 7.
19. *Tulsa Sunday World*, April 18, 1965, p. 1.
20. *Sing Out!* March 1965, p. 32.
21. *Tulsa Daily World*, April 23, 1965, p. 8.
22. *Seattle Post-Intelligence*, May 22, 1967, p. S7.
23. *San Antonio Express*, November 18, 1968, p. 15-A
24. *Time*,September 27, 1971, p. 48.
25. *Newsweek*, November 4, 196l.
26. *Fact*, 110 West 40th Street, New York, January-February 1965, p. 8.
27. *Chicago Tribune*, October 19, 1971, p. 20.
28. *Look*, August 27, 1963.

29. *American Opinion*, Belmont, Mass., December 1964, article, "Folk Music," by Dr. Jere Real, p. 23. According to an AP dispatch in the *Tulsa Daily World*, April 16, 1965, Joan Baez again refused to pay her total income tax which amounts to $57,330. She said, "This country has gone mad. But I will not go mad with it. I will not pay for organized murder. I will not pay for the war in Viet Nam."
30. Florence Fowler Lyons, *Report on UNESCO*, Box 215, Montrose, California, Volume V, No. 3, April-May, 1964.
31. *Newsweek*, January 10, 1966, p. 59.
32. *ibid.*, p. 60.
33. *Broadside*, 215 West 98th Street, Apt. 4D, New York, No. 52, November 20, 1964, p. 19. Steve Allen, in his latest book *Letter to a Conservative* (New York: Doubleday & Co., 1965), p. 284, 5, portrays Christian Crusade as an organization possessing a disease known as "rightist lunacy." He says, "While Mr. Noebel is apparently the first to suppose that the Beatles are part of a Red plot, there are many rightists who have claimed that such popular TV programs as 'Chivaree,' 'Shindig,' 'Hootenanny,' and 'Hullabaloo' are also a part cf a Communist plot to brainwash American youngsters with subversive propaganda in the form of folk music. As is often the case with Rightist lunacy there is — wrapped up in the 99 per cent outer shell of nonsense — 1 per cent of truth which, however distorted, deserves attention." Apart from the fact that Mr. Allen would have been more accurate to say, "Beatle music is part of a Red plot," we would, with his permission of course, invite him to read our analysis of the *ABC-TV Hootenanny Song Book* and then Challenge him to maintain his naive position. One other Allen "proof" of lunacy involves the Air Force Training Manual and its charges concerning certain Protestant clergymen and the National Council of Churches. He says these charges were "eventually shown to be false and slanderous." (p. 286,7) We would simply and unemotionally ask him, as we have asked other NCC apologists, what charges were false and slanderous?
34. *The Worker*, March 26, 1963, p. 5. According to *Sing Out!*, February-March 1966, pp. 2, 84 & 85, Pete Seeger is back on T.V. with a program called "Rainbow Quest." The series is being aired in New York on channel 47 from Newark. Sholom Rubinstein is the producer and director and according to *Sing Out!* the program is being offered to local television stations at a modest price.
35. *International Musician*, May 1965, p. 6.
36. Irwin Silber, *ABC-TV Hootenanny Song Book* (New York: Consolidated Music Publishers, 1963), p. 6.
37. Mario Savio was convicted and given 120 days in jail.

38. Pacific School of Religion *Bulletin*, 1798 Scenic Avenue, Berkeley, California, December 1964, p. 5.
39. *The Dan Smoot Report*, P.O. Box 9538, Lakewood Station, Dallas, Texas, February 8, 1965, p. 47.

CHAPTER XXVII - NOTES

1. *Newsweek*, September 20, 1965, p. 88.
2. *The Worker*, March 9, 1965, p. 5.
3. *ibid.*

CHAPTER XXVIII — NOTES

1. *Stevenson's Book of Quotations* (New York: Dodd-Mead, 1958), p. 123.
2. *Genesis* 4:21, 22.
3. *Saturday Evening Post*, May 30, 1964, p. 32.

CHAPTER XXIX - NOTES

1. *Billboard*, August 21, 1965, p. 3
2. *Sing Out!*, January, 1965, p. 7.
3. *California, Fourth Report of the Senate Fact-Finding Subcommittee on Un-American Activities*, 1948, p. 392.
4. *California, Fifth Report of the Senate Fact-Finding Subcommittee on Un-American Activities*, 1949, p. 544.
5. *Billboard*, August 21, 1965, p. 3.
6. *Sing Out!*, November 1965, p. 72. See Appendix 22 A and B.

CHAPTER XXX - NOTES

1. *Newsweek*, September 20, 1965, p. 88.
2. *Time*, September 17, 1965, p. 102.
3. For Guthrie's Communist activity see our earlier chapter entitled Pete Seeger and Woody Guthrie. For Dylan's connections to Guthrie consult Sy and Barbara Ribakove, *The Bob Dylan Story* (New York: Dell Publishing Co., 1966), pp. 24, 46 and 95.
4. Brecht was a German Communist, Lorca a Spanish pro-Communist and Yevtushenko a Russian Communist. For Dylan's association with these men's works see Sy and Barbara Ribakove, *The Bob Dylan Story*, p. 40.
5. *The Sunflower* February 23, 1966, p. 5. (University of Wichita newspaper).
6. Sy and Barbara Ribakove, *The Bob Dylan Story, p. 1.*
7. *ibid.*, p. 89.
8. *Guide to Subversive Organizations and Publications*, Dec. 1,1961, p. 90.
9. *Sing Out!*, November 1965, p. 95.
10. *Sing Out!*, February-March 1966, inside front cover.
11. House Committee on Un-American Activities, *Appendix — Part IX, Communist Front Organizations*, pp. 599, 671, 1139 and 1179.
12. Sy and Barbara Ribakove, *The Bob Dylan Story*, p. 36.
13. Josh Dunson, *Freedom in the Air*, p. 121.
14. *Sing Out!*, February - March 1964, p. 13.
15. *Life*, April 10, 1964, p. 109.
16. By comparing the comments regarding "radical" on page 97 in *Freedom in the Air* with the truth concerning Malvina Reynolds, one quickly senses that Dunson really means "Communist" by "radical."
17. Josh Dunson, *Freedom in the Air*, p. 75.
18. *ibid.*, p. 82.
19. Earl Robinson, ed.,*Young Folk Song Book*, Simon and Schuster, New York, 1963, p. 38.
20. House Committee on Un-American Activities, Volume 14, May 22, 1941, p. 8463.
21. Dunson *op. cit.*, p. 45.
22. Sy and Barbara Ribakove, *The Bob Dylan Story*, p. 67.
23. *ibid.*, p. 46.
24. *ibid.*, p. 67.
25. *Broadside*, 215 West 98th Street, New York, No. 23, March 1963, p. 15.
26. Josh Dunson, *Freedom in the Air*, p. 83.
27. House Committee on Un-American Activities, *Testimony of Walter S. Steele*, July 21, 1947, p. 105.

28. *Political Affairs*, February 1965, p. 14.
29. Ribakove, *op.cit.*, pp. 97, 98.
30. *Guide to Subversive Organizations and Publications*, December 1,1961, pp. 69,70.
31. Josh Dunson, *Freedom in the Air*, p. 85.
32. Sy and Barbara Ribakove, *The Bob Dylan Story*, p. 53.
33. *Guide to Subversive Organizations and Publications*, December 1,1961, pp. 69,70.
34. Josh Dunson, *op.cit.*, p. 84. The same conclusion is reached in the Ribakove book, p. 62, "As Folk-rock nearly displaced standard rock 'n' roll on the Top Forty charts, a vocal minority of Bob's former admirers decided that he had deliberately changed his style in order to reach more people with his message.
35. Josh Dunson, *op.cit.*, p. 85.
36. *The Albuquerque Tribune*, January 18, 1966, p. A-8.
37. Sy and Barbara Ribakove, *The Bob Dylan Story*, p. 119.
38. *ibid.*, p. 120.
39. *Des Moines Register*, February 10, 1966, p. 18. (Des Moines, Iowa)
40. *ibid.*, p. 18.
41. H.C.U.A. *Annual Report*, 1952, p. 73 and H.C.U.A., Oct. 10,1962 *Report*, p. 1480.
42. *Sing Out!*, February 1964, p. 53. *Sing Out!*, November 1964, p. 22.
43. *Broadside*, 215 West 98th Street, New York, No. 54, January 20, 1965, p. 11.
44. Sy and Barbara Ribakove, *The Bob Dylan Story*, p. 122.
45. *Broadside*, No. 63, October 15, 1965, p. 5.
46. *New York Times*, August 27, 1965, *Broadside*, No. 62, Sept. 15, 1965, p. 11.
47. *Newsweek*, September 20, 1965, p. 90.

CHAPTER XXXI - NOTES

1. *Rock Folk Song Folio* (Connecticut: Onyx Publishing Co., 1966), p. 9.
2, *ibid.*, pp. 10, 11.
3. *Rock Folk Song Folio*, p. 14.
4. *Fact*, 110 West 40th Street, New York, January-February 1965, front cover.
5. *Rock Folk Song Folio*, p. 23. Phil Ochs' album "In Concert" produced by Elektra Records contains the poems of Mao Tse-tung with the question, "Is This the Enemy?"
6. *ibid.*, p. 20.
7. *Chicago Tribune*, January 23, 1966, Section 5, page 1.
8. *Tulsa Daily World*, January 27, 1966, p. 7.
9. Josh Dunson, *Freedom in the Air*, p. 75.
10. *Tulsa Daily World*, January 27, 1966, p. 7.
11. *Sing Out!*, 165 West 46th Street, New York, May 1965, p. 19.
12. Henry David Thoreau, *Walden* (New York: The New American Library, 1963), p. 147.

CHAPTER XXXII - NOTES

1. *Billboard,* August 21, 1965, p. 12.
2. *Time,* September 17, 1965, p. 104.
3. *Billboard, op.cit.*, p. 12.
4. *Chicago American*, Sunday, October 3, 1965, p. 3, Section 1, Jack Mabley's column.
5. *Time*, September 17, 1965, p. 102.
6. *Newsweek*, September 20, 1965, p. 90.
7. *Broadside*, No. 63, October 15, 1965, p 2f.
8. *Broadside*, 44, April 30, 1964, p. 15.
9. *Newsweek*, September 20, 1965, p. 90. Instead of printing the background of Silber and Asch, *Newsweek* simply states: "Even many who dig Dylan think, like folk authority Irwin Silber, that he is 'contradicting' his 'songs of significance' by using rock style. But Moses Asch, the scholarly, fifty-nine year old director of Folkways Records, thinks Dylan 'expresses the hoped-for.'"

CHAPTER XXXIV - NOTES

1. Jeffrey Hart, "The Rebirth of Christ," *National Review*, Dec. 28, 1965, p. 1192.
2. *ibid.*, p. 1195.
3. Frank Garlock, *The Big Beat: A Rock Blast* (Greenville, South Carolina: Bob Jones University Press, 1971), p. 49.
4. *ibid.*, p. 7.

CHAPTER XXXVIII - NOTES

1. *Guide to Subversive Organizations and Publications*, December 1, 1961, p. 108.

CHAPTER XXXIX - NOTES

1. *Time*, August 20, 1965, p. 17. "Young Negroes in late-model convertibles took command of the streets, screaming 'Burn, baby, burn!' a hipster term popularized locally by 'the Magnificent Montague,' a Negro disc jockey." *Chicago Tribune*, August 16, 1965, p. 2. "The arsonists had a code phrase — 'Burn, baby burn' - according to Robert Richardson, a Negro and an advertising salesman for the *Los Angeles Times.* He reported the 'hep slogan borrowed from a disc jockey' was used by arsonists to identify themselves to others of their ilk. And when gasoline bombs were thrown, numerous teenagers would shout, 'Burn, baby, burn.'"
2. *Tulsa Tribune*, October 28,1969.
3. Jerry Rubin, *Do It!*, p. 249.
4. *Los Angeles Free Press*, November 1971.
5. *ibid.*,
6. *ibid*,

INDEX